William Wright

Contributions to the Apocryphal Literature of the New Testament

Collected and edited from Syriac manuscripts in the British Museum

William Wright

Contributions to the Apocryphal Literature of the New Testament
Collected and edited from Syriac manuscripts in the British Museum

ISBN/EAN: 9783337123437

Printed in Europe, USA, Canada, Australia, Japan

Cover: Foto ©Lupo / pixelio.de

More available books at **www.hansebooks.com**

CONTRIBUTIONS

TO THE

APOCRYPHAL LITERATURE

OF THE

NEW TESTAMENT,

COLLECTED AND EDITED FROM SYRIAC MANUSCRIPTS IN THE BRITISH MUSEUM,

WITH

AN ENGLISH TRANSLATION AND NOTES,

BY

W. WRIGHT, PH. D., LL.D.,

ASSISTANT IN THE DEPARTMENT OF MANUSCRIPTS, BRITISH MUSEUM.

WILLIAMS AND NORGATE,

14, HENRIETTA STREET, COVENT GARDEN, LONDON;

20, SOUTH FREDERICK STREET, EDINBURGH.

1865.

TO

CONSTANTIN TISCHENDORF,

THE EDITOR OF THE

EVANGELIA APOCRYPHA

AND OF THE

ACTA APOSTOLORUM APOCRYPHA,

THIS WORK IS DEDICATED

BY HIS SINCERE FRIEND

W. WRIGHT.

PREFACE.

This little volume is intended as a humble companion to the *Evangelia Apocrypha* of my learned friend Professor Dr. Tischendorf of Leipzig. What he has done in so masterly a manner for the Greek and Latin texts of the Apocryphal Gospels, I have attempted to do—I fear very imperfectly—for the Syriac texts, so far as they are accessible to me. As my manuscripts are, generally speaking, more ancient than those used by Tischendorf, my great aim has been to reproduce the text in each case as accurately as possible, and to give a close rendering into English, so that the Orientalist may be able to judge of my understanding of the document, and the Classical Scholar to compare it easily with the Greek original or the old Latin translation. Where the manuscripts are torn or otherwise illegible, I have inserted within brackets what I suppose to be the missing words or letters. All other emendations and corrections I have invariably placed at the foot of the page. I have also added a few notes, pointing out some of the more important differences between the several versions, and explaining, or at least noticing, certain difficulties; but to these notes I do not attach much value, my wish being rather to edit and translate than to annotate. If my labours are favourably received, I shall be encouraged to bring out another volume, which I have now in preparation, containing the *Apocryphal Acts of the Apostles*, such as St. John, St. Thomas, Paul and Thekla, etc.

The documents contained in this book are the following:—

I. The *Protevangelium Jacobi*, taken from the Nitrian manuscript Add. 14,484, fol. 10 rect.—fol. 12 vers. (as at present numbered). This manuscript seems, as nearly as I can judge, to belong to the latter half of the sixth century. It is a large quarto, written in two columns, in a fine, regular Esṭrangĕlā. The diacritical points were in many cases inserted by the scribe, but others have been added at a much later period by some industrious reader, and I found it impossible to make any distinction between them in print. The greater part of this apocryph has been lost, the text commencing with the words that correspond to the clause *αὐτὴ ἡ ἡμέρα κυρίου ποιήσει ὡς βούλεται* in cap. xvii. of the Greek text.

II. *The Gospel of Thomas the Israelite*, taken from the same manuscript as the preceding, fol. 12 vers.—fol. 16 vers. (as at present numbered).

III. *The Letters of Herod and Pilate*, taken from Add. 14,609, fol. 120 rect.—fol. 122 rect. This is a small quarto, written in two columns, in a good, regular Esṭrangĕlā of the sixth or seventh century. It has been partially described by my friend Dr. Land of Amsterdam in his *Anecdota Syriaca*, tom. I., prolegom., p. 19. These letters, of which Dr. Tischendorf possesses the *Greek* originals, are clearly a forgery of comparatively late date, I should say not earlier than the end of the fourth century. The quotation from Josephus, p. ܟܒ (transl., p. 17) is evidently made, not directly, but through the *Ecclesiastical History* (lib. II. cap. 10) of Eusebius, who died about A.D. 340. I need hardly point out, that, in the latter part of the letter of Pilate, the author forgets his assumed rôle altogether. Whom he means by Justin and Theodore I do not pretend to know. The passages quoted are not improbably mere inventions of his own; and he may have used the name of Justin because *Justin Martyr* cites the *Acta Pilati* in his *First Apology*, cap. 48 (edit. 1742, p. 72). As to Josephus, the passage regarding king Agrippa has no connection whatever with the rest of the letter.

IV. Under this head I have combined fragments of two recensions of the well-known *Transitus*, *Assumptio*, or Κοίμησις *beatæ Virginis*. This work is, as Ewald has already shown, most probably a production of the latter half of the fourth century. Older it certainly cannot be, partly on account of the dignity and importance which it attaches to the monastic life, and partly because of the works cited or made use of in writing it. These are, firstly, the *Testament of Adam*, which can hardly belong to an earlier period than the fourth century; and, secondly —if my conjecture (p. 60) regarding the name of ܣܝܐܢܘܣ or ܣܝܢܘܣ, *Σηϊανός*, *Sejanus*, be correct— the *Chronicle of Eusebius*.

An edition of the original *Greek* text we may

shortly expect from Dr. Tischendorf, who has discovered it in two manuscripts. Meanwhile the reader should examine the old *Latin* redaction of the work, printed in La Bigne's *Maxima Bibliotheca vett. Patrum*, tom. II. pars 2, p. 212 foll.; and the *Arabic* version, published by Enger, under the title of اخبار يوحنّا السليح، في نقلة امّ المسيح" , *id est Joannis Apostoli de Transitu beatæ Mariæ Virginis liber* (Elberfeld, 1854).

Of *Syriac* editions or redactions I have now brought to light no less than three.

The first of these is a fragment, occupying p. ܡܗ—ܠܕ of this volume. It is taken from Add. 14,484, fol. 7 vers.—fol. 9 rect. (as at present numbered). These leaves are palimpsest, but the more ancient writing is almost wholly illegible. Our text is written in a good, current hand, apparently of the tenth century. It was left unfinished by the scribe, who stopped short in the middle of fol. 9 rect. This seems to me to be the simplest form of the Syriac text, and will probably be found to approach most nearly to the Greek.

The second Syriac recension is that which I have published, with an English translation, in the *Journal of Sacred Literature* for January and April 1865. It is taken from Add. 14,484, fol. 16 rect.—fol. 45 rect., collated with Add. 14,732, which latter is a manuscript of the thirteenth century. In this recension the work has been considerably enlarged, in particular by the addition of a lengthy introduction, narrating the pretended discovery of the book, and connecting its history with the church of St. John at Ephesus and the monastery on Mount Sinai. Ewald has written a review of my edition in the *Gött. gel. Anzeigen* for 1865 (Stück 26, p. 1018 foll.), and it is worth while to quote his opinion of the value and interest of the book. "Man kann sicher behaupten erst dieses Buch sei der feste Grund für alle die unselige Marienverehrung und hundert abergläubische Dinge geworden welche seit dem fünften Jahrhunderte immer widerstandloser in die Kirchen eindringen und so viel zur Entartung und Lähmung alles besseren Christenthumes mitgewirkt haben. Das kleine Buch ist daher für die Geschichte aller Jahrhunderte des Mittelalters von der grössten Wichtigkeit, und noch heute sollte man vieles hier zu Lernende weit bestimmter beachten als gewöhnlich geschieht. Der ganze Mariencultus der Päpstlichen Kirche beruhet auf diesem Buche: man würde ganz vergeblich eine andre Grundlage für ihn suchen, trotzdem dass es durch das *Decretum Gelasii* noch einmal in früheren Zeiten aus der Reihe der Kanonischen Bücher ausgeschlossen wurde. Die drei jährlichen Marienfeste bei welchen die Griechische Kirche bis heute stehen geblieben ist und über deren Zahl nur die Päpstliche im langen Laufe der Jahrhunderte inmer weiter hinausging, sind zuerst in diesem Buche gefordert und sogar ihren Jahrestagen nach bestimmt. Der Wahn von der unbefleckten Empfängniss Maria's welcher in unsern Tagen zum Dogma erhoben ist, findet nach S. 35, 18—21 nur

once on a time, Jesus was playing, and he sowed one measure (*h*) of wheat, and reaped a hundred cōrs (*i*) and gave them to the people of the village. (XIII.) And Jesus was eight years old; and Joseph was a carpenter, and made nothing else but ploughs and yokes. And a man had ordered of him a bed of six cubits (in length). And there was not the (proper) measure in one plank of one side, but it was shorter than the other (*j*). And the boy Jesus took the measure of the wood, and laid hold, and stretched it, and made it equal to the other. And he said to Joseph his father: "Do all that thou wishest." (XIV.) And Joseph, when he saw that he was clever, wished to teach him letters; and he brought him into the house of a scribe; and the scribe said to him: "Say Alaph," and Jesus said (it). And the scribe next wanted him to say Beth; and Jesus said to him: "Tell me first what Alaph is, and then I will tell thee concerning Beth." And the scribe took and beat him; and immediately he fell down and died; and Jesus went to his family. And Joseph called Mary his mother, and spoke to her, and ordered her not to permit him to go out of the house, that those might not die who struck him. (XV.) But a scribe said to Joseph: "Hand him over to me, and I will teach him." And Jesus entered into the scribe's house, and took a roll, and was reading, not those (things) that were written, but great miracles. (XVI.) And again, Joseph had sent his son Jacob to gather sticks, and Jesus was going with him. And whilst they were gathering sticks, a viper bit Jacob in his hand. And when Jesus came near him, he did to him nothing more but stretched out his hand to

(*h*) Heb. סְאָה. (*i*) Heb. כּוֹר.

(*j*) *Literally*, its fellow.

him and blew upon the bite, and it was healed. (XVIII.) And when Jesus was twelve years old, they went to Jerusalem, as it was the custom for Joseph and Mary to go to their festival. And when they had held (*k*) the Passover, they returned to their house. And when they had turned to come (home), Jesus remained in Jerusalem; and neither Joseph nor Mary his mother knew (it), but they thought that he was with their companions (*l*). And when they came to the halting-place of that day, they were seeking among their kinsfolk and among those whom he knew. And when they did not find Jesus, they returned to Jerusalem, and were seeking him. And after three days, they found him sitting among the teachers, and hearing from them, and answering their questions; and all who were hearing were astonished, because he was bringing these teachers to silence, for he was expounding to them the parables of the prophets and the mysteries and hard sayings which are in the law. And his mother says to him: "My son, why hast thou done to us these (things)? for we were distressed and anxious, and seeking for thee." Jesus answered and said: "Why did ye seek me? Do ye not know that it is fitting for me to be in my Father's house?" The scribes and Pharisees answered and say to Mary: "Art thou the mother of this boy? The Lord hath blessed thee; for the like of this glory and wisdom in children we have neither seen nor heard that any one has spoken." And he rose (and) went with his mother, and was subject to them. But his mother was preserving all these words. And Jesus was excelling and advancing in wisdom and in grace before God and before men. Amen.

(Here) ends the Childhood of our Lord Jesus.

(*k*) *Literally*, made. (*l*) *Literally*, the people of their company.

THE

LETTERS OF HEROD AND PILATE.

THE LETTER OF HEROD TO PILATE THE HĒGEMŌN.

Herod to Pontius Pilate the Hegemōn of Jerusalem, health!

I am in great anxiety. I write unto thee these (things), that, when thou hast heard them, thou mayest grieve for me. For as my daughter, who was dear to me, Herodia, was playing on a deep (pond) of water which was frozen over, the ice broke under her, and her whole body went down, and her head was cut off, and remained on the surface of the ice. And lo, her mother is holding her head on her knees in her lap, and my whole house is in great sorrow. For I, when I heard of the man Jesus, wished to come unto thee, and to see him alone, and hear his word, if it was like to that of the sons of men. And it is certain that, because of the many evil things which I did unto John the Baptist, and because I mocked at the Messiah, lo, I am receiving a just recompense; for I have shed much blood of other people's children upon the ground. On this account, the judgments of God are just; for every man receives according to his thought. But thou, because thou hast been deemed worthy to see the God-man, on this account it is fitting for thee to pray for me. And my son Azbonius is in the agony of the hour of death. And I too am in affliction and great trial. For I have got the dropsy (*a*), and am in great distress (*b*); because I persecuted the opener of the

(*a*) *Literally*, have collected water.

(*b*) *Literally*, deficiency (of water), drought.

baptism of water, who was John. Because of these things, my brother, the judgments of God are just. And my wife too, through all the grief for her daughter, her left eye has become blind; because we wished to make blind the eye of righteousness. There is no peace to the doers of iniquities, saith the Lord. For from now great affliction is coming upon the priests and upon the writers of the law, because they delivered unto thee the Just One. For this is the consummation of the world, that they consented that the Gentiles should become heirs. For the children of light shall be cast out; for they have not observed the things which were preached concerning the Lord and his Son. Because of this, gird up thy loins and receive righteousness, being mindful, thou with thy wife, by night and by day, of Jesus; and of you Gentiles shall be the kingdom, for we the (chosen) people have mocked at the Righteous One. But if there be a place for our petition, O Pilate, because we were in power at one time, bury my household with care; for it is right that we should be buried by thee rather than by the priests, whom, after a short time, as the Scripture says, at the coming of Jesus the Messiah, vengeance shall overtake. Mayest thou be well, along with Procla thy wife! I send thee the earrings of my daughter and my own signet-ring, that they may be in thy possession a memorial of me after death; for the worms have already begun to issue forth from my body, and lo, I am receiving judgment in this world, and dreading the judgment that is to come. For in both we stand before the works of the living God; but this judgment, the one in this world, is temporary, whilst that which is to come is an everlasting judgment.

(Here) ends the letter to Pilate the Hēgemōn.

Pilate to Herod the Tetrarch, health!

Know and see, that in that day when thou deliveredst unto me Jesus, I had compassion on myself, and testified by the washing of my hands (that I was free) from (the blood of) him who rose from the grave after three days; but I did on him thy pleasure, as thou wishedst that I should join with thee in crucifying him. But now I learned from the executioners, and from the soldiers who were watching his tomb, that he rose from the grave; and above all I made quite sure of what was told me, that he was seen in the body in Galilee, with the same form, the same voice, the same doctrines, and the same disciples, having changed nothing, but preaching boldly his resurrection and the everlasting kingdom. And lo, heaven and earth were rejoicing; and lo, my wife Procla was believing (in him) through those visions which appeared to her, when thou didst send (me word) to deliver up Jesus to the people of Israel, because of their ill will (against him). And now when Procla my wife (*a*) heard that Jesus was risen, and had been seen in Galilee, she took with her Longinus the centurion and the twelve soldiers who watched the tomb, and went forth, as it were to a great sight, to welcome the person of the Messiah. And she saw him along with his disciples. And whilst they were standing in astonishment looking upon him, he looked upon them and said to them: "What is it? Do ye believe on me? Know, Procla, that in the testament which God gave to the fathers, it is said, that every body

(*a*) The Syriac text has "his wife."

which had perished, should live by means of my death, which ye have seen. And now ye see that I am alive, whom ye crucified; and many things did I bear, until I was laid in the tomb. And now, listen to me, and believe in God my Father who is with me. For I have burst (*b*) the bands of death, and have broken open the gates of Sheōl, and (it is) my coming which is to be (hereafter)." And when my wife Procla and the soldiers (*c*) heard these things, they came (and) told me, weeping, because they too had been against him, when they were plotting the evil things which they had done unto him ; so that I too upon my bed am in distress, and put on a garment of sorrow, and take to me fifty soldiers along with my wife, and go unto Galilee. And as I was going on the road, I was testifying these things, that Herod did these things with me, who planned along with me and constrained me to arm my hands against Him, and to judge the Judge of all, and to scourge the Just One, the Lord of the just. And when we drew nigh unto him, O Herod, a great voice was heard from heaven, and terrible thunder, and the earth trembled and gave forth a sweet smell, the like of which was never seen even in the temple of Jerusalem. But when I stood on the way, our Lord saw me, as he was standing and talking with the disciples. But I prayed in my heart, for I knew that this was he whom ye delivered unto me, that this was the Lord of created things, and the Creator of all. But we, when we saw him, all of us fell upon our faces before his feet. And I was saying with a loud voice: "I have sinned, Lord, in that I sat and judged Thee, that avengest all in truth. And lo, I know that Thou art God, the Son of God, and thy Manhood have I seen, but not thy

(*b*) *Literally*, opened. (*c*) *Literally*, the Romans.

Godhead. But Herod with the children of Israel compelled me to do evil unto thee. Have pity, therefore, upon me, God of Israel." And my wife in great tribulation said; "God of heaven and earth, God of Israel, reward me not according to the deeds of Pontius Pilate, nor according to the will of the children of Israel, nor according to the thoughts of the sons of the priests; but remember my husband in Thy glory." And our Lord drew nigh and raised up me and my wife and the soldiers; and I looked upon him and saw that there were on him the scars of his cross. And he said: "That which all the just fathers hoped to receive, and did not see, (thou hast seen); in thy time the Lord of time, the Son of man, the Son of the Exalted One, who is from all time, has risen from the grave, and is glorified on high by all that he has created and established, for ever and ever."

Justinus, one of the writers who were in the days of Augustus and Tiberius and Gaius (Caligula), wrote in his third discourse: "Mary the Galilæan, she who bore the Messiah, who was crucified in Jerusalem, had not belonged to a man; and Joseph did not forsake her; but Joseph remained in purity without a wife, he and his five sons by a former wife; and Mary remained without a husband."

Theodorus wrote to Pilate the Hēgemōn: "Who was the man, concerning whom there was a complaint before thee, that he was crucified by the people of Palestine? If many demanded this justly, why didst thou not agree to their just demand? (*d*) And if they demanded this unjustly, why didst thou transgress the law and order something that was far from justice?" Pilate sent him (answer): "Because he was doing signs, I did not wish to crucify

(*d*) *Literally*, their justice.

him; and because his accusers said, 'he calls himself a king,' I crucified him."

Josephus says: "When king Agrippa put on a robe that was woven with silver, and beheld the spectacles in the theatre of Cæsareia, when the people saw that his robes flashed (like lightning), they said to him: 'Till now we were afraid of thee as of a man; henceforth thou art exalted above the nature of mortals.' And he saw an angel standing over him, and he smote him as it were to death."

(Here) ends the letter of Pilate to Herod.

THE

HISTORY OF THE VIRGIN MARY,

THE HOLY MOTHER OF GOD.

To our beloved and believing brethren throughout the whole world, who are zealous after excellence, and seek the work of life, and cleave unto the love of God at all times, and are prisoners of his mercy; peace and grace be with you from God our Father, and from our Lord Jesus the Messiah, and His Holy Spirit. Amen, Amen. We make known to the children of the mystery of faith, that the Word of Life, which was with the Father, truly came into the world, and was born of a woman by a great miracle; and went about the streets as a child, to the confirmation of His incarnation; and received the education of growth, after the manner of all the sons of men; and trod the path of baptism, and of fasting, and of working of miracles, for all His true disciples; and tasted willingly of suffering, and death, and burial, without any phantasy or error; and rose with glory from the grave, without having seen corruption in Sheōl; and took upon Himself the humiliations of our race, that He might exalt us unto His Father; and ascended with victory to heaven, with great glory and a vast host of angels. And of all these things we are witnesses, and we know that our testimony is true; because we have seen with our eyes, and felt with our hands. And to every one who believes these things, there is life for ever in His Person, because He is life and truth and light. And we were thus commanded by Him, before He was raised up to heaven: "Go, teach, and baptize all nations, in the name of the Father and the Son and the Holy Spirit." Also He sent to us the gift of the Holy Spirit, as He promised when He was going up. And from that time we were scattered through all countries, to preach the Gospel of His kingdom. But Mary His mother, after all these things, was continuing in great sorrow, and was constant in prayer every hour at the tomb and Golgotha. And she was much hated by the people of the crucifiers, and many a time too they were going to kill her. And they set watchers for themselves beside the grave, and said with much eagerness: "If she goes out thither to pray, let her be stoned by you with stones, because she is a mocker at Israel." She was the daughter of Joachim, who was the seed of Nathan the son of David, of the tribe of Judah; and her mother was called Hannah; and her own name was Mary. And on a Friday she took a thurible and incense, and went forth in sorrow to the tomb. And when she had prayed for a long while, she thus spoke: "My Lord (*Rabbūlī*, רַבּוּנִי) the Messiah, whom I have in Heaven, send (and) take me from this world; for lo, the Jews want to stone me." And the moment that her prayer had gone up to heaven, the angel of the Lord came down to her, and thus he spoke to her: "Hail to thee, mother of God! for thy prayer is heard in heaven before thy Son, Jesus the Messiah; and within a few days of this time thou shalt leave this world, as thou hast asked." And when he had said these things to her, he departed from her; and a great wonder seized the watchmen who were standing and looking on, so that they said, "We can do nothing to her." But when she had returned to her house, they went into Jerusalem and said to the priests: "Mary came to-day (and) prayed beside the tomb; and we saw clearly the angel of the Lord, who was speaking with her; and for this reason we were not able even to speak to her; and now do whatever is good in your eyes." And when the Jews heard this, they spoke to the Hēgemōn of that place, whose name was Sabinus, whom Tiberius the emperor of the Romans had placed there, and said: "We beg of thee, my Lord Hēgemōn, send (and) order Mary not to go out to pray by the grave and Golgotha. It is enough for her that all Jerusalem is agitated by the child whom she bore, that there should not be strife and mischief among us and in our city because of her." The Hêgemōn says: "Do ye go and order her what ye please." And they, when they had gone to her, say to her: "Mary, remember the sins which have been committed by thee before God, and do not lead people astray and say, that he who was born of thee is the Son of God; because heaven and earth testify that he is the son of Joseph the carpenter. But enter into the synagogue, and hearken to the law of Moses. And we will lay upon thee a Torah, and absolve thee of thy sins. And we will blow a trumpet in thy ears, and thou shalt be cured of thy obstinate will. But if thou dost not agree to these things, go forth from Jerusalem, and do not go again to the tomb and to Golgotha; because the Hēgemōn has commanded thus." Mary says to them: "It was not right that ye should come to me with these words, because I will not hear your words, and will not receive your order. But this I do of my own will, for I have no desire to dwell longer in your city." And the Jews returned to their houses, because the evening arrived.

Then she called the women of her neighbourhood, and says to them: "The Jews say to me that they will not permit me to dwell in Jerusalem, and therefore I am going forth to Bethlehem to my own house. But, if there be (any) among you who wishes to go with me, let her come." For three virgins were dwelling with her constantly, who were the daughters of chief men and rulers of Jerusalem. One of whom was the daughter of Nicodemus, the friend of the Messiah, and her name was Callĕthā; by whose name is described the Church, the betrothed of the Son of God. And another was the daughter of Gamaliel, the chief of the synagogue and the teacher of the Law, and her name was Neshrā; and by the likeness of the eagle is typified the King the Messiah, who bears upon His wings the Holy Church. And the other was the daughter of a (man of) comitian (rank), of the family of Archelaus, and her name was Ṭābĕthā, for Ṭābĕthā (the good) is an epithet of the Holy Spirit, by which life is given to men and all good gifts. These were the names of the virgins who were dwelling with Mary the mother of our Lord, Callĕthā, and Neshrā, and Ṭābĕthā. And the three of them answered and said to her: "Thou knowest, my Lady, that on thy account we have left our fathers and brothers and all that we have, and with thee we wish to live, and we will not leave thee till we die." Then she stretched out her hand to heaven, and blessed them, and said to them: "My prayer will be received before my Master, whom I have in heaven; because of all the families of Israel you alone have done me pleasure." And they arose quickly, and went forth to Bethlehem. And there she prayed, and thus she said: "My Master the Messiah! hearken to the voice of Thy mother, and come to me, Thou and the Apostles, Thy disciples, that I may see ye before I die. And by this I shall know that Thou hearest me whenever I pray unto Thee." When she had finished her prayer, John was in Ephesus; and the Holy Spirit informed him, as he was going in to pray in the church of Ephesus, and said to him: "The time is near for the mother of thy Lord to depart from this world, and she desires much to see thee; but make haste and go to her to Bethlehem. And lo, I will send thither all the Apostles thy fellows." Then John prayed and said: "Our Lord Jesus the Messiah, Son of the blessed God, give my feet strength that I may go to Thy mother to Bethlehem, and see her before she dies." And when his prayer was not yet finished, the Holy Spirit placed him on a cloud of light, and he arrived speedily at Bethlehem. And when he entered into the chamber in which Mary was, he found her lying on the bed. And he drew near and kissed her on her knees, and said: "Hail to thee, mother of God; and hail to the Messiah, who was born of thee, who has deemed me worthy to behold thee. Be not grieved; because thou art departing from this world with great glory." And when she heard these (words), she was filled with great joy; and she answered and said to John: "My son, the Jews have sworn oaths, that, when I am dead, they will burn me with fire." John says to her: "Our Lord Jesus the Messiah, thy Son, standeth for thee." And the tears of both of them flowed over from weeping; and the three virgins too were standing apart and weeping. John says to her: "If thou, who art the mother of God, art so grieved because thou art leaving this world, what shall sinners do, and those who have not kept the commandments of God?" Then the Holy Spirit informed us in all the regions in which we were, and says to us: "The time is near for the mother of your Lord to leave this world; but rise, go to her to Bethlehem." To Simon (Peter) It made this known in Rome; and to Paul at Tiberias; and to Thomas in India; and to Matthew at Bērȳtus (Beirūt); and to Bartholomew in Armenia; and to Thaddæus at Laodicea; and to James in the cave of Zion. But Andrew, the brother of Simon, and James, the brother of John, and Philip, and Simon the Cananite, and Matthew, who became an apostle in the place of Judas Iscariot, these five were dead. And the Holy Spirit awoke them, and said to them: "Rise, but do not think that the resurrection is come; but on this account do ye rise, that ye may go to Bethlehem to the mother of your Lord, who is departing from the world, and asks to see you." And as we were standing (perplexed) by many thoughts, how we might go to Bethlehem, each of us from where he was, our Lord sent us swift steeds and clouds of light. And we were carried away by the Holy Spirit, and came to Bethlehem. And Mary, when she knew that we were come to her, rose up joyfully to meet us from the bed on which she was lying, and says to us: "Blessed be the Lord, who has fulfilled my desire, and sent you to me, that I may see you and rejoice before I die. Now I know that my Master will come, and I shall see Him, and then I shall die. But I wish you to tell me, who told you that I am dying, and how ye came, that ye are arrived so quickly." We all say to John: "Do thou speak first, because thou camest first." John says: "I was standing by the altar of the Lord, which is in the church of Ephesus, when the Holy Spirit announced unto me, 'The time is near for the mother of thy Lord to leave this world, but make haste, (and) go to her to Bethlehem.' And immediately"

✣ ✣ ✣ ✣ ✣

✣ ✣ ✣ ✣

✣ ✣ ✣ ✣ ✣

✣ ✣ ✣ ✣

✣ ✣ ✣ ✣ ✣

"which are more than of all of them." The unbelievers say: "Whence do ye show to us that the son of Mary is the Messiah?" The lovers of the Messiah say: "We are showing it." The Judge says: "Not with (high) words nor with disturbance are ye to speak one against another, but gently (and) from your books, for I too am desirous to know how your wisdom is." The lovers of the Messiah say: "Adam, when dying, commanded his son Seth in his testament, and said to him: 'My son Seth, lo! offerings are placed in the cave of treasures, gold and myrrh and frankincense; and the Messiah is about to come and to be taken by wicked men and to die; and through his death (there shall be) resurrection to all the sons of men; and he shall rise in three days, and shall take my body up with him to heaven. And lo! the Magi shall come from Persia, and take this testament and these offerings, and go to Bethlehem of Judah, and worship the Messiah who is born of the virgin.' And so it was. And the Magi came and brought these offerings and testament with them. And from the testament of Adam all mankind have learned to make testaments; and from the Messiah, who was born of Mary, all mankind, who were in darkness, have received light. From Adam to Seth letters were written, and fathers gave (them) to sons, and sons gave (them) to sons' sons, down to Abraham, all mankind going on and saying, 'the Messiah shall come and shall be born in Bethlehem.' We then are not ashamed of what we say." The unbelievers say: "Is the son of Mary better than Abraham, who called on God, and He opened the heavens and spoke with him as men speak one with another?" The lovers of the Messiah say: "Ye see that ye know nothing! For we, who are lovers of the Messiah, know that the Messiah, the son of Mary, created Abraham, ere yet He was formed in His mother's womb." The unbelievers say: "Is the Messiah, of whom ye are proud, better than Isaac, who became an offering, and the savour of his offering went up, and heaven and earth were gladdened by it?" The lovers of the Messiah say: "Isaac's not being slain on the altar (depended) entirely on (this), that it was about to be that the Messiah, who is (born) of Mary, should come and die for all, and save the world from error. For if Isaac had died, one offering would have been offered; but when the Messiah died, the offerings of all creatures were offered to God in Him." The unbelievers say: "Is the Messiah better than Jacob, the like of whose vision men have never seen? Who went up (and) slept on Mount Gilead, and God opened the heavens and spoke with him, and stretched a ladder from heaven to earth, so that, if he had wished, he might have gone up by it; and the angels came down to greet him." The lovers of the Messiah say: "Both Jacob, and the ladder, and the angels whom he saw, are types of the coming of the Messiah and of the mystery of His death." The unbelievers say to the lovers of the Messiah: "The ascent of Elias to heaven puts you to shame, for every thing that he says is obeyed in heaven, and every thing that he wishes is done on earth." The lovers of the Messiah say: "Elias went up in a whirlwind to this heaven in which are fixed the sun and moon, and no man worshipped him in his ascent except Elisha his disciple. But the Messiah, when He went up, went up not merely to one heaven, but He went up above all the heavens; and lo! He sits at the right hand of His Father, and all creatures that are above and below, bow their heads and worship Him and glorify Him for ever; for no man ever went up to heaven except Him who came down from it, who is the Messiah, the Son of God, who was born of Mary." The unbelievers say: "Let Moses the prophet come, and his miracles, with which he chastised Pharaoh and delivered Israel; and when Pharaoh wished to hinder Israel, when he came to the sea, Moses lifted up a dry staff and restrained the waves of the sea in heaps." The lovers of the Messiah say: "Jesus too, who was born of Mary, rebuked evil spirits, and they were scattered before Him; and to Peter, when the sea was swallowing him up, He stretched out His hand and lifted him up; and if He had not had power over the sea and the land, whence would all these have obeyed Him?" The unbelievers say: "We are not able to dispute with you, because ye are imbued with (*a*) the doctrine of the Son of Mary, and if ye were to dispute with Satan, ye would overcome him." The lovers of the Messiah say: "Ye have not said a single word in which there is conviction (*b*), nor do ye carry off the victory." The unbelievers say: "Neither David the son of Jesse, nor Elisha the son of Shaphat, who brought to life the dead after he had lain down by him in the grave, nor Enoch, who was removed and did not taste of death—there is none who is

(*a*) *Literally*, have tasted of. (*b*) *Literally*, rest.

so excellent as Jesus the son of Mary." The lovers of the Messiah say: "Neither in heaven nor on earth is is there (any) who is more excellent than Jesus, who was born of Mary, and His exalted Father, who sent Him for our deliverance, and His Holy Spirit; and thus we confess and cry out, and our children and our dead from the graves testify along with us at this time, that the Messiah, who is (born) of Mary, was about to come, and Him all creatures were expecting, in whom light arose for us, and as soon as He was born of Mary, He annihilated the power of Satan; and the like of the miracles and mighty deeds and healings and cures which He wrought, no tongue can speak, nor mouth explain, nor can those above nor those below say what the Messiah, the Son of God, did in the world."

Then the judge commanded, and six men of the unbelievers were severely scourged. And after they were scourged, the lovers of the Messiah said: "Do ye then wish to escape with impunity? (c) We will show you what we shall do. We will reveal all the frauds which have been (done) in Jerusalem, before this just Hēgemōn, whom our Lord hath sent to demand at our hands the ignominy of Jesus, whom we crucified." The judge says to the lovers of the Messiah: "Say whatever ye wish, and be not afraid." They say: "Where is the cross concealed, on which He has crucified? and where are the nails which were fixed in His hands? and the sponge, in which we offered Him vinegar? and the spear with which He was pierced? and the crown of thorns, which we placed on His head? and the robes of infamy, with which we clothed Him, where are they concealed?" The Hēge-

(c) *Literally*, to prevail.

mōn says to the unbelievers: "Speak, and disclose what they say to you." They say: "They too, my Lord, know where they are." But the judge when he saw (this), stood up on his tribunal, and made those swear who confessed our Lord, and said: "By the Messiah, who was born of Mary, and in whom ye believe, and in whom I too believe, say what ye know concerning the Messiah." Then the lovers of the Messiah cried out and said with one voice: "O wise judge! Woe to us from the judgments of the Messiah, when He comes to judge the world! Woe to us from Thy hands, Thou Son of Mary, whom we have slain! Woe to us, how we have injured Thee! And not Thee only have we injured, but also the Father, who sent Thee to the world." The Hēgemōn says: "Disclose to me, where the cross is, on which He was crucified, and the crown of thorns, and the spear with which He was pierced, and the robes which He had on." They say: "My Lord, these robes which He wore, we cast lots upon them, and they came to one; and we took them, and folded them up, and placed them beside His cross, and dug a deep hole in the ground, about thirty cubits. And we wrote upon the cross of Jesus, and placed it a little way off from the crosses of the thieves; and we placed a small stone between them, and heaped upon them earth and stones; and they were well concealed. And opposite the head of the cross of Jesus, we made an aperture hollowed out through the midst of the earth, so that a man's hand might reach the head of our Lord's cross; and when an affliction comes upon any one of us, he that is sick stretches out the tip of his finger, and if it reaches it (*viz.* the cross), he is cured. May God prolong thy days, illustrious Hēgemōn! Lo, there are ten thousand five hundred and two souls, whom we know, and whose names are written down, men, women and children, whom the cross of the Son of Mary has healed and saved from death, who are of the populace of Jerusalem. And when we see a man who is sick, we go thither with him, and he stretches out his hand through that opening and is healed. And if any one has a sick person in his house, and takes some of that dust, and goes and casts it upon him, he is healed. And whosoever was healed, we used to take a fee from him. And it was enjoined unto us, that whosoever should reveal this secret, should be cast out from among us with his whole family; and that he who revealed it should be slain. And we said among ourselves, 'If a man be questioned, let him say, we have in that place a pot of the manna, and of the water of trial, and the staff of Aaron, and these things give help to every one who goes thither.' O illustrious judge! fetch Jonadab and scourge him, because he has in his house one nail of those which we fastened in the Messiah, concealed for himself; and he has saved from death by it more than 550 souls, and has become very rich, so that he does not know what he owns. For which of the prophets and of the fathers did wonders, and healed, and brought to life, and delivered from death, like the cross of the Messiah, or like a single nail that we fastened in His hands? How much more then shall that Jesus, who was crucified upon it, give aid to every one who believes in Him? Come, let us raise up His cross from the dust in which it is hidden; and from the ends to the ends of the earth let peoples and tongues come and worship the cross of the Son of God, who gives life to all living things that believe on Him." The judge says; "Great is the thing that was concealed among you; and because ye were angry with one another, ye have revealed it. If the king hears it, he will take off all your heads. Come, show me where these nails are hidden, and where ye have made that aperture over the head of our Lord's cross." And they went and showed him. He says to them: "What shall I do for you now?" They say to him: "Command, my Lord, and let these crosses be taken up; and let the cross of our Lord be placed in the temple of Jerusalem, and be worshipped by all mankind." The Hēgemōn says: "I am not ordered by the king to do this, but I will put you to shame before all men; for I will not go near the cross of the Messiah; for He who was crucified upon it, will bring it forth from the earth in which it is hidden." And he gave orders, and brought large stones; and they heaped (them) upon the place in which these crosses were hidden, as it were ten times the height of a man, so that no help might come forth from that aperture to the children of Israel. And those who believed said to the Hēgemōn: "Give orders, my Lord, and let thirty of the chief men of the city of Jerusalem come, and scourge them, because of the ignominy of our Lord, and because they have spoken ill of the blessed (virgin) before thee." And the judge was silent, and made no answer; and the day declined; and the judge passed the night in the Prætorium in anger. And the cock crew, and the Hēgemōn went forth, he and his two young men and his son along with him; and his son had the disease of the gravel (and a disease) of the bowels. And he went and knocked at the door of my lady Mary, and her waiting-maid came out; and he said to her: "Go in and tell thy mistress, the Hēgemōn of this city wishes to worship thee." And she gave orders, and he came in and worshipped before her and kissed her feet, and cried out and said: "Hail to thee, virgin Mother of God! and hail to the Child, who was born of thee! Hail to the heavens, which bear the holy throne of thy Son, on which His Godhead is exalted. Mouth and tongue are too feeble to recount thy praises, O holy Virgin! The earth on which thou walkest, becomes heaven. The heaven that beholds thee, gives a blessing to the creatures that believe in thee. The healthy who behold thy chastity, receive gladness. The sick who come unto thee, receive help. I worship thee, Mary, the mistress of the world. Stretch out thy hand and bless me, me and also this only (child) whom God hath given (me); and pray for the souls whom I have at Rome, that I may go in peace, and see (them), and rejoice with them; and that I may carry presents and offerings, and come and worship thee, the mother of God." Now Mary was standing and praying, the censer of incense being placed before her; and when she heard the words of the judge, she finished her prayer, and turned to him, and stretched out her hand and blessed him, him and his son, and said to him, "Sit down." Now the apostles of our Lord were there in the house, and were thinking that it was day. And when they came out and looked at the sky, they saw that at that moment the cock had crowed. And the judge ran and fell at the feet of the apostles, and said to them: "Peace be with you, ye chosen (ones), who were chosen before the foundations of the world! and (hail) to your Master, who chose you to be His heralds!" The apostles say: "We have heard what thou hast done to the crucifiers, and we have prayed much for thee." The Hēgemōn says: "Enough for them is the scorn they are become before God and before men." The apostles say: "And what have they done that is not to their disgrace? But now we tell thee, that lo! it is sixteen years that we have gone forth proclaiming the gospel and the preaching of our Lord Jesus the Messiah in all regions. And when each one of us was proclaiming His preaching in the place to which he was sent, the time arrived for this blessed (one) to depart from this world. And without our perceiving it, or any one telling us, the Holy Spirit revealed to each of us, 'The time is near for the mother of thy Lord to depart from this world; go to her unto Bethlehem.' And when each of us heard (this), he was in much perplexity, because we were preaching at the ends of the earth. And each of us said to himself: 'Whence shall I get a swift steed? that I may go without delay, before she dies whilst I am going?' And when this thought arose in our hearts, the Holy Spirit made (it) known to each of us, and a cloud of light was placed in a chariot, and in the midst of the chariot was set a throne, covered with glory. And when the Holy Spirit drew near, It said to him: 'Behold the steeds that your Lord hath sent you from heaven. Rise, sit upon them, and go to His mother unto Bethlehem.' And accordingly Peter ascended with haste into the chariot, and stood in the air between heaven and earth, looking at the apostles who were coming to him. And as he was standing, the apostles came from the four quarters of the world unto him; and those who were dead, were raised, and came along with those who were alive, to worship the holy (one). Thus we came from those places in chariots guided by reins, and on clouds of glory we entered Bethlehem with troops of angels, and worshipped the blessed (one); because God, who was born of her, commanded us, who chose us before the foundations of the world, that we might be preachers concerning His living words and concerning the wonders which He showed. And He sent and fetched us according to His will, that with our testimony He might crown His mother, and we might see and assert that this is the woman who gave birth to God. And we came to Bethlehem, and they stirred up the people of Jerusalem against us. And the Holy Spirit said to us: 'Do not go anywhere, lest the Jews should think that ye are afraid of them.' And It brought us to Jerusalem, and no man saw us, and we entered in here, because we carried the holy (one) on her bed, and the Holy Spirit carried us; and glorious robes of flame were spread over us. And after we were here, our Lord willed to disclose the glory which He was preparing for His mother; and the angels of the Lord were seen going in and coming out to salute the blessed one. And there was a great tumult, that the Jews might be put to shame, and the Son of God and His mother be glorified."

These things the Apostles spoke to the judge, when he went and worshipped them. And again the judge besought the blessed one and said: "I beg of thee, my lady, that I may learn of thee, how God, who came into the world, dwelt in thy virginity." The blessed one says to him: "Hear and receive my words, and give glory to God, who sent His only (Son) from the heaven of His glory, and He dwelt in me. I do not know whence He entered into the palace of my members, but, as I was sitting in my house and making coverings for the door of the temple of the Lord, on the first day of the week, at the ninth hour, an angel opened (heaven) and descended unto me. And a light shone through the whole house in which I was sitting, and he said to me: 'Hail to thee, thou blessed among women! My Lord is with thee, and will rise from thèe (like the sun).' And a sweet odour was diffused through the whole house; and the foundations of the house too sent forth waves of odours through the whole quarter. And after the salutation with which he announced (this) to me, he departed from me. And I arose, and set forth incense, and fell on my face, and glorified the name of the grace of my Lord, that I had seen a wonder like this; for, from the time that I was born into the world, and came forth from my mother's womb, no man knew me, and I saw not the way of women. And He was born of me like a man, and was reared up like the children of Adam, and like an infant in the streets and like a child He ran about, and showed miracles and wrought wonders, and walked in the world like God, and every thing that He said to me, He began and He finished. And I saw that men were not able to do the miracles which He did. And the envious Jews took Him, and crucified Him, and slew Him; and He was placed in the grave, and raised Himself up, and rose and appeared to His disciples, working the wonders and miracles of His glorious Father; and He ascended to heaven to His Father; and if the Jews do not believe in Him, I and Joseph the carpenter and His disciples believe in Him, that He is the Messiah the Son of the living God; and I assert and believe that He who was born of me shall come and demand His blood of His crucifiers. And He used to say to me that, Hwhen e removed from the world, He would come to me with troops of angels; and as He has assembled His disciples from the four quarters, I accordingly am expecting Him to come, that I may see Him, and to place His hand on my eyes, and to take me out of the wicked world, and hide my body and carry my spirit away in safety whithersoever He pleases."

These things spoke the blessed Mary to the Hēgemōn and before the Apostles, and he believed much in Mary, and drew near and cast down his son before her and said to her: "I beg of thee, mother of God, heal this only son of mine, who is tortured by cruel diseases." And the holy one stretched out her hand, and made the sign of the cross on the boy, and spoke thus: "In the name of my Master, whom I have in heaven, let him be healed." And straightway the boy was cured by the prayer of Mary. And the judge went away from beside the holy Mary, and wrote down all the miracles and wonders which the mother of God had done. For the mouth of man is not able to recount the wonders and cures which the blessed one did in the world.

And the Hēgemōn was dismissed, and went from the city to Rome, and went in unto the Emperor and the nobles, and related to them all the miracles and wonders which Mary did in Jerusalem and Bethlehem. And the disciples of Peter and Paul went to Rome and wrote down whatever they heard from the judge, who had gone up to Rome from Jerusalem. And they also wrote letters and sent them to all who were in the West, to Mount Sinai, and Egypt, and to Thebais, and Pontus, and Asia; and they wrote in their letters that great was the glory with which she departed from this world. And they also wrote to their teachers Peter and Paul, (saying:) "When ye have buried the holy one, let the book of her glorious deeds come with you to Rome, for lo! the ends and quarters (of the world) are full of her glories, and people believe much in her, because, since the judge came from beside her, he has narrated here concerning her, and whoever confesses her, she helps him greatly and every one who calls on her.

The wonders which the blessed one wrought. She appeared on the sea, when it was troubled and raised itself to destroy all that was on it; and the sailors called on the name of the blessed one and said: "My Lady Mary, mother of God, have mercy on us;" and she rose like the sun and delivered ninety-two ships and the souls that were in them, and none of them perished. And she appeared by day on a mountain, where robbers had fallen on the brethren to slay them; and they cried out, "Mother of God, help us;" and the holy one came and smote the eyes of the robbers, and they were blinded; and these escaped and were not injured. And she appeared to a widow woman, whose son had fallen into a well of water; and she screamed out and said, "Mother of God, have mercy on me;" and the holy one came and snatched him out of the well, and gave him to his mother, and he was not hurt. And again she appeared in Rome to a man who had been sick sixteen years, and no one cured him; and he took a censer and cast into it incense, and said, "My Lady Mary, mother of God, help me;" and at that moment she appeared to him, and he was healed, and stood up, and went to the church before the whole people. And again she appeared to two women, who were going along the road, and a black snake came out upon them to devour them; and they screamed out, "Mother of God, save us!" and at that moment it split open from its head downwards, and they were not injured. And again she appeared to a merchant, who had borrowed a thousand drachms to go and trade with them; and as he was sitting, eating bread, he arose and his purse (dropped) from him (and) was lost; and he cried out, "Mother of God, help me;" and at that moment he found himself standing over his purse; and he departed rejoicing.

And whilst she was doing these things in Rome, the Apostles were beside her in Jerusalem. And when the morning of Friday dawned, the Holy Spirit revealed unto the Apostles: "Take up the holy one and go forth from Jerusalem by the road that leads out to the head of the valley beside the Mount of Olives. And lo, there are three caves, one within another; and in the innermost there is a raised seat (*or* bench) on the right hand. There go and place the holy one, until it be told you (what to do). And they arose in the morning, and took up the blessed one; and the Jews were looking on and saying: "The disciples of the seducer are carrying Mary and going away." And the blessed one was looking upon them. And the Jews made signs one to another and said: "Lo, Mary thinks that she has conquered (us), and goes forth from Jerusalem." And there was there a man whose name was Yūphanyā (Jephunneh), both tall and handsome of figure. And the elders of Israel said to him: "Come near; Yūphanyā; blow upon Mary, and she will fall down with her bed (litter); for she thinks that she has conquered and goes forth from Jerusalem." And Yūphanyā ran up with violence and cast his arms upon the litter of the blessed one that it might break, and hung on by it that it might fall, and the Jews might come and burn it. And when Yūphanyā cast his arms (on it), an angel of fire smote him with a sword of fire, and cut off both his arms from his armpits. And he was crying out and saying: "Ye Apostles of the Messiah, have pity upon me." The Apostles say: "Why callest thou on *us*? Call on my Lady Mary, whose litter thou didst wish to break." Yūphanyā says: "Mother of God, have mercy on me." The holy one says: "Give him his arms." And Peter drew near, and took up the arms of Yūphanyā; and when he had spat on one of them, he said: "In the name of Mary, cleave to thy place." And he fastened them, and he was healed. And Peter took a staff which he was holding, and gave it to Yūphanyā, and said: "Do thou too go (and) show a great miracle with this staff to the Jews; perhaps they may be ashamed; and tell of the holy one, what she hath done for thee." And Yūphanyā went and fell down before the blessed one, and said to her: "Pray for me, that I may go forth (and) preach among the Jewish tribes, and chide them for their disbelief in thee and in thy holy Son." And he began to bless the holy one in the Hebrew tongue, citing texts from the Law and from the Prophets, until the Apostles were astonished.

And Yūphanyā went away and arrived at the gate of the city, and struck the dry staff on the threshold of the gate of the city; and straightway it put out leaves and produced twigs. And the Jews saw the staff that it budded, and were ashamed. And Yūphanyā cried out and said: "Blessed is the Messiah, who was born of Mary." The Jews say: "What hath befallen thee, Yūphanyā?" But he said: "This hath befallen me, that I am become a disciple of the Son of God and of Mary His mother; for my arms were severed from me, and I begged them of her, and she gave them to me; and when Peter had spat upon them he said: 'In the name of Mary, cleave to your place;' and he made them cleave unto me, and I was healed; and he gave me this staff, which has budded. And now I believe that she gave birth to the Son of God." The Jews say to him: "Verily thou art mad, Yūphanyā." But he said: "Ay, I am mad! Come (and) see what the dry staff can do." They say to him: "What can it do?" He says: "Thus Peter commanded me: 'Every sick man on whom thou layest this staff, shall be healed.'" And Yūphanyā went in and laid it on a blind man, and he saw the light; and every sick man on whom he laid the staff, was healed. And he commanded every sick man who was cured to cry out: "Blessed be Mary, and blessed be her Holy Son." And Yūphanyā was healing all the sick and afflicted that were in Jerusalem.

And when the Apostles had gone to the caves that were at the head of the valley, they entered and found in the innermost one a seat (*or* bench) of clay, and placed the couch of the Blessed One (on it) . . . .

⁘ ⁘ ⁘ ⁘ ⁘

⁘ ⁘ ⁘ ⁘

⁘ ⁘ ⁘ ⁘ ⁘

and assemblies of spiritual beings, whose troops were without numbers, and their ranks without end, who were coming and praising, band by band; and every tongue in its own language was crying glory; and they were hovering over the blessed Mary. And the chariots were coming last, one of Moses, and one of Enoch, and one of Elias; and then the blessed chariot of our Lord was coming after them. And heaven and earth were praising on that day; and the dead, who were buried, gave glory from their graves. And a pleasant and sweet odour went forth from the highest heavens of His glory to all parts of creation. And they carried the blessed one to Paradise with this glory, and her holy body was placed there. And when she was carried up and reached the gate of Paradise, the sword that surrounds Paradise was taken away, and the holy one went in with glory that is unspeakable into Paradise, the celestials and terrestrials being intermingled. And they placed her in boundless light amid the delicious trees of the Paradise of Eden; and they exalted her with glory on which the eye of flesh is not able to gaze. And our Life-giver stretched out His hand and blessed Mary; and He was raised up from beside her to His glorious Father, and His promise is life to all those who believe in Him.

Then the twelve Apostles returned to the Mount of Olives in the same clouds of light, and went and kneeled down and prayed, thinking and saying: "Great is the glory which our eyes have beheld at the departure of the blessed one." And again they prayed and said: "Lord, give unto us that we may command the people and nations concerning the commemoration of Thy mother, that they may make unto her commemorations and offerings from year to year; because we know that every one who makes unto her an offering and takes refuge with her before Thee, when he cries unto Thee, Thou wilt answer him; for there is no other God but Thee, who art worshipped and glorified along with Thy Father and Thy Holy Spirit for ever and ever. Amen. Happy are they who make a commemoration of the mother who bore Thee; and happy are we, who have been deemed worthy to be blessed by her, and have seen glorious things. Therefore, Lord, as Thy Holy Spirit promised us and said, do Thou give us power on the last day, when Thou comest, that we may sit on twelve thrones and judge the twelve tribes of Israel, who have not believed in Thee, nor in the mother who bore Thee. And let us confess the glorious Trinity, Father and Son and Holy Spirit, for ever and ever, Amen." And may Thy mercy, Lord, and Thy grace, and Thy goodness, and the forgiveness and pardon of Thy compassion, come and be poured out on the (writer,) feeble and sinful and stained with crimes; and through the prayers of Thy mother, pardon his faults and sins; and forgive all the shortcomings of every one who participates (in his work); now, and at all times, and for ever and ever, Amen.

(Here) ends the history of the Departure of the Mother of God, the blessed mother. May her prayers be with us.

THE OBSEQUIES OF

THE HOLY VIRGIN.

⁘ ⁘ ⁘ ⁘ ⁘

⁘ ⁘ ⁘ ⁘

⁘ ⁘ ⁘ ⁘ ⁘

"AND he gave a sign to his father that he might know God. And the son answered and said to his father: 'I beg of thee, my father, if I have found grace in thine eyes, bring a little of our earnings, (*a*) and give it to this one who is afflicting my soul, that perchance he may leave me and I may not die.' Then his father brought the half of his property, and placed it before his beloved son, and answered and said with a loud voice: 'I beg of him who is afflicting the soul of my son, take these goods, and grant me the life of my son.' And after these things the boy was greatly afflicted; and again he answered and said to his father: 'My father, he who is afflicting my soul does not cease from me; perhaps what thou hast brought to him is altogether too little for him; and because he has seen that it is too little for him, he afflicts me exceedingly.' And his father arose, and brought all that he possessed, and along with it he borrowed other (property) and brought it, and placed it before his beloved son, and said with a loud voice: 'I beg of him who is afflicting the

(*a*) *Literally*, toil.

soul of my son, take all that I have, and leave me only my son.' But the boy was greatly afflicted; and when he was near death, he turned to his father and said to him: 'My father, thou seest that neither gold nor silver nor any thing else can be given for life, save a heart that is sincere towards God. Rise therefore, my father, and take these goods, and build with them places for strangers, that they may enter in and dwell and rest in them; and give also of them to the poor and orphans, and we shall find peace for our souls.' These things the son said to his father, and his life ended; and his father did all that his son had said to him. And when eight days were past, and they did not come to king Solomon, according to the covenant they had made before him, that after seven days they would go to him—and the eighth (day) passed, and the ninth, and they did not go to king Solomon—the king sent after them, saying: 'Why are ye not come, that I might settle (matters) between you, as I said unto you?' And the father of the boy answered and said: 'My lord, lo it is eight days since my son departed out of the world. Had I known he was dying, I would have given all I had to my son not to distress him; but all that he said to me, I have done.' And when Solomon heard this from the man, he said: 'The evil spirits know what is going to happen. Because of this, men say, 'It is not they who mock at us,' because they do not know the things which are said by them.' "

Then the Apostles gave their assent to what Paul said; for they were wishing him to speak again with them, that he might not press them, and they might (not) reveal to him the glorious secrets which our Lord taught. And again all the Apostles answer and say to Paul:

"Brother Paul, speak to us with words, because we hearken unto thee kindly; for our Lord hath sent thee to us to gladden us during these three days." And Paul answered and said to Peter; "Since ye have not chosen to reveal to me the great things of Jesus, yet ye will inform me, if ye go forth, what ye will preach and teach; (for) I too, would know how to teach with your doctrine." Peter says to him: "Brother Paul, this word that thou hast spoken is good. Since then thou wishest to know and hear what we are going to teach and preach to men, hear, and I will tell thee. I, if I go forth to preach, will say, that no one who does not fast all his days, shall see God." Paul said to Peter: "Father Peter, what is this word that thou hast spoken? For they will not hear thy word, but will arise and slay thee; because they are wicked, and are not acquainted with God nor with fasting." And again, Paul turned to John, and said to him: "Do thou too tell us thy doctrine, father John, that I too may so teach and preach." John says to him: "I, if I go forth to teach and preach, will say, that no one who is not a virgin all his days, is able to see God." And Paul answered and said to John: "Father John, what are these words to men who do not know God? For men who worship stones and stocks, if they hear these things from you, will throw us into and shut us up in prison." And again, Paul turned to Andrew, and said to him: "Father Andrew, do thou too tell us what is thy thought, that I too may teach and preach (it); lest perchance Peter may think that he is great and a bishop, and John also be proud of his being a virgin, and because of these things they may speak great (words)." Andrew says to Paul: "I, if I go forth to preach, will say, that no one who does not leave father and mother, and brother and sister, and children and houses, and all that he hath, and go out after our Lord, is able to see God." Paul says to Andrew: "Father Andrew, the words of Peter and John are light compared with thine, for thou severest every one from the earth in one moment. Who will hear your words at this time, and lay a heavy burden on himself?" And Peter and Andrew answered and say to Paul: "Paul, friend of our soul, tell us how thou desirest that we should go forth and preach? Paul says to them: "If ye will hearken unto me, do these things, and let us devise such things as they are able to do, because they are of recent origin and know not the truth; and let us say to them these things: 'Let every man take his wife, that they may not commit adultery; and let a woman take her husband, that she may not commit adultery.' And let us appoint for them one or two days in the week, and let us not be very hard upon them, lest they become remiss and turn away. But, if they fast to-day and become a little weary, they will persevere to the time and say: 'To morrow we will not fast.' And if they come to the time for eating, and find a poor man and give to him, they will say: 'For what do we fast, if we do not give to the poor,' and they will know God in their hearts. And let us also say to them: 'Let him who is feeble, fast till the sixth hour; and let him who is able, till the ninth; and him who is able, till evening.' And when we have given them to drink as it were with milk, and have turned them towards us, then we will speak to them great and glorious things, words that will be useful to them."

Then all the Apostles murmured, and would not agree to the words of Paul. And as all the Apostles were sitting before the entrance of the tomb of Mary, and disputing about the words of Paul, lo, our Lord Jesus the Messiah came from heaven with the angel Michael, and sat among the Apostles, as they were disputing about the word of Paul. And Jesus answered and said: "Hail to thee, Peter the bishop, and hail to thee, John the virgin, ye who are my heirs! And hail to thee Paul, thou adviser of good things! Verily I say unto thee, Peter, that thy counsels were at all times detrimental, thine and Andrew's and John's. But I say unto you that ye should receive those of Paul; for I see that the whole world shall be caught in the net of Paul, and it shall prevent (*or* anticipate) them. And then, after these things, your maxims (*or* opinions) shall become known in the latter times." And our Lord turned to Paul and said to him: "Brother Paul, be not grieved that the Apostles, thy fellows, have not revealed to thee the glorious secrets; for to them have been revealed the things that are on earth, but to thee I will teach the things that are in heaven."

And after these things our Lord made a sign to Michael, and Michael began to speak with the voice of a mighty angel. And angels descended on three clouds; and the number of angels on each cloud was a thousand angels, uttering praises before Jesus. And our Lord said to Michael: "Let them bring the body of Mary into the clouds." And when the body of Mary had been brought into the clouds, our Lord said to the Apostles that they should draw near to the clouds. And when they came to the clouds, they were singing with the voice of angels. And our Lord told the clouds to go to the gate of Paradise. And when they had entered Paradise, the body of Mary went to the tree of life; and they brought her soul and made it enter into her body. And straightway our Lord dismissed the angels to their places.

And after these things the Apostles say to our Lord: "Lord, Thou didst say to us, when Thou wast with us, when we besought Thee that we might see the grave of Mary, that it would be well for us; and Thou didst say to us, 'If ye wish to see this, abide till the day of the departure of Mary, and I will lead you and ye shall see dreadful things.

The dreadful place of torment which the Disciples begged of our Lord that they might see.

And when these things were said by the blessed Apostles, our Lord made a sign with his eyes, and a cloud snatched away the Apostles and Mary and Michael, and our Lord along with them, and carried them to where the sun sets, and left them there. And our Lord spake with the angels of the pit, and the earth sprang upwards, and the pit was revealed in the midst of the earth. And our Lord gave place to the Apostles, that they might look, as they were wishing. And when they drew near and looked into the pit, those who were in the pit saw Michael; and there was a great weeping and groaning; and they answered and say to Michael: "Michael, chief of the angels, Michael our strength, Michael our general, hast thou prevailed to-day in thy contest on our behalf? For thou hast forgotten us during all this lapse of time. Why dost thou not beg on our behalf from our Lord, that he would grant us a little respite from torment." And as soon as Mary and the Apostles saw (this), they fell on the ground because of the distress of those who were in the pit. And our Lord raised them up and said to them: "O ye

Apostles, rise and learn; for I told you beforehand that ye would not be able to endure the sight of these things. If I had conveyed you to that outer place where there is not a breath of mankind, and where there are many torments which differ from one anoth er, what would have become of you ?" Then Michael spoke to those who were in the pit, and said to them: "My sons, the Lord liveth, the Lord liveth; He liveth who is about to come to judge the dead and the quick; He liveth who hath power over all creatures; for there are twelve hours in the day and twelve in the night, and these are nnmbered with praise, and offering goeth up to God; and the angels fall down and worship His grace, and intercede for all creation, and for all mankind. And the angel who is set over the waters, drew near and besought God, saying: 'Let the fountains of waters increase because of the race of men; for they are Thy image and Thy likeness, O Lord. On this account I beseech Thee to hear me, for I am Thy minister. Let thy mercy be upon the waters, and let them increase over the whole earth.' "

⁘ ⁘ ⁘ ⁘ ⁘

⁘ ⁘ ⁘ ⁘

⁘ ⁘ ⁘ ⁘ ⁘

" 'and I will place them in a secret place under the hand of thy power, that they may not find them. And when I have done this, they will not be able to flee and leave them; for we have heard that Joseph, when he was dying, made the children of his people swear that, when they were going up, his bones should go up along with them; and when I have done this, they will not be able to flee, unless they take them along with them, and they will remain under thy power in Egypt.' And after these things,

Pharaoh, king of Egypt, arose, and ordered that a pit should be (made) in the midst of the river. And he took the bones of Joseph, and placed them in a . . . box, and smeared it with bitumen . . . , and inscribed the name of Joseph in a roll, (writing) 'These are the bones of Joseph.' And he put the roll in the box, and commanded that it should be placed in the centre of the pit in the middle of the river. And when Pharaoh went in, he laid hard work upon the children of Israel, and said to them that they should go forth. And the children of Israel answered and say to Moses: 'Let us go forth first to the bones of our brother Joseph, because he made our fathers swear that his bones should go up along with the children of Israel.' But Moses went, and did not find them; for the children of Israel did not know that Pharaoh had taken them away from them. And when they did not find them, they rent their garments and wept bitterly; and they groaned and cried unto God, and Moses along with them: 'Lord God of our fathers, why hast Thou forsaken Thy people? For Thou didst turn unto us; and after Thou didst turn, Thou hast turned away Thy mercy from us, and we are become like a desert land, which has not seen water.' And after a long time, the river was laid bare. And when it was laid bare and had passed away, the children of Israel cried unto the Lord and say: 'The sin and folly of Thy people, O Lord, Thou hast remembered; on this account Thou hast concealed the bones of our brother Joseph, that we might remain in this bondage for ever. And now turn unto us, O Lord, and deliver Thy people from the slavery of Pharaoh.' And when these things were said by Moses and by the whole people, I came and spoke, I Michael the angel, and said to Moses: 'Moses, Moses, God hath heard your groan. Rise and go to the river, and smite the waters with thy staff, and the hidden treasure shall be laid bare before thee.' What thinkest thou, Mary? As soon as Moses smote the river, did not the box in which Joseph was placed, appear and come to the dry land? And Moses opened it, and found the roll in which was written, 'These are the bones of Joseph'; and he took them and conveyed them to their land unto their fathers. And after a long time . . . . .

⁂ ⁂ ⁂

them according to their wish. And He sent by the hand of the Apostles to them (to ask,) were these things not so? And He said: "These are the shepherds of the house of Israel, who are praying for the sheep, that they may be sanctified and made glorious before the sons of men; and themselves they are not able to sanctify, because they exalt themselves like the strong. Did I not give them many signs?" And the Apostles said: "Lord, lo, they beseech and pray and repent, and kneel upon their knees. Why dost Thou not hear them?" Our Lord says unto them: "I too was willing to hear them, but there is deception in them, (as) ye too know." And when Jesus wished to show the Apostles for what reason He did not hear them, He took them up to a mountain, and let them become hungry. And when the Apostles had gone, they asked of Him and say to Him: "Lord, we are hungry; what have we then to eat in this desert?" And Jesus said to them, to go to the trees which were before them. And He said to them: "Go to those trees which are over-against us, whose branches are many and fair and beautiful at a distance, and from them ye shall get food." And when the Apostles went, they did not find fruit on the trees. And they returned to Jesus and say: "Good Teacher, Thou didst send us to those trees which are over-against us, and we went and found on them no fruit, but only branches, which were fair and beautiful, but there was no fruit on them." And Jesus said to them: "Ye have not seen them, because the trees grow straight upwards. Go therefore at once, because the trees are bending themselves, and ye shall find on them fruit, and get yourselves food." And when they went, they found the trees bending down, but they did not find fruit upon them. And they returned again to Jesus in great distress, and say to Him: "What is this, Teacher, that we are mocked? For at first Thou didst say to us, 'Ye shall find trees which are straight, and there is fruit on them;' and we found none. Why are we mocked? But it is fitting that Thou shouldest teach us, what this is that has happened; for we think that what Thou didst wish to teach us is false; for by a visible power the trees were laid hold of and bent down. If this be a temptation, make known to us what it is." And Jesus said to them: "Go and sit under them, and ye shall see what it is that abides on them, but ye shall not be able to bend them again." And when the Apostles went and sat under the trees, straightway the trees threw down stinking worms. And the Apostles came again to Jesus and say to him: "Teacher, dost Thou wish to lead us astray, or to turn us away from this . . . ?"

⁂ ⁂ ⁂ ⁂ ⁂ ⁂

NOTES.

THE PROTEVANGELIUM JACOBI.

The Greek text to which reference is made in the following notes, is that of Tischendorf, *Evangelia Apocrypha*, Leipzig, 1853, pag. 31 foll.

Chap. XVII. ܥܠ ܚܡܪܗ, reading *τὸν ὄνον αὐτοῦ*, with Tischendorf's MS. A.; otherwise the translator would have used ܐܬܢܗ (אתון, اتان) instead of ܚܡܪܗ (חמור, حمار).—The clause *καὶ ἠκολούθει Ἰωσήφ* is wanting in the Syriac.—ܨܒܐ ܕܢܦܘܩ. All the Greek MSS. have *χειμάζει αὐτήν*. Our Syrian either translated very loosely, or he had before him some such reading as *ἐθέλει προελθεῖν*. — The whole of the last sentence, *καὶ κατήγαγεν αὐτὴν κ. τ. λ.*, is wanting in the Syriac.

Chap. XVIII. The text of this chapter is much shorter in the Syriac than in the Greek, the entire latter portion, from *Ἐγὼ δὲ Ἰωσὴφ περιεπάτουν* onwards, being compressed into a single sentence, which may have run thus: *Ἐγὼ δὲ Ἰωσὴφ περιεπάτουν, καὶ εἶδον τὰ πάντα ἔκθαμβα· καὶ πάντα ὑπὸ θῆξιν ἐλύετο καὶ τῷ δρόμῳ αὐτῶν διελαύνετο.*

Chap. XIX. About the middle of this chapter the Syriac text is again much shorter than the Greek. The translator seems to have read: *καὶ ἦν νεφέλη φωτεινὴ ἐπισκιάζουσα τὸ σπήλαιον, ἕως οὗ ἐφάνη τὸ βρέφος. κ. τ. λ.*.—ܡܕܡ ܕܗܢܐ ܟܝܢܐ ܠܐ ܣܦܩ ܠܗ, i.e. *ὃ οὐ χωρεῖ ἡ φύσις αὕτη*, as in Tischendorf's MS. B.—ܚܝ ܗܘ ܡܪܝܐ ܘܐܠܐ, *Ζῇ κύριος ὁ θεός, ἐὰν μὴ ἴδω, οὐ μὴ πιστεύσω ὅτι παρθένος ἐστι.*

Chap. XX. ܚܘܝ ܢܦܫܟܝ, "show thyself," is a very loose rendering of *σχημάτισον σεαυτήν*. Probably the translator had a different reading in his MS., the more so as the same words occur again in the following clause, ܐܠܐ ܚܘܝ ܢܦܫܟܝ ܕܐܢ

ܒܬܘܠܬܐ ܐܢܬܝ, which has no equivalent in any of Tischendorf's MSS.—ܕܣܝܡܐ ܠܟܝ, ἐπίκειταί σοι.—ܘܩܪܒܬ ܘܚܙܬ, perhaps καὶ προσελθοῦσα εἶδεν ὅτι παρθένος ἐστι.—ܐܠܗܐ ܐܢܬ, ὁ θεός μου, omitting τῶν πατέρων.—The Syriac presents no trace of the clause ἀλλὰ ἀπόδος με τοῖς πένησιν (or τοῖς γονεῦσί μου ;) nor is there anything in the Greek MSS. to correspond to the words ܡܛܠ ܕܫܘܠܡܢܘܬܐ ܕܗܘܬ ܠܝ ܒܝܬ, a little farther on.

CHAP. XXI. ܘܩܪܐ ܠܪ̈ܒܝ ܟܗ̈ܢܐ ܘܫܐ. Apparently καὶ καλέσας τοὺς ἀρχιερεῖς, ἀνέκρινεν αὐτοὺς λέγων, Ποῦ γέγραπται περὶ τοῦ βασιλέως ὅτι γεννᾶται.—The clauses οὕτως γαρ γέγραπται· καὶ ἀπέλυσεν αὐτούς are wanting in the Syriac.—ܘܐܬܐ ܟܘܟܒܐ ܘܩܡܘ. The Greek MSS. all have the singular, referring, as we should naturally expect, to *the star*.—ܘܥܠܘ ܠܐܡܗ ܘܟܠ, καὶ ἰδόντες τὸ παιδίον μετὰ τῆς μητρὸς αὐτοῦ Μαριάμ, πεσόντες προσεκύνησαν αὐτῷ, καὶ προσήνεγκαν αὐτῷ δῶρα, χρυσὸν καὶ σμύρναν καὶ λίβανον.

CHAP. XXII. ܐܝܟ ܙܒܢܐ ܕܐܟܬܒ ܡܢ ܡܓܘ̈ܫܐ, κατὰ τὸν χρόνον, ὃν ἠκρίβωσε παρὰ τῶν μάγων, exactly as in Tischendorf's MS. N.—ܘܠܝܬ ܗܘܐ ܐܬܪܐ, καὶ οὐκ ἦν τόπος, omitting ἀποκρυφῆς with Tischendorf's MS. D.—ܘܢܘܗܪܐ ܪܒܐ ܘܟܠ καὶ τὸ ὄρος ἐκεῖνο διέφαινε αὐτοῖς φῶς μέγα.

CHAP. XXIII. ܠܗܝܟܠܐ, apparently reading, with Tischendorf's MS. C. εἰς τὸ θυσιαστήριον κυρίου, or εἰς τὸν ναὸν κυρίου. —ܘܐܡܪ ܕܡܠܟܐ ܘܐܬܕܟܪ ܠܗ. Read ܘܐܡܪ ܠܗ λέγων.—ܐܦ ܠܐ ܝܕܥ ܐܢܬ οὐκ οἶδας, لا أعلم.—The Syriac has the clause καὶ ἀπῆλθον οἱ ὑπηρέται καὶ ἀπήγγειλαν αὐτῷ, which is omitted in some of the Greek MSS.—ܣܗܕ ܗܘ ܐܠܗܐ, μάρτυς ὁ θεὸς ὅτι ἐκχέεις μου τὸ αἷμα.—ܙܟܝܐ and ܕܠܐ ܥܘܠܬܐ seem to be a double rendering of the word ἀθῷον, and there is nothing to correspond to the words εἰς τὰ πρόθυρα τοῦ ναοῦ κυρίου.

CHAP. XXIV. In the Syriac the words κατὰ τὸ ἔθος are placed after ἀπῆλθον, οἱ ἱερεῖς being omitted.—ܘܚܕ ܠܒܬܪ

ܡܩܕܫܐ, *εἰσῆλθεν εἰς τὸ ἁγίασμα.* ܕܡܐ ܕܐܫܬܕ ܘܩܒܝܥܐ ܐܝܟ ܟܐܦܐ, *τὸ αἷμα κείμενον καὶ πεπηγός ὡσεὶ λίθος.*—

The whole of the following passage, from *καὶ ἀκούσας τὸν λόγον ἐφοβήθη* to *λίθον γεγενημένον,* is omitted in the Syriac.—The words *καὶ τρεῖς νύκτας* are wanting, as in Tischendorf's MSS. B, F[a], F[b]; but the reading ܝܘ̈ܡܬܐ ܣܓܝ̈ܐܐ, "*many* days," does not occur in any of the Greek MSS.

CHAP. XXV. ܒܡܘܬܐ ܡܪܝܪܐ, *πικρῷ θανάτῳ,* as in Tischendorf's MSS. G. and H.—The words *τὴν δωρεὰν καὶ* are wanting in the Syriac, as well as the whole of the last sentence, from *ἔσται δὲ ἡ χάρις* onwards.

THE GOSPEL OF THOMAS THE ISRAELITE.

THE Greek text to which reference is made is again that of Tischendorf, *Evang. Apocryph.* p. 134 foll., especially his *Evang. Thomæ Græce A.*—The first chapter of the Greek is altogether wanting in the Syriac.

CHAP. II. Compare the *Pseudo-Matthæi Evang.*, ch. xxvi and xxvii, and the *Evang. Thomæ Latinum*, ch. iv.—The words ܘܥܒܕ ܠܗܘܢ ܩܢ̈ܩܠܐ most nearly correspond to the *quibus singulis fecit araciunculas* (*aratiunculas*) of the Pseudo-Matth. —The Syriac omits the clause *καὶ λόγῳ μόνῳ ἐπέταξεν αὐτά.*—ܘܓܒܠ ܡܢ ܪܦܬܐ ܘܥܒ, as in the MSS. Par. and Vind., in which *ἐκ τῆς χείλεως* or *ὕλεως* seems to be a blunder for *ἐκ τῆς ἰλύος* or *εἰλύος.*—The Greek has nothing equivalent to the words ܘܦܠܚܗ ܟܠ ܢܦܫ.—The words ܡܕܡ ܐܠܡ ܕܐܡܪ seem, as stated at p. ܐܓ, note *c*, to express the *ἅμα τῷ λόγῳ* of Tischendorf's text B. (cap. iii., last line but one). The Pseudo-Matth., ch. xxvii., has *ad vocem imperii sui.*—ܐܙܠܘ ܦܪ̈ܚܘ ܘܙ. Here again the Syriac follows the MS. Par., *ὑπάγετε πετάσθητε καὶ μέμνησθέ μου ζῶντες.* Similarly in Tischendorf's text B. *ὑπάγετε πετάσθητε καὶ μιμνήσκεσθέ μου ζῶντα.*—In the last sentence the Syriac has "a Pharisee," whereas the Greek A. mentions "the Jews," and B. "Joseph."

CHAP. III. Compare the *Pseudo-Matth.*, ch. xxvi. and xxviii., and the *Evang. Thomæ Lat.*, ch. iv.—ܥܡ ܝܫܘܥ, "with Jesus." The Greek has "with Joseph."—The Syriac text omits all the abusive epithets of the Greek and Latin.

CHAP. IV. Compare the *Pseudo-Matth.*, ch. xxix., and the *Evang. Thomæ Lat.*, ch. v.—ܥܡ ܐܒܘܗܝ, "with his father." The two Greek texts have διὰ τῆς κώμης and μέσον τῆς πόλεως; the Latin combines both readings, *cum Joseph per villam.*—ܗܢܐ ܛܠܝܐ ܐܝܬ ܠܟ, as in the MS. Par. σὺ τοῦτο τὸ παιδίον ἔχων.—Instead of δίδασκε, the Syriac has the verb in the plural, and stops short at εὐλογεῖν.

CHAP. V. Compare the *Pseudo-Matth.*, ch. xxix., and the *Evang. Thomæ Lat.*, ch. v.— ܘܫܪܒܝܢ is doubtless (as suggested at p. ܟܒ, note *d*) a mistake for ܘܫܪܝܢ. The Greek A. has καὶ πάσχουσιν οὗτοι, and the Pseudo-Matth. *multi dolentes.* —The words subsequently put in the mouth of Jesus differ considerably from those in any of the Greek and Latin recensions; and the Syriac omits the passage καὶ οἱ ἰδόντες ἐφοβήθησαν . . . . . . ἐποίησεν ὁ 'Ιησους.—ܗܘܦܐ ܠܟ ܘܐܦ. The Syriac text is by no means clear, but the translator seems either to have omitted μὴ before εὑρίσκειν, or to have confounded it with με. The clause οὐκ οἶδας κ. τ. λ. is also wanting.

CHAP. VI—VIII. Compare the *Pseudo-Matth.*, ch. xxx. and xxxi., and the *Evang. Thomæ Lat.*, ch. vi.—ܐܘ ܠܡܠܟܐ ܚܒܝܫܐ. The Greek and Latin texts represent Zacchæus as filled with surprise, instead of anger, at the sayings of Jesus.—ܕܢܬܪܕܐ ܠܐܡܬܕܪܫܘ ܘܫܐ, as in the Pseudo-Matth., *tu non vis filium tuum tradere ut doceatur scientia humana et timore?* etc.—ܘܡܚܒܐ ܡܫܟܚ ܘܫܐ. Pseudo-Matth., *et si quis est qui possit hunc infantem tenere et docere?*—ܠܡܚܐ ܠܝܠܕܐ ܕܢܘܪܐ ܘܫܐ
The nearest approach to this in the other texts is in the *Evang. Thomæ Lat.*, where we read: *numquid creditis, parvus erit*

parvulus iste?—ܚܒܪܐ ܗܘܐ ܝܫܘܥ ܘܐܡܪ ܠܗܘ ܡܠܦܢܐ. ܘܫ. This passage agrees substantially with the *Pseudo-Matth.*, ch. xxx., from *Auditis Jesus quæ dixerat Zachyas* to the end. Instead, however, of ܘܡܠܟܐ ܗܘ ܕܐܡܪܬ ܘܫ., we find there merely: *Ipse enim potest qui dignus est.*—ܘܐܡܪ ܠܕܒܝ ܡܠܦܢܐ ܠܝܫܘܥ. ܘܫ. In this passage the agreement with the Greek and Latin texts is less close. The whole description of the letter A is omitted, and the subsequent speech of Zacchæus much shortened. The difficult sentence about the "smith's anvil," (in which read "can teach," instead of "can learn,") has no exact equivalent in any one of them. The nearest approach to it is in the *Pseudo-Matth.*, where we read as follows: "Jesus autem dixit ad didascalum Levi ut quid me percutis? In veritate scias quia ipse qui percutitur magis docet percutientem se quam ab eo doceatur. Ego enim te possum docere quæ a te ipso dicuntur. Sed hi omnes cæci sunt qui dicunt et audiunt, quasi æs sonans aut cimbalum tinniens, in quibus non est sensus eorum quæ intelliguntur per sonum illorum." There is also something similar in the *Evang. Thomæ Lat.* (p. 162), *Me autem oportet te docere*, etc.

Chap. ix. Compare the *Pseudo-Matth.*, ch. xxxii., and the *Evang. Thomæ Lat.*, ch. vii.—ܒܝܘܡܐ ܕܫܒܬܐ, as in the Pseudo-Matth., *et cum esset ibi una sabbati.*

Chap. x. of the Greek text, corresponding to ch. viii. of the *Evang. Thomæ Lat.*, is wanting in the Syriac, as also in the *Pseudo-Matth.*

Chap. xi. Compare the *Pseudo-Matth.*, ch. xxxiii., and the *Evang. Thomæ Lat.*, ch. ix.—ܒܪ ܫ̈ܢܝܢ ܫܒܥ. The Greek and Latin texts all have "six years of age," instead of "seven."

Chap. xii. Compare the *Pseudo-Matth.*, ch. xxxiv., and the *Evang. Thomæ Lat.*, ch. x. The Syriac text is shorter than even the former. It agrees, however, with the Greek in reading "100 cors," instead of "three."

Chap. xiii. Compare the *Pseudo-Matth.*, ch. xxxvii., and

the *Evang. Thomæ Lat.*, ch. xi. The Syriac text is again shorter and simpler than any of the others.

Chap. xiv. Compare the *Pseudo-Matth.*, ch. xxxviii., and the *Evang. Thomæ Lat.*, ch. xii. The difference between these and the Syriac text is great, but less than between the latter and the Greek. According to the Greek, the teacher only falls down in a swoon (ἐλιποθύμησε).

Chap. xv. Compare the *Pseudo-Matth.*, ch. xxxix, and the *Evang. Thomæ Lat.*, ch. xiii. The text of these as, well as of the Greek, is far longer than the Syriac, to which the following are the corresponding passages. *Μετὰ δὲ χρόνον τινὰ ἕτερος πάλιν καθηγητής, γνήσιος φίλος ὢν τοῦ Ἰωσήφ, εἶπεν αὐτῷ, Ἄγαγέ μοι το παιδίον εἰς τὸ παιδευτήριον· ἴσως ἂν δυνηθῶ ἐγὼ μετὰ κολακείας διδάξαι αὐτὸ τὰ γράμματα. . . . . Καὶ εἰσελθὼν θρασὺς εἰς τὸ διδασκαλεῖον εὗρε βιβλίον κείμενον ἐν τῷ ἀναλογίῳ, καὶ λαβὼν αὐτὸ οὐκ ἀνεγίνωσκε τὰ γράμματα τὰ ἐν αὐτῷ, ἀλλὰ ἀνοίξας τὸ στόμα αὐτοῦ ἐλάλει πνεύματι ἁγίῳ, καὶ ἐδίδασκε τὸν νόμον τοὺς περιεστῶτας.*

Chap. xvi. Compare the *Pseudo-Matth.*, ch. xli., and the *Evang. Thomæ Lat.*, ch. xiv. The latter agrees very closely with the Syriac, though, like the Greek and the *Pseudo-Matth.*, it adds to the narrative the death of the snake: *et vipera mortua est, καὶ το θηρίον ἐρράγη.*

Chaps. xvii. and xviii. of the Greek text are wanting in the Syriac.

Chap. xix. Compare the *Evang. Thomæ Lat.*, ch. xv., the second paragraph; and also the *Pseudo-Matth.* ch. xl[e]., according to the text of Tischendorf's MS. B. The Greek text agrees closely with the Syriac.

THE LETTER OF HEROD TO PILATE.

Page ܠ., line 18. ܐܙܒܘܢܝܘܣ, *Azbonius.* Perhaps *Zenobius* was the name intended by the writer. We have no notice of any such son of Herod Antipas, nor does this name appear at all in the genealogical lists of the family of Herod.

Page ܟܛ, line 17. ܦܪܘܩܠܐ, *Πρόκλα*, *Procla* or *Claudia Procula*. See Tischendorf, *Evang. Apocrypha*, p. 274, in the *Evang. Nicodemi, pars I. B., ch. IV.* *Τότε ἦλθε μηνυτὴς ἀπὸ τῆς Πρόκλης τῆς γυναικὸς Πιλάτου πρὸς αὐτόν.*—In this same line I have printed ܩܕ̈ܫܐ, because the word is distinctly so written in the MS. The dictionaries give the form ܩܕܫܐ; e. g. Add. MS. 7203. (شنوف) اقرطة شنوف ܩܕ̈ܫܐ شنف ܩܕ̈ܫܐ.

THE LETTER OF PILATE TO HEROD.

PAGE ܟܐ, line 2. ܛܛܪܟܐ is a not uncommon form in MSS., instead of the more accurate ܛܛܪܪܟܐ (Matth. xiv. 1; Luke iii. 19, ix. 7).—Line 18. ܠܘܢܓܝܢܘܣ. The author follows that tradition which gives the name of *Longinus* to the centurion who presided over the execution, not to the soldier who pierced our Lord's side with the spear. See Fabricius, *Codex Apocryphus Novi Test.*, 2nd ed., t. iii, p. 472.—Last line. Instead of ܕܒܝ, the more correct orthography would be ܕܒܝ.

Page ܟܒ, line 1. This appears to be a quotation from the *Testament of Adam*, from which I have given an extract in a subsequent note.

Page ܟܓ, line 15 foll. I must confess my ignorance as to the Justin and Theodore whom the writer cites as contemporaries of Pilate. The passage of Josephus may be found in the *Antiquities*, xix. 8, 2; but our author seems to have taken it from Eusebius, *Hist. Eccles.*, ii. 10.

THE HISTORY OF THE VIRGIN MARY.

PAGE ܟܕ, line 14. ܕܠܐ ܡܚܫܒܘܬܐ ܡܕܡ, "without any phantasy." The writer alludes to the doctrines of the older *Docètæ*, not to those of Julian of Halicarnassus (ܝܘܠܝܢܘܣ ܦܢܛܣܝܐ), the contemporary and opponent of Severus of Antioch.

Page ܢܒ, line 18. ܪܒܘܠ. On the use of this word in our book, I think it as well to quote the remarks of Ewald in the *Gött. gel. Anz.* 1865, *Stück* 26, p. 1027. "Dass die gerade in diesem Syrischen Buche so oft vorkommende Anrede ܪܒܘܠ *Rabûl* an Christus, wie der Herausgeber andeutet, nur im Lautwechsel von רַבּוֹנִי sich unterscheidet ist zwar gewiss: allein man muss doch dabei vorzüglich beachten dass nach dem beständigen Sprachgebrauche dieses Buches nur Maria ihren Sohn so anredet und sonst so nennt, wenn sie aber zu Anderen über ihn redet dann einfach ܪܒܘܟܘܢ *euer Herr* (oder *Meister*) sagt. Dieser Unterschied der sich durch die ganze Sprache des Buches hindurchzieht muss seinen Grund haben: und wir thun dabei wohl zu bemerken dass auch in demselben Buche des N. Ts, z. B. bei Markus oder bei Johannes, die Anrede *ῥαββονί* oder vielmehr wie die bessere Lesart nicht nur Joh. 20, 16 sondern auch Marc. 10, 51 lautet *ῥαββουνί* mit der gewöhnlichen *ῥαββί* só wechselt dass jene die bei weitem seltenere ist und doch nicht etwa eine Steigerung des Begriffes enthalten kann. Denn eine solche Steigerung wäre an sich hier untreffend, und dazu übersetzt Johannes in seinem Evangelium beide Anreden gleichmässig mit *διδάσκαλε*. Darum ist es durchaus wahrscheinlich dass die längere Aussprache nichts als das Klein- oder vielmehr das Zärtlichkeitswort wiedergiebt welches im Aramäischen überhaupt weit näher liegt als im Griechischen. Dann erklärt sich auch warum nach unserm Buche bloss Maria ihren Christus so anredet; und ebenso leuchtet nun ein warum das Wort im Evangelium des Johannes nur einmal und zwar im Munde eines Weibes erscheint."

Page ܠܕ, line 8. ܣܒܝܐܢܘܣ. In the text published by me in the *Journal of Sacred Literature* for January and April 1865, the name is written ܣܒܝܢܐ and pointed in the younger of the two MSS. ܣܶܒܝܳܢܶܐ, *Sebiane* or *Seviane*. Probably the writer had read in Eusebius (*Chronicorum Canonum libri duo*, ed. Mai and Zohrab, p. 371) of *Sejanus*, the favourite of Tiberius, and either imagined him to have been governor of Palestine, or thought that his name would do as well any other: *Σηϊανὸς ἔπαρχος Τιβερίου Καίσαρος περὶ τελείας ἀπωλείας τοῦ ἔθνους τῶν Ἰουδαίων πολλὰ συνεβούλευσεν τῷ Καίσαρι, ὡς Φίλων ἱστορεῖ ἐν τῷ β′.*

Page ܠ, line 20. ܒܪܬܗ ܕܩܘܡܝܛܝܢܐ. In the other text he is called ܛܘܒܝܐ ܩܘܡܝܛܝܢܐ, "Tobia the comitian" (*κομητιανός*).

Page ܠܒ, line 15—21. The list of apostles in the other text (*Journal of Sacred Literature* for January 1865, p. ܝܗ, and for April 1865, p. 137) differs both as to their number, their names, and the places where they were. Here we have thirteen: there only twelve; viz. John, Simon Peter, Paul, Thomas, Matthew, James, Bartholomew, Andrew, Philip, Luke, Simon the Cananite, and Mark. Matthew, instead of being at Berytus, is placed ܒܦܢܘܣ, for which Ewald would read ܒܦܠܘܣ = *ἐν πλοίῳ*, ܒܐܠܦܐ (*Gött. gel. Anz.* 1865, *Stück* 26, p. 1025); Bartholomew is in the Thebaid, ܒܬܒܐܝܣ, instead of in Armenia; and James is stated to have been in Jerusalem, sitting in the church of Zion, ܒܥܕܬܐ ܕܨܗܝܘܢ. It is not impossible that ܒܡܥܪܬܐ may be merely a corruption of ܒܥܕܬܐ.

Page ܠܓ, line 17. The corresponding passage in the other text may be found in the *Journal of Sacred Literature* for January 1865, at p. ܝܒ, or for April 1865, at p. 144.—Line 19. I have translated ܒܡܡܠܠܬܐ by "with (high) words"; but the fact is that ܒܡܡܠܠܬܐ is nothing but a corruption of ܒܡܥܬܐ "with clamour," as we read in the other text.

Page ܠܕ, line 3. In the *Testament of Adam*, ܕܕܝܬܝܩܐ ܕܐܒܘܢ ܐܕܡ, Add. 14,624 (ninth century), fol. 8 vers. and foll., we read as follows (fol. 9 vers. ܐܡܪ ܐܕܡ ܠܫܝܬ ܒܪܗ. ܫܡܥܬ ܒܪܝ ܕܐܝܬ ܐܠܗܐ ܠܡܠܟܐ ܡܢ ܒܬܪ ܕܬܒܥܐ. ∴ ܘܡܢ ܡܬܬܠܬܐ ܡܬܬܟܠܝܢ. ܘܠܥܠ ܦܠܓܘܬܐ ܘܬܫܠܡܬܐ ܐܝܟ ܕܬܒܥܐ.

ܘܪܒܐ ܐܢܬ ܠܥܕܬܐ ܀ ܀ ܘܫܒܩܬ ܐܬ̈ܘܬܐ ܘܬܕܡܪ̈ܬܐ ܥܠ
ܐܪܥܐ. ܀ ܢܚܡܠܟ ܥܠ ܚ̈ܝܠܟܐ ܕܗܡܣܐ. ܀ ܒܐܝܟܐ ܐܝܟܐ ܒܪ̈ܘܚܐ
ܘܫ̈ܠܝܢ ܀ ܢܦܪ ܠܚ̈ܝܠܟܐ ܘܩܝܣܡ ܀ ܡܨܠܘܬ ܫܡ̈ܝܢܐ. ܀ ܡܢܕܥܐ
ܪ̈ܒܒܐ ܀ ܡܫܬܡܥ ܠܫ̈ܪܝܐ ܀ ܦܬ̈ܘܚܐ ܡܥܠܠܝܢ. ܀ ܩ̈ܦܘܦܐ
ܡܬܒܪܝܢ ܀ ܡܥ̈ܪܬܐ ܢܚܘܫ ܀ ܠܐܣ̈ܝܪܐ ܡܥܕܪ ܀ ܕܠܒܪ
ܠܒ̈ܢܝܐ ܀ ܢܚܡ ܠܥܒ̈ܕܐ ܀ ܡܛܠ ܕܗܘ ܐܡܪ ܗܘܐ ܠ
ܒܦܪ̈ܕܝܣܐ ܒܗ ܢܦܠܬ ܡܢ ܦܐܪܐ ܕܐܘܣܐ ܗܘܐ ܒܗ ܡܘܬܐ.
ܐܕܡ ܐܕܡ ܠܐ ܬܕܚܠ. ܝܗܒܬ ܕܬܗܘܐ ܐܠܗܐ. ܐܠܗܐ
ܚܙܐ ܐܢܐ ܠܟ. ܠܘ ܚܙܪ ܗܝܟܐ ܐܠܐ ܒܬܪ ܕܚܙܢܐ ܘܦܠܚܐ
ܕܚ̈ܙܢܐ. ܠܡܘܬܐ ܢܥܠܡ ܐܢܐ ܠܟ. ܘܐܟܠܐ ܠܗ ܗܘܐ
ܘܪܡܘܬܐ ܠܥ̈ܒܕܝܟ ܀ ܘܚܝܘܬ ܘܐܬܚܪܪܬ ܠܗ. ܒܠ ܡܢܝܐ ܡܢܝ ܀
ܘܐܡܪ ܠܗ ܒܠ ܕܥܒܕܬ ܩ̈ܠܐ ܣܘܦܐ. ܡܐܟܘܠܬܟ ܠܣܘܦܐ
ܬܗܘܐ ܘܬܠܝܢ. ܘܒܬܪ ܘܒܠܝܐ ܥܠܝܠ ܗ̈ܘܝܢ ܚܠܦܝܟ ܪ̈ܘܚܐ.
ܡܛܠ ܕܡܢ ܠܗܢ ܐܬܓܢܒܬ. ܘܠܐ ܥܒܕ ܐܢܐ ܠܟ ܕܬܬܠܐ
ܒܢܘܠ ܀ ܡܛܠܬܟ ܡܢ ܡܪܝܡ ܒܬܘܠܬܐ ܡܬܠܕ ܐܢܐ ܀
ܡܛܠܬܟ ܡܘܬܐ ܛܥܡ ܐܢܐ : ܘܠܒܫܬ ܚ̈ܫܘܬܐ ܒܢܝܠ
ܐܢܐ. ܀ ܀ ܡܛܠܬܟ ܝܩܝܪܐ ܫܘܬܐ ܚܒܝܒ ܐܢܐ. ܘܬܠܝܢ
ܡܛܠܬܟ ܐܢܐ ܒܗܘܢ ܀ ܘܒܬܪ ܬܠܬܐ ܝܘ̈ܡܝܢ ܕܩܝܡܬܐ ܐܢܐ
ܒܗ ܡܢܘܪܐ ܀ ܀ ܡܢܣܩ ܐܢܐ ܠܦܪ̈ܕܝܣܐ ܕܠܒܥܕܢ ܡܢܟ.
ܘܡܬܬܒ ܐܢܐ ܠܟ ܡܢ ܡܫܝܚܐ ܕܐܠܗܘܬܝ. ܘܚܙܐ ܐܢܐ
ܠܟ [b]ܐܠܗܐ ܐܝܟ ܕܝ[ܠܟ ܐܢܬ] ܀ ܘܢܦܩ ܐܢܐ ܡܢ ܐ . . . .

[a] Read ܢܚܘܫܝ (?).

[b] I have added this word. Compare above, ܐܠܗܐ ܚܙܐ ܐܢܐ ܠܟ.

ܒܗܝܡܢܘܬܐ ܘܗܒ . . . . ܠܝ ܘܠܬܠܡ̈ܝܕܝܟ ܕܐܬܝܗܒܬܗ̇،
ܒܐܘܢܬܐ ܕܫܡܝܐ. ∴ ܫܡܥܬ ܒܪ، ܫܡܥܬ. ܕܢܐܬܐ ܠܦܘܩܕܢܐ
ܘܢܦܩ ܠܥܠܡܗ̇ ܐܪܒܥܐ ܡܛܠ ܒ̈ܢܬ ܩܕܡ ܐܝܫܘܥ (fol. 10, a.)
ܕܡܛܠ ܛܠܝܐ ܕܠܚܘܕܐ ܫܘܬܟ ܘܡܛܠܗ ܠܡܫܝܚܐ ܐܝܫܘܥ. ܒܗ̇،
ܕܡܢ ܐܡܬܟ ܗܘܐ ܐܬܒܪܢܘ ܫܠܡܐ. ܘܒܬܪ ܠܦܘܩܕܢܐ ܬܗܘܡ
ܬ̈ܢܝܢܐ ܠܝܣܘܗ ܕܒܠܒܐ. ܥܠܬܐ ܬ̈ܠܬܝܢ ܕܬ̈ܢܝܢܐ ∴ ܘܗܝܕܝܢ
ܢܦ̇ܘܐ ܘܦܩܘܗ ∴ ܘܐܢܐ ܫܡܥܬ ܒܣܘܦܗ ܕܬܫܡܫܬܐ ܗܕܐ.
ܘܟܬܒܬ ܐܢܐ ܘܡܟܪܘܗ، ܡܢ ܬ̈ܪܝܢ ܦܪ̈ܨܘܦܐ ܠܗܘܦܠ
ܦܬܝܬܐ ܡܪܟܒܬܐ ܕܐܬܟܬܒܬ ܥܠ ܐܪܥܐ. ܕܫܡܥܗ̇ ܝܫܘܥ.
ܘܐܬܠܘ، ܐܝܟ ܡܢ ܡܠܐܟ̈ܐ ܘܫ̈ܠܝܚܐ ܕܫܡܝܐ. ܡܛܠ
ܕܒܝܠܕܗ ܕܐܠܗܐ ܐܬܒܪ،. ܘܝܫܟ ܫܡܫܐ ܘܗܘܦܪܐ.
ܘܦܝܘܐ ܚܡܝܠܢܐ ܫܡܫܐ ܡ̈ܢܗܬܐ. ܘܐܬܡܢܗ̇ ܠܕܝܬܝܩܐ.
ܘܡܫܡܗ̇ ܒܡܫܪܬ ܐܢܫ̈ܐ ܒܡ ܡܘܪ̈ܒܢܐ ܕܐܢܦܩ ܐܝܟ ܡܢ
ܦܪܕܝܣܐ. ܕܗܒܢܐ ܘܡܘܪܐ ܘܠܒܘܢܬܐ ∴ ܘܐ̈ܬܝܢ ܩܕܡ ܬ̈ܠܬܐ
ܬ̈ܗܘܒܢܐ ܘܣܓܕܝܢ ܠܗܘܢ ܘܬ̈ܫܠܡܘܢ ܠܗܘܢ ܠܒܪ ܐܠܗܐ
ܠܬܫܠܘܡ ܕܝܗܘܒܐ ܠܡܒܪܬܐ ∴

Page ܠܐ, line 9. ܐܫܬܐ ܓܒܪ̈ܝܢ, "six men." The other text has "four," and the Arabic translation "forty."

Page ܡܒ, line 9. ܫܪܪ، ܘܫܠܡ. I am strongly inclined to think that the correct reading is ܫܪܪ ܘܫܠܡ, (as in the MS. A. of the other text, p. ܕܡ, last line,) "everything that He said to me turned out true and was fulfilled."

Page ܡܗ, line 16. ܘܠܐܣܝܐ, "and to Asia," *i.e.* the Roman province, of which Ephesus was the chief city.

Page ܡܛ, line 12. For the corresponding passage in the other text, see the *Journal of Sacred Literature* for January 1865, p. ܫ, and for April, p. 150.

ERRATA.

Page ܝܕ, line 22. For ܒܠ read ܟܠ.

" ܟܘ, line 7. For ܠܝܠ read ܠܟܠ.

" ܟܚ, line 3. Here the MS. has ܐܦܪܐܠ.

" ܟܒ, line 13. Read ܘܡܫܡܫܢܘܬܗ.

" ܠ, line 7. Read ܕܡܫܡܫܢܘܬܗܘܢ.

" ܡܙ, line 5. Insert the letter 'v' after ܠܗܘܢ.

" ܡܗ, line 5. Read ܠܡܫܝܚܘܬܐ.

" 9, line 5. Read "can teach."

" 23, line 10. For "Matthew" substitute "Matthias."

ܘܡܬܪܥܝܢ. ܐܠܐ ܕܝܢ ܢܘܗܪܐ ܐܝܬܘܗܝ. ܐܘܕܥ ܠܝ ܡܢܐ
ܗܝ ܗܕܐ. ܘܐܡܪ ܠܗܘܢ ܫܡܥܘܢ. ܕܠܐ ܘܬܒܘ ܬܫܡܫܬܗܘܢ
ܘܣܝܡ ܐܢܬܘܢ ܕܡܢܐ ܐܝܬܘܗܝ، ܡܕܡ ܕܐܡܪ ܥܠܝܟܘܢ
ܘܠܐ ܡܬܒܥܝܢ ܐܢܬܘܢ ܠܗܘܢ ܬܘܒ ܡܬܪܥܝܢ. ܘܟܕ ܐܙܠܘ
ܥܠ̈ܝܡܐ ܘܬܒܥܘ ܬܫܡܫܬ ܐܠܗܝܬ. ܡܫܡܫܐ ܐܠܗܝܐ ܥܒܕܘ
ܬܘ̈ܕܝܬܐ ܕܦܘܪܩܢ. ܘܐܬܘ ܬܘܒ ܥܠ̈ܝܡܐ ܠܘܬ ܫܡܥܘܢ ܘܐܡܪܝܢ
ܠܗ. ܡܠܦܢܢ. ܕܬܠܡܝܕܐ ܡܢ ܓܒܝܬ ܐܘ ܬܫܡܫܬܢ ܠܝ ܡܢ
ܗܕܐ ⁘ ⁘ ⁘ ⁘

⁘ ⁘ ⁘ ⁘

⁘ ⁘ ⁘ ⁘ ⁘

⁘ ⁘ ⁘ ⁘

ܐܦ ܐܢܬܘܢ ܕܚܝܢ ܐܢܬܘܢ ܘܗܝ ܕܒܗ ܥܘܕܐ ܕܢܘܕܐ
ܐܢܘܢ ܠܥܠܝܡܬܐ ܡܛܠ ܐܝܕܐ ܚܠܬܐ ܠܐ ܥܒܕ ܠܗܘܢ
ܐܦ ܗܘ ܐܢܘܢ ܠܛܘܪܐ ܣܝ. ܘܥܒܕ ܠܗܘܢ ܕܢܚܙܘܢ ܘܗܝ
ܐܝܠܝܢ ܥܠܝܡܬܐ ܒܗ ܒܗܘ ܘܐܡܪܝܢ ܠܗ. ܡܪܝ، ܒܚܝܢ
ܐܝܟܢ. ܡܢܐ ܗܘܝܠ ܐܝܬ ܠܝ ܕܐܬܚܙܐ ܒܡܥܒܪܢܐ ܗܢܐ.
ܘܐܡܪ ܠܗܘܢ ܥܘܒܕ. ܕܢܗܘܘܢ ܠܐܝܠܝܢ ܕܡܘܗܒܘܢ.
ܘܐܡܪ ܠܗܘܢ. ܕܐܝܠ ܠܗܠܝܢ ܐܝܠܝܢ ܕܠܗܘܒܠ. ܗܠܝܢ
ܕܦܬܝܢ ܘܦܩܝܕܘܢ ܘܥܒܝܕܝܢ ܘܥܒܕܝܢ ܡܢ ܪܘܚܐ.
ܘܡܢܗܘܢ ܡܬܗܕܝܢ ܐܢܬܘܢ ܘܗܝ ܐܝܠܝܢ ܥܠܝܡܬܐ ܠܐ
ܐܥܒܕ ܒܗܘܢ ܦܐܪܐ ܒܐܝܠܢܐ. ܘܗܦܟܘ ܠܗܘܢ ܥܘܒܕ
ܘܐܡܪܝܢ. ܡܠܦܢܐ ܛܒܐ. ܥܒܕܬ ܠܝ ܠܗܠܝܢ ܐܝܠܝܢ
ܕܠܗܘܒ[ܠ] ܘܐܝܠ ܐܝܟܢ ܘܠܐ ܐܥܒܕ ܚܢ ܒܗܘܢ
ܦܐܪܐ. ܐܠܐ ܐܢ ܗܘܒܐ ܕܗܕܝܢ ܘܥܒܝܕ ܘ[ܦ]ܐܪܐ
ܠܝܬ ܒܗܘܢ ܘܐܡܪ ܠܗܘܢ ܥܘܒܕ. ܠܐ ܚܙܝܬܘܢ ܐܢܘܢ
ܡܛܠ ܕܠܒܠ ܛܪܝܡ ܗܘܘ ܐܝܠܢܐ. ܘܠܐ ܗܘܝܠ ܡܚܙܝܐ
ܡܛܘܠ ܕܐܝܠܢܐ ܡܪܚܝܢ ܢܦܫܗܘܢ. ܘܡܥܒܕܝܢ ܐܢܬܘܢ
ܒܗܘܢ ܦܐܪܐ ܘܡܬܗܦܟܝܢ ܐܢܬܘܢ ܘܗܝ ܐܝܠܝܢ ܐܥܒܕܘ
ܐܢܘܢ ܠܐܝܠܢܐ ܕܡܪܚܝܢ. ܘܠܐ ܐܥܒܕܘ ܒܗܘܢ ܦܐܪܐ.
ܘܗܦܟܘ ܬܘܒ ܠܗܘܢ ܥܘܒܕ ܒܒܥܬܐ ܪܒܬܐ ܘܐܡܪܝܢ ܠܗ.
ܡܢܐ ܗܝ ܗܕܐ ܡܠܦܢܢ. ܕܐܬܒܥܝܬ ܣܝ. ܒܡܕܒܪܬܐ
ܐܡܪܬ ܠܝ ܒܪܝ ܕܡܥܒܕܝܢ ܐܢܬܘܢ ܐܝܠܢܐ [ܕܐܬ]ܪܝܡܘ
ܘܐܝܬ ܒܗܘܢ ܦܐܪܐ. ܘܠܐ ܐܥܒܕܘܢ. ܠܡܢܐ ܡܬܒܥܝܬܘܢ
ܣܝ. ܐܠܐ ܦܫܩ ܕܬܠܦ ܠܝ ܡܢܐ ܗܝ ܗܕܐ ܕܗܘܬ.
ܐܢܫܝܢ ܒܪܝ ܗܒܝܢ ܐܢܫܝܢ ܕܒܟܠ ܚܕ ܡܢܗܘܢ ܕܒܥܘܬ ܕܬܠܦ
ܠܝ. ܡܢ ܚܝܠܐ ܒܪܝ ܕܡܬܚܙܝܐ [ܡܢܬ]ܠܒܒܝܢ ܐܝܠܢܐ

ܘܗܟܢܐ ܐܬܬܩܦ ܚܠܝܡ ܡܪܢܐ. ܘܦܢܐ ܠܗܕܡܝܢ ܡܢ ܫܘܚܒܪܗ
ܕܦܘܪܩܢ̈ ܘܟܕ ܗܠܝܢ ܡܬܐܡܪ̈ܢ ܗܘ̈ܝ. ܡܢ ܡܘܫܐ ܘܡܢ
ܢܒܝܐ ܟܠܗ. ܐܢܐ ܐܝܬܝ ܘܡܠܠܬ. ܐܢܐ ܡܫܬܐܠ
ܡܠܐܟܐ ܘܐܡܪܬ ܠܗ ܠܡܘܫܐ. ܡܘܫܐ ܡܘܫܐ̇ ܫܡܥ
ܐܠܗܐ ܐܒܗ̈ܬܟܘܢ ܩܘܡ ܘܙܠ ܠܘܬ ܢܘܪܐ. ܘܡܫܚ
ܒܫܘܦܪܟ ܠܡܫܝܐ. ܘܗܫܡܬܐ ܡܫܦܠܢܬܐ ܬܬܦܠܚܐ ܡܕܡܝܢ.
ܡܢܐ ܗܦܟܬ ܡܢܝܢ. ܠܐ ܡܫܢܐ ܕܡܫܝܚܐ ܡܘܫܐ ܠܢܘܪܐ
ܐܬܟܠ ܗܘ̇ ܐܝܢܐ ܕܗܘܝܢ· ܗܘ̣ܐ ܒܗ ܘܗܘܐ ܘܐܬܦ̣ܐ
ܠܒܝܫܐ. ܘܦܬܝܚܗ ܡܘܫܐ ܘܐܫܟܚ ܡܫܠܡܬܐ ܕܚܬܝܒ ܒܗ̇.
ܕܗܠܝܢ ܒ̈ܢܝܐ ܕܝܘܣܦ ܐܢܘܢ. ܘܫܒܩ ܐܢܘܢ ܘܐܙܠ
ܐܢܘܢ ܠܐܪܥܗܘܢ ܠܘܬ ܐܒܗ̈ܬܗܘܢ ܘܡ[ܢ ܟܬܒ] ܕܗܢܐ
ܫܠ[ܡܐ] ܐܫܬܠܡܬ ...... ܐܢܘܢ̈ ...... •

ܐܢܘܢ ܐܝܟ ܕܒܝܫܘܬܗܘܢ̈ ܘܫܪܪ ܒܗ ܥܠܝܡܐ ܠܗܘܬܗܘܢ̈
ܠܐ ܗܘܝܢܐ ܗܘ̈ܘ. ܘܐܦܢܝ ܕܗܠܝܢ ܕ̈ܒܗܬܐ ܕܒܢܝ ܐܝܣܪܝܠ.
ܕܒܟܝܢ ܥܠ ܚܛ̈ܗܐ ܕܢܬܚܣܝܘܢ ܕܢܬܚܫܒܘܢ ܗܝܟ ܩܕܡ
ܐܒܗܐ. ܘܠܢܦܫܗܘܢ ܠܐ ܡܚܟܡܝܢ ܕܚܫܘܢ. ܡܛܠ
ܕܡܒܟܝܢ ܢܦܫܗܘܢ ܐܝܟ ܒܢܝܐ. ܠܐ ܐܬܬܘ̈ܬܐ ܗܘܝܬ
ܠܗܘܢ ܦܘܠܚܢ̈ܬܐ. ܘܫܠܝܚܐ ܐܡܪ ܡܢ ܗܘ ܐ ܡܦܣܝܢ
ܘܡܫܠܝܢ ܘܬܚܝܢ. ܘܥܠ ܒܥܒ̈ܕܗܘܢ ܒܪܝܢ. ܠܡܢܐ ܠܐ
ܫܡܥܬ ܠܗܘܢ ܐܡܪܬ ܠܗܘܢ ܡܪܢ ܐܦ ܐܢܐ ܦܪܥܐ
ܗܘܝܬ ܕܐܫܡܥܟ. ܐܢܘܢ ܐܠܐ ܡܦܠܚܢܘܬܐ ܐܝܬ ܒܗܘܢ.

ܕܗܠܝܢ ܠܒ̈ܢܘܗܝ، ܒܚܝܗܘܢ ܢܣܒܘܢ ܘܡܢܐ ܕܒܪܬ ܠܗ
ܗܕܐ ܠܐ ܡܬܚܫܒܝܢ ܕܢܗܘܘܢ؛ ܐܠܐ ܐܢ ܫܡܥܘ ܐܢܘܢ
ܒܡܘܬܗܘܢ؛ ܘܦܬܚܝܢ ܠܗܘܢ ܬܪܥܐ ܫܠܝܚܝܢ ܒܡܪ̈ܝܡ. ܘܡܢ
ܒܬܪ ܗܠܝܢ. ܡܢ ܦܪܘܩܢ ܡܠܟܐ ܕܡܪ̈ܝܡ. ܘܦܩܕ ܕܢܗܘܐ
ܫܦܝܪܐ ܟܠܗ ܢܘܗܪܐ. ܘܩܒܠ ܐܢܘܢ ܠܒ̈ܢܘܗܝ، ܕܝܘܣܦ.
[ܘ]ܗܘ ܐܢܘܢ ܒܐܪܥܐ . . . . ܦܐ. ܘܫܡܥܗ ܒܒܘܦܪܐ
. . . . . . ܘܚܙܝܬ ܫܡܥܗ [ܕܝܘܣܦ ܒ]ܡܓܠܬܐ. ܗܢ . . . .
[ܗܠܝܢ] ܠܒ̈ܢܐ ܕܝܘܣܦ ܐ[ܢܘ]ܢ. ܘܗܘ] ܠܡܓܠܬܐ
ܒܐܪܥܐ. ܘܦܩܕ ܕܢܬܬܗ[ܡ] ܒܡܓ̈ܠܬܗ ܕܫܦܝܪ[ܐ] ܟܠܗ
ܢܘܗܪܐ. ܘܟܕ ܟܠ ܦܪܘܩܢ ܐܘܪܚ ܦܘܠܚܢܐ ܡܫܐ ܟܠ ܒ̈ܢܝ
ܐܣܪܐܝܠ ܘܐܡܪ ܠܗܘܢ ܕܢܗܘܘܢ. ܘܟܠܗ ܒ̈ܢܝ ܐܣܪܐܝܠ
ܘܐܡܪܝܢ ܠܗ ܠܡܠܟܐ. ܢܗܘܘܢ ܠܘܬ ܠܒ̈ܢܘܗܝ، ܕܝܘܣܦ
ܐܢܫ ܡܢ ܡܠܟܘܬܐ. ܡܛܠ ܕܐܘܡܝ ܗܘܐ ܠܐܒ̈ܗܝܢ. ܕܢܗܘܘܢ
ܠܒ̈ܢܘܗܝ، ܒܡܗܘܢ ܕܒ̈ܢܝ ܐܣܪܐܝܠ. ܐܝܟ ܕܝܢ ܡܠܟܐ ܘܠܐ
ܐܫܟܚܘ ܐܢܘܢ. ܠܐ ܓܝܪ ܢܕܥܝܢ ܗܘܘ ܒ̈ܢܝ ܐܣܪܐܝܠ ܕܐܝܟܢ
ܐܢܘܢ ܦܪܘܩܢ ܡܫܝܚܢ ܘܟܕ ܠܐ ܐܫܟܚܘ ܐܢܘܢ. ܬܠܝܘ
ܡܫ̈ܝܚܝܢ ܘܒܟܘ ܡܪܝܪܐܝܬ. ܘܐܬܬܢܝܘ ܩܕܡ ܠܘܬ
ܐܠܗܐ. ܘܡܘܟܐ ܒܡܗܘܢ؛ [ܡܪܢܐ] ܐܠܗܐ [ܕ]ܐܒ̈ܗܝܢ
ܠܡܠܟܐ [ܕ]ܒܡܠܟܘܬܗ، ܠܒܢܝ. ܐܬܦܬܚܬ ܚܕ ܟܠܝܢ. ܘܡܢ
ܒܬܪ ܕܐܬܦܬܚܬ: ܐܦܬܚܬ ܕܝܚܝܢ ܡܢ. ܘܗܘܘ ܐܝܟ
ܐܪܒܥܐ ܕܝܘܡܬܐ ܕܠܐ ܚܙܬ ܫܡܫܐ. ܘܡܢ ܒܬܪ ܕܝܘܡܐ
ܦܬܚܝܢ. ܐܬܓܠܝ ܢܘܗܪܐ. ܘܟܕ ܐܬܓܠܝ ܘܚܙܐ. ܟܠܗ ܠܘܬ
ܡܪܢܐ ܒ̈ܢܝ ܐܣܪܐܝܠ ܘܐܡܪܝܢ. ܫܠܡܐ ܠܡܠܟܐ ܘܠܡܠܟܘܬܗ
ܕܒܢܝ ܡܪܢܐ ܐܬܒܪܝܬ. ܡܛܠ ܗܢܐ ܠܓܒܝܬ ܠܒ̈ܢܘܗܝ،
ܕܝܘܣܦ ܐܢܘܢ. ܕܢܗܘܐ ܒܗܕܐ ܒܒܪܘܬܐ ܒܒܪܝܐ ܠܟܠܗ.

[ܘ]ܐܬܠܒܫ݁ ܡܢܡܘܬ ܒܢܝ [ܘ]ܐܡܪܬ ܠܗܘܢ ܕܠܐ ܡܫܡܫܝܢ
ܐܢܬܘܢ [ܕ]ܬܗܡܢܘܢ ܡܢܐ [ܕ]ܚܝܬܘܢ ܡܠܝܢ. ܐܠܐ ܒܢܝ
ܐܘܟܠܬܟܘܢ ܠܗܘ ܐܬܪܐ ܒܪܝܐ. ܐܝܟܢܐ [ܕ]ܐܦ ܠܐ
ܢܫܬܐ [ܕ]ܩܢܐ ܐܢܫܐ ܐܝܬ. [ܘ]ܬܗܘܢ ܐܝܬ ܬܫܡܫܬܐ
[ܘ]ܟܢܫܐ ܕܡܫܠܡܝܢ ܡܢ ܕܫܘܪܐ. ܡܢ [ܗ]ܘܐ ܗܘܐ
ܡܢܗܘܢ [ܗ]ܘܝܘ ܡܠܠ ܡܫܬܐܠ [ܠܗ]ܠܝܢ ܕܫܡܫܬܐ ܘܡܬܡܪ
[ܠ]ܗܘܢ. ܩܢܝ. ܚܕ ܡܢܗ [ܡ]ܪܐ ܚܕ ܡܢܗ [ܡ]ܪܐ. ܚܕ ܡܢܗ
ܗܘ ܕܫܬܝܢ ܕܝܗܘܢ ܠܩܢܝܬܐ ܘܠܢܘܪܐ. ܚܕ ܡܢܗ ܗܘ ܕܫܠܝܛ
ܥܠ ܟܠ ܒܢܝܢ. ܡܛܠ ܕܬܫܡܫܬܐ ܫܡܝܢ ܐܝܬ ܒܗ ܗܘ ܒܝܘܡܐ
ܘܬܫܡܫܬܐ ܒܠܠܝܐ. ܘܗܠܝܢ ܡܬܡܢܝܢ ܒܬܫܒܘܚܬܐ
ܘܗܠܟܐ ܕܒܝܬܐ ܠܐܠܗܐ. ܘܢܦܠܝܢ ܡܠܐܟܐ ܘܣܓܕܝܢ ܠܗ
ܠܡܪܗܘܢ. ܘܡܫܒܚܝܢ ܚܝܠ ܒܠܗ ܒܪܝܬܐ. ܘܟܠ ܒܠܗ
ܐܢܫܘܬܐ. ܘܡܠܐܟܐ ܕܒܫܡܝܐ ܒܠ ܩܢܝܐ. ܦܪܝ ܘܡܫܒܚ
ܠܗ ܠܐܠܗܐ ܒܪ ܐܕܡ. ܕܢܬܬܪܘܢ ܡܟܝܟܐ ܕܩܢܝܐ
ܡܛܠ ܒܥܘܐ ܕܩܢܝ ܐܢܫܐ. ܡܛܠ ܕܐܠܗܘܬܐ ܐܢܘܢ ܘܕܫܒܘܚܬܐ
ܡܢܗ. ܡܛܠܗܢܐ ܡܫܒܚ ܐܢܐ ܠܟ ܕܬܫܒܚܬܐ ܕܡܫܒܚܢܘܬܐ
ܐܢܐ. ܢܫܒܚܘܢ ܝܫܘܥ ܥܠ ܩܢܝܐ ܕܬܫܒܘܚܬܐ ܒܟܘܠܗ
ܒܪܝܬܐ ܘ.ܘ.ܘ.ܘܘ

⁘ ⁘ ⁘ ⁘ ⁘

⁘ ⁘ ⁘ ⁘

⁘ ⁘ ⁘ ⁘ ⁘

(fol. 5) ܘܐܘܕܥ ܐܢܘܢ ܒܐܬܪܐ ܠܦܢܝܐ ܬܫܥܝܬ ܐܕܡ
ܕܫܠܡܝܢ. ܕܠܐ ܢܫܡܥܘܢ ܐܢܘܢ ܘܡܢܐ ܕܒܒܝܬ ܗܕܐ.
ܠܐ ܡܫܡܫܝܢ ܕܒܪܝܘܢ ܘܢܦܩܘܢ ܐܢܘܢ ܫܡܫܝܗܘܢ. ܒܢܝ
ܠܗܘܢ ܒܪ ܡܢܐܬ. ܕܐܘܡܢ ܗܘܐ ܠܟܢܝ ܒܡܫܗ. ܕܡܫܐ

(fol. 4) ܡܪܢ ܠܒܢ̈ܝܐ ܕܫܒ̈ܝܠ ܠܘܬ ܦܬܚܗ ܕܦܪܕܝܣܐ.
[ܘ]ܒܗ ܟܠܗܘܢ ܠܦܪܕܝܣܐ. ܐܝܟ ܦܓܪܗ̇ ܕܡܪܝܡ ܠܘܬ ܐܠܗܐ
ܕܚ̈ܝܐ. ܘܐܬܬܘ ܠܢܦܫܗ̇ ܘܐܟܠܘܢ ܠܗ ܦܓܪܗ̇. ܘܡܫܝܚܐ
ܡܪܢ ܫܪܐ ܠܡܠܐ̈ܟܐ ܠܕܘܟ̈ܝܬܗܘܢ ܘܡܢ ܒܬܪ ܗܠܝܢ
ܐܡܪܝܢ ܫܠܝ̈ܚܐ ܠܡܪܢ ܡܪܝܐ. ܐܒܓܪܬ ܠܝ ܒܗ ܒܗܢ ܗܘܘܬ.
ܒܗ ܐܦܣܩܢ ܕܢܣܒܐ ܠܦܓܪܗ̇ ܕܡܪܝܡ ܕܝܠܕܬ ܠܝ. ܘܐܒܓܪܬ
ܠܝ ܐܢ ܗܕܐ ܒܚܝܠܝܢ ܕܬܫܡܫܢ: ܗܘܘ ܠܗܘܢܐ ܕܡܦܩܢܗ̇
ܕܡܪܝܡ. ܘܫܡܥ ܐܢܐ ܠܟܘܢ ܘܫܬܩܘܢ ܫ̈ܠܝܚܐ ܀

ܬܐܪܐ ܕܫܠܐ ܕܬܫܒܘܚܬܐ ܕܟܠܗ ܫ̈ܠܝܚܐ ܡܢ ܡܪܢ ܕܫܡܥܘܢ.
ܘܒܗ ܗܠܝܢ ܡܬܐܡܪ̈ܢ ܗ̇ܘ ܡܢ ܫܠܝܚܐ ܦܘܠܘܣ. ܪܒܐ
ܡܪܢ ܒܒܢ̈ܘܗܝ. ܘܒܢܝܢܐ [ܣܠܩܬ] ܐܝܟ ܠܫ̈ܠܝܚܐ
ܘܠܡܪܘ[ܡ] ܘܠܡܠܟܘܬܐ. ܘܡܪܢ ܒܥܡܗܘܢ ܘܐܡܪ[ܠܗ]
ܐܝܟ ܠܟܠܒܐ ܕܟܪ[ܒ] ܫܡܫܐ. ܘܐܪܦܣܬ [ܐܝܟ] ܬܡܢ.
ܘܟܠܠ ܡܪܢ ܒܡ ܡܠܐ̈ܟܐ ܕܒ[ܫܝܬܐ.] ܘܫܪܘܬ ܐܪܒܐ
ܠܟܠ ܘܐܬܟܠ ܦܫܬܐ ܟܠ[ܘ] ܐܪܒܐ. ܘܡܪܢ ܗܘ[ܒ]
ܐܬܪܐ ܠܫܠܝܚ[ܐ] ܕܢܣ[ܒܪܘܢ] ܐܝܟ ܕܟܬܝܒ ܗܘܘ. [ܘܒܗ]
ܡܪܒ ܘܐܬܕܡܘ ܒܚܝ[ܬܐ] ܗ̇ܘ ܫܘ ܠܡܠܟܘܬܐ ܗ̇ܘܢ
ܕܒܚܝܬܐ ܘܗ[ܘܐ] ܒܒܢܝܐ ܪܒܐ ܘܫܟ[ܬܐ.] ܘܒܢܘ
ܘܐܡܪܝܢ ܠܡܠܟܘ[ܬܐ.] ܡܠܟܘܬܐ ܪܡܐ ܡܠܐ̈[ܟܐ] ܡܠܟܘܬܐ
ܫܠܝ ܡܠܟܘ[ܬܐ] ܪܒ ܫܠܝ. ܘܐܒܬ ܘܡܪ[ܝ] ܒܬܫܒܘܚܢ
ܫܠܒ[ܝܢ.] ܠܚܒܬ ܠܝ ܚܢ ܒܘܠ[ܗ] ܗܢܐ ܢܘܓܪܐ. ܠܡܪ[ܐ]
ܠܗ ܒܓܒܬ ܫܠܦܡ ܡܪ[ܝ] ܡܪܢ ܕܢܬܠ ܠܝ ܥ[ܠ ܢܒ]ܐܥܐ
ܡܢ ܐܘܠܝܢܐ. [ܘ]ܡܫܝܚܐ ܕܢܚܬ ܡܪܝܡ ܘܫܠܝܚܐ. ܢܚܠܘ
ܒܠ ܐܪܒܐ ܡܢ ܒܡܬܐ ܕ[ܗ]ܠܝܢ ܕܒܦܫܬܐ. [ܘ]ܡܪܢ
ܐܡܝܢ ܐܝܟ [ܘ]ܐܦܪܘܬ ܠܗܘܢ. ܐܘ [ܬ]ܠܝܬܐ ܘܒܗܘܢ

ܬ̈ܠܐ ܕܡܨܝ̈ܕܬܐ ܠܗܘܢ .ܘ.ܘ ܘܘ ܗܘܝܢ ܙܠܦܐ ܟܠܗܘܢ
ܥܠܝ̈ܡܐ ܘܠܐ ܐܬܦܠܣܘ ܠܬ̈ܠܝܗܘܢ ܕܦܘܠܘܣ. ܘܐܝܟ
ܕܐܬܟܡ ܡܢܟ ܬܪܥܗ ܕܡܫܪܐ ܕܡܪܩܝܘܢ ܟܠܗܘܢ ܥܠܝ̈ܡܐ
ܘܐܬܚܕܝܘ ܥܠ ܬ̈ܠܝܗܘܢ ܕܦܘܠܘܣ. ܗܐ ܡܪܩܝܘܢ ܡܫܒܚ
ܡܟܝܟܐ ܐܬܐ ܡܢ ܫܡܝܐ ܠܡ ܡܢ ܓܒ[ܪܐܝܠ] ܡܠܐܟܐ.
ܘܐܬܒ ܥܒܕ ܥ̈ܠܝܡܐ. ܗܢ ܕܝܢ ܥܠ ܡܠܬܗ ܕܦܘܠܘܣ. ܘܚܙܝܐ
ܘܐܡܪ ܡܫܒܚ. ܥܠܡ ܠܝ ܦܬܓܡܐ ܐܦܣܛܘܠܐ. ܘܥܠܡ ܠܝ
ܡܫܝܚ ܒܬܘܠܐ. ܕܐܬܝܠܕ ܒܝܕ ܢܒܝ̈ܘܬܗ. ܘܥܠܡ ܠܝ
ܦܘܠܐ ܡܠܘܟܐ ܕܡܫܝ̈ܚܘܬܐ. ܐܝܟܢ ܕܝܢ ܐܡܪܝܢܐ ܠܝ ܦܬܓܡܐ.
ܕܡܬܠܝܢ ܒܡܠܟ ܡܬ̈ܠܐ ܗܘܘ.‧ ܕܠܝ ܘܕܐܝܬܝܗܘܢ
ܘܕܗܘܝܢ. ܐܡܪܝܢܐ ܠܟܘܢ ܕܝܢ ܕܕܦܘܠܘܣ ܢܬܩܒܠܘܢ. ܚܙܐ
ܐܝܟ ܥܠ ܕܒܘܠܗ ܒܠܒܐ ܒܡܫܝܚܘܬܗ ܗܘ ܕܦܘܠܘܣ
ܡܬܝܩܪ. ܘܗܘ ܡܫܒܚܐ ܠܗܘܢ ܘܗܘܝܢ ܡܢ ܒܬܪ ܗܠܝܢ.
ܢܬܝܕܥܘܢ ܦܬܟܪ̈ܝܗܘܢ ܠܣܪܬܐ ܕܕܝܢܐ. ܘܐܬܦܬܚ ܡܪܝܢ
ܠܗܬ ܦܘܠܘܣ ܘܐܡܪ ܠܗ. ܐܝܟ ܦܘܠܐ ܠܐ ܠܐ ܬܬܟܝܢ ܕܠܐ
ܟܠܗ ܠܝ ܥܠܝ̈ܡܐ ܣܓܝ̈ܐܝܢ ܕܝܢ ܫܡܝ̈ܢܐ. ܠܗܘܢ ܕܝܢ
ܐܬܟܠܝ ܗܠܝܢ ܕܒܐܪܥܐ. ܠܝ ܕܝܢ ܐܠܗܝ ܗܠܝܢ ܕܒܫܡܝܐ.
ܘܡܢ ܒܬܪ ܗܠܝܢ ܢܦܩ ܠܗ ܡܪܝܢ ܠܡܫܡܥܘ. ܘܒܟܠܐ
ܡܫܡܥܘ ܒܟܠܐ ܕܡܠܐܟܐ ܡܫܠܡܐ. ܘܚܝܠܘ ܒܢ̈ܝܢܐ
ܬܠܬ. ܡܠ̈ܐܟܐ. ܘܡܫܝܚܐ ܕܡܠ̈ܐܟܐ ܕܒܢ̈ܝܢܐ ܕܚܙܐ ܚܙܐ ܐܝܟ
ܡܢܗܘܢ ܐܠܦ ܡܠ̈ܐܟܝܢ ܡܫܡܫ[ܝܢ] ܩܕܡܘܗܝ. ܕܦܫ[ܛ]
ܘܐܡܪ ܡܪܝܢ ܠܡܫܡ[ܥܘ] ܕܦܬܓܡܗ ܕܡܪܩܝܘܢ ܢܬܠ[ܘܢ]
ܠܬ̈ܪܝܢ ܒܢ̈ܝܢܐ. ܘ[ܒܪ] ܥܠ ܦܬܓܡܗ ܕܡܪܩܝܘܢ ܠܒ̈ܢܝܢܐ. ܐܡܪ
ܡܪܝܢ ܠܥܠܝ̈ܡܐ. ܕܢܬܩܪ[ܒܘܢ] ܠܗܬ ܒ̈ܢܝܢܐ. ܘܒ[ܪ] ܐܬܘ
ܠܗܬ ܒܢ̈ܝ[ܐ]! ܡܪܩܝܘܢ ܗܘܘ ܒܟܠ[ܐ] ܕܡܠ̈ܐܟܐ ܘܐܡܪ

ܥܒܕ ܠܐܒܐ ܘܠܐܡܐ. ܘܠܐܚܐ ܘܠܐܚܘܬܐ ܘܩܪܝܒܐ
ܘܚܬܢܐ. ܘܟܠ ܡܕܡ ܕܐܝܬ ܠܗ ܘܢܦܩ ܒܬܪ ܡܪܢ. ܠܐ
ܡܫܟܚ ܕܢܗܘܐ ܠܐܠܗܐ. ܐܡܪ ܠܗ ܦܘܠܘܣ ܠܐܢܕܪܐܘܣ.
ܐܟܘܬ ܐܢܕܪܐܘܣ. ܩܠܝܠ ܐܚܝ ܫܠܡܘܗܝ، ܕܦܛܪܘܣ ܘܕܝܘܚܢܢ
ܡܢ ܗܠܝܢ ܕܠܝ. ܠܟܠ ܐܢܫ ܒܪ ܦܪܨܘܦܗ، ܡܢ ܐܪܒܥܐ
ܟܢܘܫܐ ܫܠܝܚܐ. ܡܛܠ ܒܪ ܫܡܥ ܫܠܝܚܘܗܝ ܟܘܠܗܘܢ ܒܗܢܐ ܙܒܢܐ.
ܘܗܐܡܪ ܟܠ ܢܦܫ ܡܗܝܡܢܐ ܗܝܡܢܘܬܐ. ܘܒܢܘ ܦܛܪܘܣ
ܘܐܢܕܪܐܘܣ ܘܐܡܪܝܢ ܠܦܘܠܘܣ. ܦܘܠܐ ܙܒܢܐ ܕܢܦܫ. ܐܡܪ
ܠܝ ܕܐܡܪܢܐ ܒܟܠ ܕܢܦܩ ܘܢܛܪ ܀.܀.܀ ܀ ܐܡܪ ܠܗܘܢ
ܦܘܠܘܣ. ܐܢ ܫܡܥܝܢ ܐܢܬܘܢ (fol. 3) [ܠ]ܗ ܗܠܝܢ ܒܒܝܬ.
ܘܬܫܡܫ ܫܠܝܐ ܗܠܝܢ ܕܡܫܡܫܝܢ ܕܢܒܝܘܗܝ ܡܛܠ ܕܫܪܬܐܝܬ
ܐܢܘܢ. ܘܠܐ ܡܢܝܢ ܙܕܩܐ. ܘܢܐܡܪ ܠܗܘܢ ܗܠܝܢ. ܕܒܟܠ
ܐܢܫ [ܠ]ܐܢܬܬܗ ܢܐܚܘܕ. [ܕ]ܠܐ ܢܦܘܩܘܢ ܘܐܢܬܬܐ
ܠܒܥܠܗ ܬܐܚܘܕ ܕܠܐ [ܬ]ܦܘܩ. ܘܢܗܘܐ ܠܗܘܢ [ܡ]ܘܗܒܐ
ܬܪܝܢ ܦܪܨܘܦ ܒܒܝܬܐ. ܘܠܐ ܢܬܦܢܐ ܒܠܒܗܘܢ ܠܗ. ܕܠܐ
[ܕ]ܬܦܪܘܢ ܘܢܫܦܩܘܢ [ܐ]ܠܐ ܐܢ ܢܨܒܝܢ [ܡܢ]ܗܝ. ܘܠܒܢܝ
ܟܠܗ. [ܡ]ܦܩܝܢ ܠܒܢܝܐ. ܘܗܘܝܢ [ܬ]ܘܒ ܐܡܪܝܢ ܕܠܡܢ
[ܠ]ܐ ܢܨܒܝܢ. ܘܐܢ [ܐ]ܬܘ ܠܒܢܝܐ ܕܠܒܫܘܢ
[ܘ]ܢܫܒܩܘܢ ܡܫܡܫܢܐ [ܘ]ܢܬܠܘܢ ܠܗ. ܗܘܝܢ ܐܡܪܝܢ. ܠܡܢ
ܢܨܒܝܢ ܐܢ ܠܡܫܡܫܢܐ ܠܐ [ܢ]ܗܘܫܢ[ܢ.] ܘܢܕܒܘܢ
ܠܐܠܗܐ ܒܠܒܗܘܢ ܘܬܘܒ ܢܐܡܪ ܠܗܘܢ ܕܐܢܫܐ ܕܠܐ
ܢܗܘܐ ܒܕܡܘܬܐ ܠܥܠ ܫܡܝܐ. ܘܐܢܫܐ ܕܡ[ܫ]ܚ ܒܕܡܘܬܐ
ܠܬܚܬ. ܘܐܢܫܐ ܬܘܒ ܕܡܫܟܚ ܒܕܡܘܬܐ ܠܐܪܥܐ. ܘܗܘܐ
ܕܐܫܟܚ ܚܝܝ ܐܢܘܢ ܐܝܟ ܕܫܠܝܚܐ ܗܘܦܝܢ ܐܢܘܢ
ܠܗܬ[ܢ] ܗܕܝܢ ܡܬܠܠܝܢ ܚܝ ܠܗܘܢ ܕܪܒܘܬܐ ܘܫܒܝܚܘܬܐ.

ܕܡܫܒܚ ܘܬܬܕܟܪܘܢ ܕܟܠ ܢܦܫܢ ܐܢܬܘܢ ܕܬܬܒܪܘܢ
ܘܬܠܦܘܢ. ܐܝܟ ܐܦ ܐܢܐ ܕܐܡܪ ܐܠܦ ܒܘܠܦܢܟܘܢ.
ܐܡܪ ܠܗ ܦܛܪܘܣ. ܐܚܝ ܦܘܠܐ. ܗܕܐ ܡܠܬܐ ܕܐܡܪܬ
ܥܡܝܩܐ ܗܝ. ܡܛܠ ܕܐܦ ܕܬܕܟܪ ܒܒܢܬ ܘܕܬܫܬܒܚ ܗ̇ܝ
ܕܬܬܕܟܪ ܐܢܫ ܕܠܐ ܘܒܟܪ ܠܒܢܝܢܫܐ ܥܒܕ ܘܐܡܪ ܠܝ.
ܐܢܐ ܐܝܟ ܫܠܝܚܐ ܕܐܡܪ ܫܡܪܝܢܝ. ܕܟܠ ܕܠܐ ܗ̇ܘܐ
ܫܒܩܐ ܠܟܘܢ ܡܢܬܗܘܢ. ܠܐ ܫܘܐ ܠܗ ܠܐܠܗܐ. ܫܡܪ ܠܗ
ܦܘܠܘܣ ܠܦܛܪܘܣ. ܐܟܘܬ ܦܛܪܘܣ. ܡܢܐ ܗܝ ܗܕܐ ܡܠܬܐ
ܕܐܡܪܬ. ܕܠܐ ܠܡܠܬܟ ܫܡܥܝܢ. ܘܫܡܥܝܢ ܘܡܛܠܝܢ ܠܝ.
ܡܛܠ ܕܒ̈ܢܝܐ ܐܢܘܢ ܘܠܐ ܡܫܡܥܝܢ ܒܗ ܒܐܠܗܐ. ܘܐܦܠܐ
ܒܦܘܡܐ. ܘ.ܘ.ܘܘ ܘܘ ܘܐܬܦܢܝ ܬܘܒ ܦܘܠܘܣ ܠܘܬ
ܝܘܚܢܢ ܘܐܡܪ ܠܗ. ܐܡܪ ܠܝ ܐܦ ܐܢܬ ܡܠܦܢܝ ܐܟܘܬ
ܝܘܚܢܢ. ܕܗܟܢ ܐܦ ܐܢܐ ܐܠܦ ܘܐܡܪ. ܐܡܪ ܠܗ ܝܘܚܢܢ.
ܐܢܐ ܐܝܟ ܢܦܫܐ ܐܠܦ ܘܐܡܪ ܫܡܪܝܢܝ. ܕܟܠ ܕܠܐ ܗ̇ܘܐ
ܬܘܠܐ ܒܠܒܟܘܢ ܡܢܬܗܘܢ. ܠܐ ܡܬܚܙܐ ܕܢܚܙܐ ܠܐܠܗܐ.
ܘܡܢܐ ܦܘܠܘܣ ܘܐܡܪ ܠܗ ܠܝܘܚܢܢ. ܐܟܘܬ ܝܘܚܢܢ ܡܢܐ
ܗ̈ܢܝܢ ܗܠܝܢ ܡ̈ܠܐ. ܠܐܢܫܐ ܕܠܐ ܚܙܝܢ ܠܐܠܗܐ. ܟܠ
ܐܢܫܐ ܓܝܪ ܕܫܟܝܢ ܠܫ̈ܘܦܐ ܘܠܡܫܝܚܐ. ܐܝܟ ܫܡܥܝܢ
ܡܠܟܘܢ ܗܠܝܢ. ܪܚܝܡ ܠܝ ܘܫܡܥܝܢ ܠܝ ܒܬܐܘܪܝܐ. ܘ.ܘ.ܘ.ܘܘ ܘܘ
ܘܐܬܦܢܝ ܬܘܒ ܦܘܠܘܣ ܠܘܬ ܐܢܕܪܐܘܣ ܘܐܡܪ ܠܗ. ܐܟܘܬ
ܐܢܕܪܐܘܣ. ܐܡܪ ܠܝ ܐܦ ܐܢܬ ܡܢܐ ܗܝ ܡܫܬܒܚܘܬܟ. ܕܐܦ
ܐܢܐ ܐܠܦ ܘܐܡܪ. ܕܕܠܡܐ ܢܡܪ ܠܗ ܦܛܪܘܣ ܕܪܒܐ
ܐܝܬܘܗܝ ܘܐܦܣܩܘܦܐ. ܘܝܘܚܢܢ ܬܘܒ ܫܠܝܚ ܕܒܬܘܠܐ
ܗܘ. ܘܡܛܠ ܗܠܝܢ ܡܬܒܠܠܝܢ ܙܘܓ̈ܬܐ. ܐܡܪ ܠܗ ܐܢܕܪܐܘܣ
ܠܦܘܠܘܣ. ܐܢܐ ܐܦ ܢܦܫ ܐܢܐ ܐܠܦ ܫܡܪܝܢܝ. ܕܟܠ ܕܠܐ

ܘܒܝܬ ܒܗܘܢ ܕܗܝܡ̈ܢܘܬܐ ܠܐܦ̈ܩܝܢܐ. ܕܢܦܠܘܢ ܘܢܬܚܪܪܘܢ
ܘܢܬܬܢܝܚܘܢ ܒܗܝܢ. ܘܗܟܢ ܬܘܒ ܡܢܗܘܢ ܠܡܦܩܢܐ
ܘܠܬܬ̈ܠܡܐ. ܘܢܥܒܕ ܢܣܒܐ ܠܢܦ̈ܫܬܐ. ܗܠܝܢ ܐܡܪ ܒܪܐ
ܠܐܒܘܗܝ. ܘܫܠܡܬ ܢܦܫܗ. ܘܐܒܘܗܝ ܚܒܫ ܟܠ ܡܕܡ
ܕܐܡܪ ܠܗ ܒܪܗ ܀ . ܀܀ ܘܟܕ ܒܬܪ ܬܫܥܝܬܐ ܗܕܐ ܡܘܬܢ.
ܘܠܐ ܐܬܬ ܝܪܚ ܫܠܝܚܘܗܝ ܒܠܒܫܐ ܐܝܟ ܡܢܗܐ ܕܐܡܘܢܐ
ܡܕܡܘܬܗ. ܕܟܬܪ ܥܡܡܐ ܩܕܡܝܢ ܢܐܬܘܢ ܠܐܦܘܗܝ.
ܘܒܬܪ ܕܡܬܚܢܐ ܘܬܫܡܫܬܐ. ܘܠܐ ܐܬܘܢ ܠܘܬ ܫܠܝܚܐ
ܫܠܝܚܘܗܝ. ܫܪܪ ܒܬܪܗܘܢ ܡܠܟܐ ܒܗ ܐܡܪ. ܠܡܢܐ ܠܐ
ܐܬܝܬܘܢ ܕܐܡܪܬܐ ܒܝܘܡܢܐ. ܐܝܟ ܕܐܡܪܬ ܠܟܘܢ
ܘܒܢܝܐ ܐܒܘܗܝ ܕܗܘܐ ܦܠܛܐ ܘܐܡܪ ܡܪܝ. ܗܐ ܬܡܢܝܐ ܠܗ
ܩܕܡܝܢ ܠܒܪܝ ܕܝܬܒ ܡܢ ܒܠܚܘܕ. ܐܠܐ ܒܪܝ ܢܦܩ ܗܘܐ
ܕܡܐܢܬ ܠܗ. ܒܠ ܕܐܝܬ ܠܝ ܢܩܒ ܗܘܬ ܠܗ ܠܒܪܝ. ܕܠܐ
ܐܚܘܝܘܗܝ. ܐܠܐ ܒܠܚܘܕ ܕܐܡܪ ܠܝ ܒܒܥܬ ܀ . ܀ . ܀܀
ܘܟܕ ܫܡܥܘ ܫܠܝܚܘܗܝ ܗܕܐ ܡܢ ܒܪܐ ܗܘ. ܐܡܪ. ܕܡܕܡ
ܫܪܝܐ ܕܗܘܐ. ܡܛܠ ܗܢܐ ܐܡܪܝܢ ܩܕܝܫܐ. ܕܠܝܬ ܐܢܫ
ܗܠܝܢ ܕܡܬܚܫܒܝܢ ܒܝ. ܡܛܠ ܕܠܐ ܝܕܥܝܢ ܗܠܝܢ ܕܡܬܐܡܪܢ
ܡܢܗܘܢ. ܗܕܝܢ ܐܬܦܢܝܘ ܫܠܝܚܐ ܠܡܕܝܢܬ ܕܐܡܪ
ܦܘܠܘܣ. ܒܚܝܢ ܗܘܘ ܠܗ ܒܪܝ ܕܬܘܒ ܢܡܠܠ ܒܡܕܡܘܬ ܕܠܐ
ܢܐܬܘܢ ܐܢܘܢ ܘܢܟܠܘܢ ܠܗ ܐܦܪܐ (fol. 2) ܫܠܝܚܐ
ܕܐܠܦ ܦܛܪܘܣ. ܘܒܢܘ ܬܘܒ ܒܠܗܘܢ ܫܠܝܚܐ ܘܐܡܪܝܢ
ܠܗ ܠܦܘܠܘܣ. ܐܚܘܢ ܦܘܠܘܣ. ܡܛܠ ܒܡܢ ܒܢ̈ܝܐ. ܡܛܠ
ܕܡܬܒܥܐܝܬ ܫܡܥܝܢ ܚܢܢ ܠܟ. ܫܪܪܟ ܒܪܝ ܡܢ ܠܘܬ
ܕܬܒܥܐ ܠܝ ܒܗܠܝܢ ܬܠܬܐ ܩܕܡܝܢ. ܘܒܢܝܐ ܦܘܠܘܣ ܘܐܡܪ
ܠܦܛܪܘܣ. ܡܛܠ ܕܠܐ ܝܕܥܬܘܢ ܕܬܦܠܘܢ ܠܝ ܘܪܒܘܬܗ

܀ ܀ ܀ ܀ ܀

܀ ܀ ܀ ܀

܀ ܀ ܀ ܀ ܀

ܠܗ̇.[a] ܘܩܪܒ ܐܬܐ ܠܐܒܘܗܝ ܕܢܣܒ ܠܐܠܗܐ. ܘܒܟܐ
ܘܐܡܪ ܒܪܐ ܠܐܒܘܗܝ. ܡܛܠ ܐܢܐ ܠܝ ܐܒܝ. ܐܢ
ܐܫܟܚܬ ܪ̈ܚܡܐ ܒܒܢܝܟ. ܐܝܬܐ ܘܠܠ ܡܢ ܠܐܘܬܟ.
ܘܗܒ ܠܗܢܐ ܕܐܬܠܝ ܠܢܦܫ. ܕܐܡܪܬ ܥܒܕ ܠܝ ܘܠܐ ܡܟܐܬ
ܐܢܐ. ܗܝܕܝܢ ܐܒܘܗܝ ܐܝܬܝ ܦܠܚܘܗ ܕܢܩ̈ܦܘܗܝ. ܘܗܟܢ
ܩܕܡ ܒܪܗ ܝܚܝܕܐ. ܘܒܟܐ ܘܐܡܪ ܒܩܠܐ ܪܡܐ. ܦܬܚܐ
ܐܢܐ ܡܢ ܗܘ ܕܐܬܠܝ ܠܢܦܫܗ ܕܒܪܝ. ܗܒ ܠܝ ܗܠܝܢ ܢܦܩ̈ܬܐ.
ܘܫܒܘܩ ܠܝ ܢܦܫܗ ܕܒܪܝ. ܘܡܢ ܒܬܪ ܗܠܝܢ. ܐܬܬܠܝ ܠܗ
ܚܠܦܐ ܡܬܪܐܬ. ܘܒܟܐ ܬܘܒ ܘܐܡܪ ܠܐܒܘܗܝ. ܐܒܝ.
ܠܐ ܥܠܬܐ ܡܢ ܗܘ ܕܐܬܠܝ ܠܢܦܫ. ܒܪܐ ܡܢܒܪ ܕܢܗܘܪ ܠܗ
ܡܕܡ ܕܐܬܬܠܝ ܠܗ. ܘܥܠ ܕܒܟܐ ܕܢܗܘܪ ܠܗ: ܬܠܝ ܠܝ
ܡܬܪܐܬ. ܘܩܡ ܐܒܘܗܝ ܘܐܚܕܗ, ܥܠ ܕܡܢܐ ܩܘܦܐ.
ܘܟܦܬܗ ܐܣܘ̈ܪܐ ܐܝܟ ܘܐܚܕܗ. ܘܗܟܢ ܩܕܡ ܒܪܗ
ܝܚܝܕܐ. ܘܐܡܪ ܒܩܠܐ ܪܡܐ. ܦܬܚܐ ܐܢܐ ܡܢ ܗܘ ܕܐܬܠܝ
ܠܢܦܫܗ ܕܒܪܝ. ܗܒ ܠܝ ܥܠ ܡܕܡ ܕܐܝܬ ܠܝ. ܘܥܠܘܗܝ ܠܒܪܝ,
ܫܒܘܩ ܠܝ. ܗܘ ܕܝܢ ܚܠܦܐ ܡܬܐܬܠܝ ܗܘܐ ܡܬܪܐܬ. ܘܡܢ
ܩܪܒ ܠܡܕܒܚܬ. ܐܬܦܢܝ ܠܘܬ ܐܒܘܗܝ, ܘܐܡܪ ܠܗ. ܐܒܝ
ܫܪܐ ܐܝܬ ܕܠܐ ܕܗܒܟܐ ܘܠܐ ܒܫܘܦܐ ܘܠܐ ܡܕܡ ܐܫܪܝܡ
ܡܥܒܕ ܡܬܗܦܟ ܣܠܩ ܢܦܫܐ. ܐܠܐ ܐܢ ܠܒܟܐ ܕܦܫܝܛ
ܠܘܬ ܐܠܗܐ ܀ ܘܡܢ ܗܒܠ ܐܒܝ. ܘܗܒ ܗܠܝܢ ܢܦܩ̈ܬܐ

[a] Add. 14,484, fol. 1, rect.

THE OBSEQUIES

OF THE

THE HOLY VIRGIN.

ܠܥܠܡ ܥܠܡܝܢ ܐܡܝܢ. ܘܪ̈ܚܡܝܟ ܡܪܢ ܘܚܢܢܟ ܘܦܘܪܩܢܟ.
ܘܚܘܣܝܐ ܘܫܘܒܩܢܐ ܕܚܛܗ̈ܝܢ ܕܝܠܢ. ܢܗܘܘܢ
ܘܢܫܦܥܘܢ ܥܠ ܡܚܝܠܐ ܘܚܛܝܐ ܘܡܣܬܡܟܢܐ ܒܩ̈ܫܝܬܐ.
ܘܒܨ̈ܠܘܬܗ̇ ܕܝܠܕܬܟ: ܢܛܪܐ ܚ̈ܘܒܘܗܝ ܘܫ̈ܦܠܘܗܝ.
ܘܫܒܘܩ ܟܠܗܘܢ ܚܘ̈ܒܝܗܘܢ ܕܟܠ ܡܢ ܕܐܫܬܘܬܦ. ܗܫܐ
ܘܒܟܠܙܒܢ ܘܠܥܠܡ ܥܠܡܝܢ ܐܡܝܢ.
ܫܠܡܬ ܬܫܒܘܚܬܐ ܕܥܠ ܫܘܒܚܗ̇ ܕܝܠܕܬ ܐܠܗܐ ܐܡܐ
ܡܒܪܟܬܐ. ܨܠܘܬܗ̇ ܥܡܢ ⁘

ܬܡܢ. ܘܟܕ ܐܙܕܢܩܬ ܘܦܬܚܬ ܬܪܥܗ ܕܦܪܕܝܣܐ. ܥܢܝܐ
ܕܦܪܢܣܐ ܠܦܪܕܝܣܐ ܐܬܦܬܚܬ. ܘܦܬܚܬ ܡܢ ܒܬܫܒܘܚܬܐ ܕܠܐ
ܡܬܡܠܠܐ ܠܦܪܕܝܣܐ. ܟܕ ܫܠܝܛܝܢ ܥܡܝܩܐ ܘܐܪ̈ܝܟܐ.
ܘܦܩܕܗ ܒܢܘܡܘܣܐ ܕܠܐ ܡܬܗܦܟܝܢ: ܒܢ̈ܝܗ ܐܢ̈ܫܐ ܛ̈ܠܝܐ
ܕܦܪܕܝܣܐ ܕܟܝܢ. ܘܢܝܫܗ ܒܥܘ ܕܠܐ ܡܘܬܐ ܚܢܢܐ
ܕܟܡܘܪܐ ܬܝܪ̈ܐ ܒܗ. ܘܩܒܠ ܦܐܣܝܢ ܐܝܟܢ ܘܦܪܩܗ
ܠܡܪܝܡ. ܘܡܢ ܠܘܬܗ ܐܬܟܠ ܠܘܬ ܐܒܘܗܝ ܡܫܡܫܢܐ.
ܘܐܬܘܗܝ ܡܫܠܡܢܘܬ ܫܢ̈ܝܐ ܠܚܠܡܘܢ ܐܚܝܢ ܕܡܗܝܡܢܝܢ
ܒܗ. ܀ ܘܗܢܝܢ ܡܦܩܢ ܬ̈ܠܝܬܐ ܬܪ̈ܥܝܢ ܠܦܠܘܪܐ ܕܐܢ̈ܫܬܐ
ܒܗܝܢ ܒܒܢ̈ܝܐ ܕܢܘܦܪܐ. ܘܐܝܠܝܢ ܘܗܡܢ ܒܘܪ̈ܟܐ ܘܢܨܠܘܢ.
ܟܕ ܡܬܢܨܒܢ ܗܘܘ ܘܐܬܦܬܚܘ. ܪ̈ܒܢ ܗܘ ܫܘܒܚܐ ܕܢܟܝ̈
ܚ̈ܫܢ ܒܡܦܩܢܗ ܕܠܘܚܐ. ܘܐܘܒܕ ܢܟܝܢ ܘܐܥܒܪܘ. ܡܢ
ܗܒ ܠܢ ܕܢܦܩܐ ܠܚܬ̈ܡܐ ܘܠܦܬܘܪ̈ܐ ܡܛܠ ܕܘܒܪܢܗ ܕܐܡܪܬ:
ܕܢܘܦܘܢ ܥܒܕܝܢ ܠܗ ܕܘܒܪ̈ܐ ܘܬܘܕ̈ܝܬܐ ܡܢ ܥܝܐ ܠܥܝܢܐ.
ܡܛܠ ܕܡܒܝܢ. ܕܥܠ ܕܥܒܕ ܠܗ ܬܘܕܝܬܐ ܘܡܬܥܒܕ ܒܗ
ܡܕܒܪܢܝܬܐ: ܡܢܐ ܕܦܪܥ ܠܝ ܥܒܕܐ ܐܢܬ ܠܗ. ܡܛܠ ܕܠܝܬ
ܐܠܗܐ ܐܚܪܢ ܠܒܪ ܡܢܟ ܕܢܬܥܒܕ ܐܢܬ ܘܡܫܬܒܚ. ܟܡ
ܐܒܘܢ ܘܢܦܫܢ ܡܕܡܝܐ ܠܚܠܡ ܚܠܡܝܢ ܐܡܝܢ. ܀ ܫܘܒܚܐ
ܒܪ ܠܐܠܗܐ ܕܥܒܕܢ ܕܘܒܪܢܗ ܕܐܒܐ ܕܠܒܫܬ. ܘܠܐ ܫܘܒܚܐ
ܕܐܬܝܗܒ ܕܢܬܥܒܕ ܡܢܗ: ܘܢܨܝܢ ܥܒܕܝܘܬܐ. ܡܛܠ
ܡܢ ܐܢܬ ܕܐܫܬܘܬ ܠܢ ܪܘܚܐ ܡܕܡܝܐ ܘܐܡܪ: ܗܒ ܠܢ
ܫܘܠܛܢܐ ܠܢܘܗܪܐ ܐܚܪܢܐ ܕܐܬܐ ܐܢܬ ܒܗ: ܕܢܩܒܠ ܟܠ
ܬܪ̈ܥܝܢ ܒܦܪܘܩܘܬܐ. ܘܢܦܘܩ ܬܪ̈ܥܝܢ ܥܡ̈ܠܐ ܕܐܢܫܐ ܟܠ:
ܕܠܐ ܗܡܝܢܘ ܒܟ ܘܠܐ ܒܐܠܗܐ ܕܠܝܬ. ܘܢܘܕܐ
ܠܛܠܝܘܬܐ ܡܫܒܚܬܐ. ܐܝܟܐ ܘܒܪܐ ܘܪܘܚܐ ܡܕܡܝܐ.

ܘܦܫܩܐ. ܗܘ ܕܝܢ ܐܡܪ. ܐܝܟ ܡܫܒܚܐ ܥܒܕܬ. ܗ̇ܘ ܢܕܪܘ ܡܫܠܐ
ܟܒܪ ܫܘܠܡܐ ܡܣܬܟܐ. ܐܡ̈ܪܝܢ ܠܗ ܡܢܗܘܢ ܟܒܪ. ܐܡܪ
ܗܟܢܐ ܦܩܕܢ ܫܘܠܡܗ. ܕܟܠ ܒܪܢܫܐ ܕܡܐܟܠ ܐܝܬ ܟܠܗܘܢ،
ܗܢܐ ܫܘܠܡܐ ܡܬܒܠܥ. ܘܟܠ ܘܦܫܩܐ ܘ[ܦ]ܫ ܟܠ
ܩܕܡܐ ܘܢܝܪܐ ܢܬܗܪܐ. ܘܟܠ ܒܪܢܫܐ ܕܡܐܟܠ ܗܘܐ ܠܗ
[ܫܘܠܡܐ] ܡܬܒܠܥ ܗܘܐ. ܘܡܦܩܕ [ܗܘܐ] ܠܟܠ ܒܪܢܫܐ
ܕܢܐܟܘܠ ܗܘܐ. ܕܡܢ ܕܒܪܝܬܐ ܗܝ ܡܢܝܢ ܘܒܪܝܫ
ܠܒܬܪ ܡܢܝܢܐ. ܘܡܐܟܘܠܬܐ ܗܘܐ ܘܦܫܩܐ ܟܠܗܘܢ ܒܪܢܫܐ
ܘܡ̈ܠܝܟܐ ܕܐܝܬ ܗܘܐ ܒܐܘܪܫܠܡ. ܘܟܕ ܐܘܠܘ ܥ̈ܠܝܡܐ
ܗܠܝܢ ܠܡܕܝܢܬܐ ܕܐܝܬ ܒܪܝܫ ܢܣܠܝܢ. ܟܠܗ ܐܢܫܝܐ ܒܗܝ
ܒܗܬܐ ܡܢܠܒܬܐ ܕܢܠܝܐ. ܘܫܒܩܗ ܠܒܪܗ ܕܠܘܒܢܬܐ

⁘ ⁘ ⁘ ⁘ ⁘

⁘ ⁘ ⁘ ⁘

⁘ ⁘ ⁘ ⁘ ⁘

(fol. 452) ܒܗܢܝܐ ܟܠ ܥܡܘܗ. ܘܟܒ̈ܫܐ ܕܪ̈ܘܚܢܐ ܕܠܘܬ ܩܢܝܢ
ܠܒܪ̈ܢܫܘܬܗܘܢ ܘܠܐ ܗܘܐ ܠܒܪ̈ܢܫܘܬܗܘܢ. ܕܐܬܝܢ ܗܘܘ
ܘܡܬܚܫܒ ܟܠ ܬܐܓܪܬܐ ܒܬܐܓܪܬܗ. ܘܟܠ ܠܥܝܢܐ ܒܥܝܢܗ
ܘܚܫܝܢ ܗܘܘ ܬܫܒܘ: ܘܡܪܢܫܝܢ ܠܟܠ ܡܢܗ ܕܠܘܒܢܬܐ
ܡܢܝܢ. ܘܡܒ̈ܪܟܬܐ ܬ̈ܝܬܝܢ ܗܘ̈ܝ ܐܘ̈ܚܕܬܐ. ܚܕܐ ܕܡܗܝܡܢܐ.
ܘܚܕܐ ܕܫܠܡܐ. ܘܚܕܐ ܕܐܠܗܐ. ܘܗܢܝܢ ܡܒܪܟܬܐ ܒܪܟܬܐ
ܕܡܢ̈ܝܢ ܐܬܬܠܐ ܗܘܬ ܒܬܪ̈ܝܗܘܢ. ܘܡܬܚܫܒ ܫܡܥܝܐ
ܘܐܪܒܥܐ ܒܗܘ ܘܩܒܐ. ܘܒܢ̈ܝܢܐ ܕܡܢܝܢ ܗܘܘ ܡܢܗ ܫܘ
ܡܢ ܡܕܝ̈ܢܬܗܘܢ. ܘܢܦܩ ܓܒܪܐ ܗܢܝܐ ܘܒܗܘܢܐ ܡܢ ܥ̈ܒܪ
ܫܡܥܝܐ ܕܐܬܢܝܗ: ܠܟܠܗܘܢ ܐܬܘ̈ܬܐ ܕܒܪܝܬܐ. ܘܐܘܟܠܘܗ
ܠܒܪܢܫܘܬܐ ܠܒܪ̈ܢܫܐ ܒܗܘ ܫܘ. ܘܐܬܬܩܝܡ ܒܟܪܗ ܫܘ

ܡܦܝܣܢܐ. ܢܬܒܥ ܐܠܗܐ ܕܢܦܩ[f] ܥܠ. ܐܡܪ̈ܢܐ ܡܩܕܫܬܐ ܗ̇ܢܝ
ܠܗ ܕܪ̈ܚܡܘܗܝ. ܘܢܩܪܒ ܩܘܪܒܢܗ ܘܢܫܩܠ ܕܪ̈ܚܡܘܗܝ ܕܡܦܝܣܢܐ.
ܘܡܢܐ ܕܐܝܬ ܒܝܫ ܡܢܗܘܢ ܐܡܪ. ܒܫܡܗ ܕܡܪܢ ܐܬܕܟܪܘ
ܒܕܘܒܬܟ: ܘܪ̈ܓܫ ܐܝܟܢ ܘܐܬܚܝܠܘ. ܘܢܫܩܠ ܦܐܪ̈ܘܗܝ
ܫܦܝܪܐ ܕܠܒܝܟ ܗܘܐ. ܘܗܒ ܠܗ ܠܡܦܝܣܢܐ ܘܐܡܪ. ܗܠ
ܐܦ ܐܢܬ ܬܗܘܐ ܢܛܠܐ ܕܟܐ ܒܫܘܦܪܐ ܗܢܐ ܠܡ̈ܕܝܢܬܐ.
ܥܒܪ ܚܕܬܐ. ܘܐܫܬܒܚ ܥܠ ܡܩܕܫܬܐ ܗܢܐ ܚܕܬܐ ܠܝ.
ܘܐܙܠ ܡܦܝܣܢܐ ܢܦܠ ܩܕܡ ܪ̈ܓܠܘܗܝ ܘܐܡܪ ܠܗ. ܢܛܪ ܥܠ
ܕܐܬܦܘܩ ܐܚܪܢ ܒܕܡ̈ܘܬܐ ܬܕܡܝܐ. ܘܐܬܚܢܢ ܒܗܘܢ
ܒܐܝܠܝܢ ܕܦܩܕܬ ܒܗܝ ܘܣܠܩܬ ܡܕܝܢܐ. ܘܫܪܝ ܡܩܪܒ ܠܗ
ܠܡܫܝܚ ܒܠܚܘܕ ܒܢܝܢܐ. ܟܕ ܫܟܝܚܐ ܗܘܐ ܬܫܡܫܬܐ[g] ܡܢ
ܐܘܪܚܬܐ ܘܡܢ ܢܟܝܬ ܒܕܡܐ ܕܬܪܨܘ ܗܘܘ ܓܠܝܢܐ ÷ ܘܐܙܠ
ܗܘܐ ܡܦܝܣܢܐ ܘܡܠܟܐ ܠܬܪ̈ܥܐ ܕܡܕܝܢܬܐ. ܘܩܒܫ ܫܘܦܪܐ
ܡܢܝܢܐ ܠܐܣܛܘܦܘܬܐ ܕܬܪ̈ܥܐ ܕܡܕܝܢܬܐ: ܘܟܪ̈ܫܟܬܗ
ܐܩܪܒ ܦܐܪ̈ܐ ܘܟܒܪ ܥܒ̈ܘܕܐ. ܘܫܕܪ ܡ̈ܘܗܒܐ ܠܫܘܦܪܐ
ܕܐܩܪܒ ܒܗ̇ܘܢܗ. ܘܩܪܐ ܡܦܝܣܢܐ ܘܐܡܪ. ܒܪܝ ܗܘ
ܡܫܝܚܐ ܕܐܬܓܠܝ ܡܢ ܒܪܝܟ. ܐܬ̈ܪܟ ܡܕܝܢܬ. ܒܢܝܢܐ
ܕܩܕܝܫܝܢ ܡܦܝܣܢܐ. ܗܘ ܕܝܢ ܐܡܪ. ܗܢܝܢܐ ܕܩܕܝܫ ܕܐܬܬܠܡܕܬ
ܠܒܪܐ ܕܐܠܗܐ ܘܠܡܪܝܢ ܐܚܕܗ. ܕܐܬܦܫܛܘ ܟܠ ܕܪ̈ܚܡ.
ܘܫܒܩܬ ܐܢܘܢ ܟܠܗܝܢ ܘܩܒܠܬ ܐܢܘܢ ܠܝ. ܘܡܢܐ ܕܐܝܬ
ܦܐܪ̈ܘܗܝ ܒܗܘܢ ܐܡܪ. ܒܫܡܗ ܕܡܪܢ. ܡܢܗܘܢ ܕܒܗ
ܠܕܘܒܬܟܘܢ. ܘܪ̈ܓܫ ܐܝܟܢ ܠܝ ܘܐܬܚܝܠܬ. ܘܗܒ ܠܝ
ܫܘܦܪܐ ܗܢܐ ܕܐܩܪܒ ܘܗܘܐ ܡܫܝܚܝܢ ܐܒܝ. ܕܗܘ ܢܠܒܫ
ܠܒܪܐ ܕܐܠܗܐ ÷ ܐܡܪ̈ܢܝܢ ܠܗ ܗ̈ܕܝܐ. ܡܫܝܚܐ ܥܒܕܬ

[f] Better ܢܦܩܘܢ. [g] MS. ܬܫܡܫܬܐ.

ܒܢܘܗ. ܘܐܬܠܠ܆. ܝܠܕܬ ܐܠܗܐ ܟܪܝܗܐ. ܘܟܕ ܒܡܟܬܒܬܐ
ܐܡܬܚܡ ܦܐܡ ܠܟܠ ܡܢ ܒܢܘܗ̇ ܘܐܙܠ ܟܕ ܢܫܐ. ܀ ܘܟܕ
ܗܠܝܢ ܦܩܕܬܐ ܗܘܬ ܒܪܘܚܐ܆ ܥܠܝܡܬܐ ܠܬܠܬܗܝܢ ܗܘܘ
ܒܐܘܪܫܠܡ. ܘܟܕ ܢܓܗ̇ ܨܦܪܐ ܕܝܘܡ ܚܕܒܫܒܐ܆ ܟܠܗ̇
ܠܗܘܢ ܪܘܚܐ ܕܩܘܕܫܐ ܠܥܠܝܡܬ̈ܐ ܕܢܦܩܘ ܠܡܕܒܪܐ ܘܫܩܘܠܘ
ܡܢ ܐܘܪܫܠܡ. ܒܐܘܪܚܐ ܕܢܦܩܐ ܠܛܘܪ ܢܣܒܐ ܟܠ ܚܕ
ܦܘܪ̈ܢܝܬܐ. ܘܗܐ ܐܝܬ ܬܡܢ ܬܘܠܬܠܐ° ܡܚܒ̈ܠܝܢ. ܚܙܐ ܟܠܗ
ܣܝܐ. ܘܟܕܝ ܟܢܘܫܬܐ ܐܝܬ ܡܢ ܦܠܚܘܬܐ ܡܢ ܡܫܝܚܐ ܬܡܢ
ܕܠܐ ܡܬܒܣܝܢ ܠܡܕܒܪܐ܆ ܒܪܡܫܐ ܕܡܬܬܚܙܐ ܠܟܘܢ.
ܘܦܩܕ ܒܨܦܪܐ ܘܫܩܠܘ ܠܦܘܪܢܣܬܐ܆ ܘܩܕܡܐ ܫܪܝܢ ܗܘܘ
ܘܡܚܪܝܢ. ܬܠܬܝܢ ܕܝܢ ܡܠܦܢܝܬܐ ܠܦܘܪܫܢ ܠܡܒܪܝܢ
ܘܐܙܠܝܢ. ܘܗܝ ܦܘܪܢܣܬܐ ܒܢܘܗ ܚܙܐ ܗܘܬ. ܘܩܪܒܘ
ܩܕܡܝܗ ܚܕ ܠܚܕ ܘܐܡܪܝܢ. ܗܐ ܦܩܕܬ ܡܪܝܢ. ܕܩܪܒܬ
ܘܐܙܠܬ ܡܢ ܐܘܪܫܠܡ. ܘܐܝܬ ܗܘܐ ܬܡܢ ܒܬܪܐ ܚܕ
ܣܦܝܢܐ ܫܡܗ ܗܘܐ. ܘܪܡ ܘܫܦܝܪ ܒܡܘܬܒܗ. ܘܐܦܩܪܘ
ܠܗ ܩܕܡܐ ܕܐܣܛܪܛܠ. ܘܩܪܒ ܣܦܝܢܐ ܦܩܕ ܒܡܪܝܢ
ܘܬܦܠ ܡܢ ܒܪܘܚܗ܆ ܕܡܦܪܬ ܕܪܦܬ ܘܢܦܩܬ ܡܢ ܐܘܪܫܠܡ.
ܘܪܗܛ ܣܦܝܢܐ ܒܫܐܦܐ ܘܡܛܐ ܕܪ̈ܒܘܗܝ. ܟܠ ܒܪܘܚܗ
ܕܦܘܪܢܣܬܐ ܐܝܟ ܕܬܦܩܕ. ܘܐܬܦܠܠ ܒܗ ܕܬܦܠܚ ܘܢܐܬܝܢ
ܩܕܡܝܐ ܢܘܚܡܗ. ܘܟܕ ܣܦܝܢܐ ܝܕܥܐ ܕܪ̈ܒܘܗܝ. ܘܢܦܪܐ
ܕܢܘܪܐ ܡܢܝܫܗ ܒܣܦܝܢܐ ܕܢܘܪܐ. ܘܦܠܚ ܬܪ̈ܡܗܘܢ ܕܪ̈ܒܘܗܝ
ܡܢ ܥܒܕܘܗܝ. ܘܟܠܠ ܗܘܐ ܘܐܡܪ. ܥܠܝܡܘܗܝ ܕܡܫܝܚܐ
ܐܬܪܢܝܢܢ ܟܠ. ܐܡܪܝܢ ܥܠܝܡܬܐ. ܠܡ ܠܡܪܢ ܦܪܐ ܐܢܫ.
ܦܪ ܠܡܪܬܗ ܡܪܝܡ. ܕܥܒܕܬ ܕܬܬܟܢܫ ܒܪܘܚܗ܆. ܀ ܐܡܪ

[e] Read ܙܒܠ.

ܕܐܬܒܠܟܠܘ[z] ܘܝܘܡ ܕܢܦܠ ܟܠ ܕܐܝܬ ܒܗ. ܘܦܢܘ ܐܠܦܐ
ܒܥܡ ܦܘܠܚܢܝܬܐ ܘܐܡܪܘ. ܡܪܢ, ܡܪܝܡ ܢܛܪܟ ܐܠܗܐ
ܙܒܢܝܢ[a] ܟܠܗܝܢ. ܘܕܚܝܠܬ ܐܝܟ ܥܒܕܬܐ ܘܦܪܝܫܬ ܬܫ̈ܥܝܢ ܘܬܪ̈ܬܝܢ
ܫ̈ܢܝܢ: ܘܢܦܩܬܐ ܕܟܫ̈ܝܢ ܘܠܐ ܐܝܟ ܡܢܗܘܢ ܡܪܝܡ ܀
ܘܐܬܒܝܢܬ ܒܐܣܟܡܐ ܕܠܦܘܪܐ. ܕܢܓܠܘ ܓܢ̈ܒܐ ܥܠ ܫ̈ܢܝܐ
ܕܢܦܠܠܘܢ ܐܢܘܢ. ܘܡܛܘ: ܢܛܪܬ ܐܠܗܐ ܓܒܪ̈ܝ[b] ܠܝ. ܘܐܬܦܬܬ
ܡܢ ܡܒܝܢܬ ܥܠ ܚܢܝܘܬܢ ܕܓܢ̈ܒܐ ܘܐܬܓܒܪܘ. ܘܦܠܛܘ
ܟܠܗܘܢ ܘܠܐ ܐܬܢܟܝܘ. ܀ ܘܐܬܒܝܢܬ ܠܐܢܬܬܐ ܚܕܐ
ܐܪܡܠܬܐ ܕܢܦܠ ܒܪܗ ܒܒܐܪܐ ܕܡ̈ܝܐ: ܘܐܒܠܠܬ ܘܐܡܪܬ.
ܢܛܪܬ ܐܠܗܐ ܙܒܢܝܢ ܟܠܗܝܢ.[c] ܘܐܬܦܬܬ ܡܕܝܢ ܘܫܩܠܬܗ ܡܢ
ܒܐܪܐ. ܘܝܗܒܬܗ ܠܐܡܗ ܘܠܐ ܐܬܢܟܝ. ܀ ܘܬܘܒ
ܐܬܒܝܢܬ ܒܪܘܡܐ ܠܓܒܪܐ ܚܕ ܕܓܪܫܗ ܗܘܐ ܥܬܬܟܣܪܐ
ܬ̈ܠܝܢ. ܘܠܐ ܐܢܫ ܐܩܝܡܗ. ܘܥܒܠ ܦܪܥܐ ܘܐܪܓܙ ܒܗ
ܒܦܘܡܐ ܘܐܡܪ. ܡܪܢ, ܡܪܝܡ ܢܛܪܬ ܐܠܗܐ ܓܒܪܝܢ. ܘܒܗ
ܒܫܥܬܐ ܐܬܒܝܢܬ ܠܗ ܘܐܬܐܣܝ. ܘܩܡ ܐܙܠ ܠܒܝܬܐ ܡܕܡ
ܟܠܗ ܚܡܝܐ. ܀ ܘܬܘܒ ܐܬܒܝܢܬ ܠܬܪ̈ܬܝܢ ܢܫ̈ܐ ܕܬܪܝܠܢ ܗ̈ܘܝ
ܒܐܘܪܚܐ. ܘܢܦܩ ܥܠܝܗܝܢ ܚܘܝܐ ܐܘܟܡܐ ܕܢܓܠܟ ܫ̈ܢܝܢ.
ܘܐܬܠܠ: ܐܡܪܗ ܕܐܠܗܐ ܦܪܘܩ ܠܝ. ܘܒܗ ܒܫܥܬܐ ܦܩܕ
ܡܢ ܪܥܝܗ ܘܠܬܒܢ. ܘܠܐ ܐܬܢܟܝܘ[d]. ܀ ܘܐܬܒܝܢܬ ܬܘܒ
ܠܓܒܪܐ ܬܓܪܐ ܕܢܦܩ ܬ̈ܠܬ ܕܪ̈ܡܘܣܝ ܕܢܚܫܐ ܘܢܬܬܓܪ
ܒܗܘܢ. ܘܟܕ ܢܦܩ ܕܢܬܚܘܠ ܠܫܡܝܐ ܡܢ ܘܐܒܕ ܡܢܗܘܢ

[z] Read ܕܐܬܒܠܒܠܘ.

[a] Better ܙܒܢ̈ܝܢ.

[b] Better ܓܒܪ̈ܝܢ.

[c] Better ܙܒܢ̈ܝܢ ܟܠܗܝܢ.

[d] Better ܐܬܢܟܝ̈.

ܡܙܡܢ ܘܐܡܪ ܠܗ̇. ܛܘܒܐ ܐܢܬܝ ܡܪܬܝ ܝܠܕܬ ܐܠܗܐ ܐܦ،
ܠܗܢܐ ܒܪܐ ܚܫܘܫܐ ܕܐܝܬ ܠܝ. ܕܡܫܬܢܩ ܡܢ ܒܘܪܗܢܐ
ܒܩܘܡܐ. ܘܦܨܝܬܝ ܐܢܫ̈ܗ ܡܢ ܡܘܬܐ ܘܐܩܝܡܬܝ ܠܗܠܝܢ ܘܗܘܘ
ܐܦܨܝܬܝ. ܒܫܡܗ ܕܪܒܘܠܐ ܕܐܝܬ ܠܝ ܒܫܡܝܢ ܢܬܐܡܪ.
ܘܡܫܝܪܐ ܐܬܒܝܠ ܦܠܚܐ ܗܘ ܒܝܠܬܗ ܕܡܪܝܡ. ܘܐܙܠ
ܕܢܒܥܐ ܡܢ ܝܕ ܡܢܚ ܡܪܝܡ. ܘܡܣܒ ܒܠܗܘܢ ܚܝܠܐ
ܘܬܕܡܪ̈ܬܐ ܕܥܒܕܬ ܗܘܬ ܝܠܕܬ ܐܠܗܐ. ܀ ܠܐ ܓܝܪ ܡܨܝܐ
ܦܘܡܐ ܕܒܪܢܫܐ ܕܢܫܬܥܐ ܚܝܠܐ ܘܬܗܘܪ̈ܬܐ ܕܥܒܕܬ
ܦܘܫ ܒܫܠܡܐ. ܀ ܐܝܩܘܢܐ ܕܡܢ ܐܒܓܪ، ܘܐܙܠ ܡܢ
ܡܕܝܢܬܐ ܠܪܗܘܡ. ܘܟܕ ܝܕܥ ܦܠܚܐ ܡܢܘܪ̈ܗܐ. ܘܬܘܒ
ܠܗܘܢ ܒܠܗܘܢ ܚܝܠܐ ܘܬܕܡܪ̈ܬܐ ܕܥܒܕܬ ܡܪܝܡ
ܒܐܘܪܫܠܡ ܘܒܟܠܗ ܝܗܘܕ. ܘܐܙܠܘ ܬܠܡܝܕܐ ܕܦܠܚܘܗ̇
ܘܦܘܠܘܣ ܠܪܗܘܡ ܘܡܠܦܘ ܡܢܗ ܕܥܒܕܘ ܡܢ ܕܢܒܥܐ ܕܫܠܡ
ܠܪܗܘܡ ܡܢ ܐܘܪܫܠܡ. ܘܡܠܦܘ ܐܦ ܗܢܘܢ ܐܟܘܬܗ
ܘܫܪܪܘ ܠܟܠܗܘܢ ܕܐܝܬ ܒܡܕܝ̈ܢܬܐ ܥܡܡ̈ܐ. ܠܦܘܪ ܗܘܝ
ܘܠܐܝܓܦܛܘܣ ܘܐܦ ܠܬܪܝܐ. ܘܠܦܘܢܛܘܣ ܘܠܐܣܝܐ.
ܘܡܠܦܘ ܒܐܟܣܢܝܘܬܗܘܢ ܕܐܒ ܗܘ ܓܒ ܕܦܨܬ ܒܗ ܡܢ
ܒܠܒܐ ܗܢܐ. ܘܡܠܦܘ ܬܘܒ ܐܦ ܠܪ̈ܘܚܢܝܗܘܢ ܕܦܘܪܣ
ܘܦܘܠܘܣ. ܕܐܝܟ ܕܢܦܩܬܗܘܢ ܠܡܫܝܚܐ: ܒܬܪܐ ܕܐܬܩܢܘܗ̇
ܢܫܬܐ ܒܡܠܟܘܬ ܠܪܗܘܡ. ܡܛܠ ܕܗܘܐ ܡܠܝܢ ܗܘ̈ܦܟܐ ܘܦܘܫܩܐ
ܡܢ ܬܫܒܘܚܬܗ. ܘܦܬܚ ܒܢܒ̈ܝܐ ܗܘܝܘ ܒܗ. ܡܛܠ ܕܡܢ
ܒܗ ܐܬܩܐ ܕܢܒܝܐ ܡܢ ܠܘܬܗ ܐܫܬܢܝ ܗܕܝܐ ܡܠܟܘܬܗ.
ܘܟܠ ܕܫܘܕܐ ܒܗ̇ ܦܠܐܝܬ ܡܟܕܪܐ ܠܗ: ܘܠܟܠ ܕܦܪܥܐ
ܠܗ. ܬܕܡܪ̈ܬܐ ܕܦܪܘܩ ܠܡܟܝܢܬܐ: ܐܬܝܠܕܬ ܒܢܦܫܐ

ܘܡܢ ܒܬܪ ܫܠܡܐ ܕܩܘܪܒܢܐ ܫܪܝ ܡܢ ܠܘܬܗ. ܘܦܩܕܗ ܘܩܘܡܬ
ܒܩܘܪܒܐ ܘܢܦܠܬ ܥܠ ܐ̈ܦܐ ܘܣܓܕܬ ܠܫܡܝܐ ܕܐܠܗܘܬܗ
ܕܡܫܝܚܐ: ܕܣܥܪܬ ܕܐܝܟ ܗܕܐ ܬܕܡܘܪܬܐ. ܘܐܬܐ ܡܢ ܒܗ
ܐܬܦܢܝܬ ܒܫܠܡܐ ܘܢܦܩܬ ܡܢ ܒܝܬܗ ܕܐܣܝܐ. ܓܒܪܐ ܠܐ
ܢܓܥܘܢ. ܘܠܐ ܐܢܘܫܐ ܕܢܫܐ ܫܡܥܬ. ܘܐܬܦܠܓ ܡܢܗ ܐܝܟ
ܒܪܢܫܐ. ܘܐܝܟ ܩ̈ܢܐ ܐܕܡ ܐܬܪܒܝ. ܘܐܝܟ ܡܠܘܐܐ ܒܥܝܬ
ܫ̈ܘܩܐ. ܘܐܝܟ ܥܒܪܐ ܥܩܒ ܘܒܢܘ ܫ̈ܒܠܐ ܘܗܦܟ
ܬܕܡ̈ܪܬܐ. ܘܝܗܒ ܒܫܠܡܐ ܐܝܟ ܐܠܗܐ. ܘܥܠ ܕܐܣܒܪ
ܠܗ ܓܒܪ ܘܥܒܕ. ܘܫܪܝܬ ܕܒܬܘܢܝܐ ܠܐ ܐܣܓܝܘ ܕܢܕܟܪܘܢ
ܫ̈ܒܠܐ ܕܒܚܪ. ܘܐܝܬܝܘܗܝ ܡ̈ܪܕܝܐ ܢܦܩܘ̈ܬܐ ܘܙܡܪܘܗܝ
ܘܫܒܚܘܗܝ. ܘܐܬܬܩܝܡ ܒܗ ܡܕܝܢܬܐ. ܘܢܒܥ ܗܘ ܠܥܠܡܗ.
ܘܦܫ ܘܐܬܒܢܝ ܠܬܠܡ̈ܝܕܘܗܝ. ܒܪ ܦܘܬ ܬܕܡ̈ܪܬܐ ܘܫ̈ܒܠܐ
ܕܐܚܘܗܝ ܡܣܒܪܢܐ. ܘܗܠܝܢ ܠܫܡܥܢܐ ܒܥܘ ܠܘܬ ܐܚܘܗܝ.
ܘܐܝܟ ܡܫܪܐ ܠܗ ܡܩܘܡܢܝܢ ܒܗ: ܘܐܬܐ ܘܐܘܣܦ ܢܦܫܐ
ܘܬܠܡ̈ܝܕܐ ܡܗܝܡܢܝܢ ܒܗ. ܕܝܘܚܢܢ (fol. 451) ܘܟܗܢܐ ܡܫܝܚܐ
ܒܪܗ ܕܐܠܗܐ ܚܝܐ. ܘܐܫܪܝܬ ܘܡܠܟܘܬܗ ܕܐܬܦܠܓ
ܡܠܟܐ.[y] ܗܘ ܐܬܐ ܘܬܒܥܐ ܕܒܗ ܡܢ ܬܠܡ̈ܝܕܘܗܝ. ܘܠܐ ܐܚܪ̈ܢ
ܗܘܐ ܕܡܢܐ ܕܦܠܛܝ ܡܢ ܚܠܡܬܐ. ܗܘ ܘܒܢ̈ܝܐ ܕܫܠܝܚܐ
ܐܬܐ ܠܘܬܗ. ܘܐܝܟ ܕܓܒܪ ܠܬܠܡܝܕܘܗܝ. ܡܢ ܐܪ̈ܒܥ ܦܢܝ̈ܢ:
ܗܘܝܐ ܡܦܘܪܫܐ ܐܝܟܐ ܠܗ ܕܐܬܐ. ܘܫܪܝܐ ܐܝܟܐ ܠܗ.
ܘܦܩܐܡ ܐܝܟܗ ܥܠ ܚܕ ܘܩܘܡ ܠܝ ܡܢ ܚܠܡܐ ܒܝܫܐ.
ܘܡܫܩܘܪ ܠܗ ܠܚܪܝ ܘܡܥܘܪܒ ܠܗ ܠܪܘܚ ܠܐܠܗܐ ܕܐܝܬ
ܠܗ ܡܫܝܚܐ. ܗܠܝܢ ܐܦܪܢܬ ܡܪܝܡ ܠܡܫܝܚܘܬܐ ܠܐܚܪܢܝܐ
ܘܡܢܡ ܥܠܝܡܐ. ܘܗܘܝܢ ܦܝܫ ܒܡܪܝܡ. ܘܒܪ ܚܕܐ ܠܒܪܗ

[y] Read ܥܒܕ.

ܘܫܪܪ ܐܢܬ ܠܝ ܐܡܝܢ ܒܚܝܠܗ: ܕܒܡܗܝܡܢܘܬܟ ܢܬܠܠܗ ܠܐܠܗܐ.
ܘܫܒܚܐ ܘܐܡܪ: ܕܗܕܐ ܗܝ ܐܝܬܝܬܐ ܕܡܠܟܘܬ ܠܐܠܗܐ.
ܘܐܬܝܕܥ ܠܡܫܬܠܡܢܘ. ܘܥܒܕܘ ܚܠܝܢ ܠܟܠ ܐܘܪܫܠܡ. ⁘
ܘܪܘܚܐ ܕܩܘܕܫܐ ܐܡܪܬ ܠܝ: ܕܠܐ ܬܬܒܗܠܘܢ ܠܕܘܟܐ.
ܕܠܡܬܐ ܦܬܓܡ ܡܩܕܫ ܕܡܫܝܚܐ ܕܢܠܡ ܐܢܬܘܢ ܡܢܗܘܢ.
ܘܐܬܓܠܝܬ ܠܐܘܪܫܠܡ ܘܠܐ ܚܙܐ ܠܝ ܐܢܫ. ܘܚܠܦ ܠܡܪܟܒ
ܡܛܠ ܕܠܒܝܫܝܢ ܗܘܘ ܠܡܫܝܚܘܬܐ ܒܪܘܚܐ. ܘܠܝ ܠܒܝܫܐ ܗܘܬ
ܪܘܚܐ ܕܩܘܕܫܐ. ܘܡܫܪܝܢ ܗܘܘ ܚܠܝܢ ܢܚܬܐ ܥܡܝܩܐ
ܕܫܠܡܘܬܐ. ܘܡܢ ܕܗܘܘ ܗܪܟܐ. ܝܗܒ ܡܪܢ ܕܢܬܠܐ
ܥܠ ܝܫܘ̄ ܕܢܬܒܥ ܠܐܒܘܗܝ. ܘܐܬܝܗܒܘ ܡ̈ܠܐܟܘܗܝ ܕܡܪܢܐ
ܕܢܐܠܝܢ ܘܢܦܩܝܢ ܠܥܠܡܗ ܕܡܠܟܘܬܐ. ܘܗܘܘ ܪܘܚܐ
ܦܬܓܡܐ ܕܢܒܝܘܬܗ ܡܩܕܫܐ. ܘܢܬܟܒܫ ܒܪܗ ܕܐܠܗܐ ܗܘ
ܘܢܬܠܬܗ. ⁘ ܗܠܝܢ ܐܡܪܬ ܥ̈ܠܝܡܐ ܠܢܒܝܐ ܒܗ ܐܘܠ ܦܓܪ.
ܠܗܘܢ. ܘܬܘܒ ܐܦܝܣ ܕܢܒܐ ܠܡܠܟܘܬܐ ܘܐܡܪ. ܒܗܐ
ܐܝܟܐ ܡܫܝܚܐ ܡܪܬܝ ܕܢܦܠ ܡܠܟܝ ܕܐܝܟܢܐ ܒܪܐ
ܒܬܘܠܘܬܝ ܐܠܗܐ ܕܐܝܬܘܗܝ ܠܥܠܡܐ. ܐܡܪܬ ܠܗ
ܠܡܫܝܚܘܬܐ ⁘ ܫܒܚ ܘܦܩܕ ܟܠ. ܘܗܘܐ ܬܫܒܘ ܠܐܠܗܐ:
ܕܫܪܪ ܠܡܫܝܚܗ ܡܢ ܫܡܝܐ ܕܐܝܩܪܗ ܘܦܪܩ ܒܗ. ܘܠܐ ܢܬܒܥܐ
ܡܢ ܐܝܟܐ ܓܠ ܠܥܢܬ ܫܪܒܐ. ܐܠܐ ܒܗ ܢܬܟܐ ܐܝܟܐ
ܒܒܢܬܝ. ܘܢܒܥܐ ܐܝܟܐ ܥ̈ܘܦ ܬܪܥܐ ܕܗܝܟܠܗ ܕܡܪܝܐ.
ܒܫܒܥܒܥܐ ܒܬܫ̈ܒܚ ܥ̈ܡܡ. ܦܬܚ ܓܒܪܐ ܘܫܒܚ ܠܗܬ.
ܘܕܢܚ ܢܘܗܪܐ ܒܥܠܡ ܒܢܬܐ ܕܢܬܒܥܐ ܗܘܘܬ ܒܗ: ܘܐܡܪ
ܠܝ. ܫܠܡܠܡ ܒܪܡܫܬ ܒܢ̈ܝܐ. ܡܪܝ ܒܟܒܝ ܘܡܢܝ ܕܢܢ. ⁘
ܘܡܚܝܐ ܪܘܚܐ ܒܗܘܢܝܢ ܒܥܠܡ ܒܢܬܐ. ܘܐܦ ܐܦ̈ܘܗܝ
ܕܒܢܬܐ ܟܠܝܠܐ ܕܗܘܪܡܝܐ ܩ̈ܦܝܡ ܗ̈ܘ ܠܥܠܡ ܥܒܒܘܬܐ.

ܘܒܪܘܬܘܬܗ ܕܡܪܢ ܫܘܒܚ ܡܫܝܚܐ ܒܥܠ ܩܢܘܡ. ܘܟܕ
ܠܡܫܝܚ ܡܢ ܩܕܡ ܒܪܘܬܗ ܒܗܘ ܐܬܪܐ ܕܠܝܬ ܕܠܗ
ܐܫܬܕܪ: ܐܬܩܢܝܢ ܙܒܢܐ ܕܬܫܠܡ ܠܡܫܝܚܘܬܐ ܗܘܐ ܡܢ
ܒܠܚܘܕ ܗܢܐ. ܘܟܕ ܠܐ ܙܒܢܝܢ ܘܠܐ ܐܝܟ ܐܘܪܒ
ܠܝ: ܢܘܚܐ ܕܣܘܕܥܐ ܓܠܐ ܠܡܫܝܚ ܚܕ ܡܢܝ. ܕܐܡܗ
ܕܐܠܗܐ ܢܦܠ ܠܗ ܙܒܢܐ ܕܬܫܠܡ ܡܢ ܒܠܚܘܕ ܗܢܐ. ܘܠ
ܠܘܬܗ ܠܟܬܝܒܬܐ. ܘܟܕ ܝܗܒ ܠܡܫܝܚ ܡܢܝ ܦܩܕ ܒܡܢܝܢܘܬܐ
ܦܘܐ. ܡܛܠ ܕܟܢܘܫܝܐ ܕܒܢܝܬܐ ܡܢܝܢ ܦܘܡ. ܘܐܡܪܢ
ܠܡܫܝܚ ܡܢ ܒܬ ܠܗ ܠܢܦܫܗ. ܕܡܢ ܐܡܟܐ ܠܝ ܙܒܢܐ ܘܠܠܝ
ܢܐܠ ܕܠܐ ܬܘܕܝܬܐ. ܡܢ ܩܕܡ ܕܫܒܝܬܐ ܒܟ ܢܐܠ ܐܒܐ.
ܘܟܕ ܗܢܐ ܫܘܥܒܐ ܦܠܛ ܒܠ ܙܒܢܝ: ܢܘܚܐ ܕܣܘܕܥܐ
ܐܘܪܒܗ ܠܡܫܝܚ ܡܢܝ. ܘܒܢܝܐ ܕܢܘܦܪܐ ܦܢܝܐ ܒܡܕܒܪܬܐ.
ܘܒܝܬ ܡܕܒܪܬܐ ܦܢܡ ܒܢܘܦܐ ܕܒܢܝܡ ܒܬܥܒܘ. ܘܡܟܐ
ܕܒܢܝܬܗ ܢܘܚܐ ܕܣܘܕܥܐ ܐܡܢܪܐ ܠܗ. ܗܐ ܙܒܢܐ ܕܥܕܪ
ܠܟܘܢ ܡܕܒܘܢ ܡܢ ܫܡܝܐ. ܣܘܡܘ ܦܝܓܘ ܒܠܫܘܢ ܘܐܠܘ
ܓܪ ܐܡܗ ܠܟܬܝܒܬܐ. ܘܗܟܢܐ ܐܬܦܠܓ ܦܐܪܘܣ
ܒܡܕܒܪܬܐ ܘܦܩ ܒܠ ܐܐܪ ܒܬ ܫܡܝܐ ܠܐܪܒܝ. ܒܟ
ܢܐܪ ܠܬ̈ܠܡܝܕܐ ܕܐܬܘܢ ܓܐܕܘܗܝ. ܘܟܕ ܦܘ ܦܐܪ ܐܬܘ
ܬ̈ܠܡܝܕܐ ܡܢ ܐܪ̈ܒܥ ܦܢܝܬܗ ܕܒܠܚܘܕ ܠܘܬܗ. ܘܕܚ̈ܠܝܢ
ܗܘܘ ܐܬܒܢܝܘ ܘܐܬܘ ܒܟ ܗܠܝܢ ܕܢܒܝܢ ܠܡܕܒܪܬܗ
ܕܣܘܕܥܬܐ. ܗܟܢܐ ܐܬܘܢ ܡܢ ܐܬܪ̈ܘܬܐ ܗܠܝܢ ܒܡܕ̈ܒܪܬܐ
ܕܡ̈ܕܒܪܐ ܘܒܢ̈ܝܢܐ ܕܥܘ ܓܠܝܢ ܠܟܬܝܒܬܐ ܒܟ ܒܢ̈ܝܐ
ܕܬ̈ܠܡܝܕܐ ܘܦܓܪܝܢ ܠܡܫܝܚܘܬܐ. ܡܛܠ ܕܐܠܗܐ ܕܐܬܘܠܐ
ܡܢܗ ܦܘܫ ܠܝ: ܕܦܘ ܒܒܢܐ ܠܝ ܡܢ ܩܕܡ ܬܪ̈ܒܝܬܗ ܕܒܠܚܘܕ.
ܕܢܣܘܐ ܒܪܘܢܐ ܒܠ ܡ̈ܠܘܗܝ ܫܒܝܬܐ ܘܒܠ ܬܕ̈ܡܪܬܐ ܕܢܒܘܢ.

ܕܢܦܫܐ ܘܦܠܛܝܢ: ܐ̈ܘ ܒܬܘܠܬܐ ܩܕܝܫܬܐ. ܐܪܒܥܐ ܕܝܢ
ܕܡܬܠܒܫܐ ܐܢܬܝ، ܒܠܒܘܫ ܥܡܛܢܐ ܬܗܘܡܐ. ܥܡܛܢܐ ܕܝܢ ܕܥܢܢܐ
ܠܗ ܒܡܘܪܒܝܬܐ ܬܬܠ ܠܒܪ̈ܝܬܐ ܕܒܗ ܡܫ̈ܝܚܝܢ. ܫ̈ܠܝܚܐ
ܕܢܣܒ ܠܒܣܡܘܬܗ ܢܦܩܘܢ ܚܕ̈ܘܬܐ. ܒܪ̈ܡܫܐ ܕܝܢ ܕܐܬܝܢ
ܠܘܬܗ ܢܦܩܘܢ ܒܡܕ̈ܪܝܐ. ܦܓܥ ܐܢܝܢ ܠܗ ܡ̈ܪܝܡ:
ܡܪܬܗ ܕܥܠܡܐ. ܦܓܥܬ ܡܚܝܒ ܘܦܪ̈ܩܝܢ. ܠܝ ܐܦ ܠܗܢܐ
ܡܣܒܪܐ ܕܐܝܟ ܐܠܗܐ. ܘܐܦ ܟܠ ܢܦ̈ܩܬܐ ܕܐܝܟܢ ܠ
ܒܙܒܢ: ܕܐܙܠ ܒܥܠܡܐ ܘܐܚܘܝܐ ܒܗܘܢ. ܘܐܦܠܐ
ܐܘܪܚܐ ܘܡܘܪ̈ܒܢܐ ܘܐܬܬܐ ܐܫܟܚܬ ܠܗ ܝܠܕܬ ܐܠܗܐ.
ܡܪܝܡ ܕܝܢ ܡܬܢܚܐ ܗܘܬ ܘܡܬܒܠܝܐ ܟܕ ܚܙܩ ܦܘܪܫܢܐ
ܕܫܘ̈ܡܗܐ ܡܕܡܢ. ܘܟܕ ܥܒܕܬ ܫ̈ܠܡܘܗܝ ܕܕܝܢܐ. ܫܠܡܬ
ܠܒܝܬܗ. ܘܐܬܚܒܝܬ ܥܡ ܐܝܕܘܗܝ ܘܦܪܢܣܬ ܐܢܫܗ ܘܡܪ̈ܟܒܬܗ
ܠܗ ܘܠܒܪܗ. ܘܐܡܪܬ ܠܗ ܗܟܢ ܠܝ. ܫ̈ܠܝܚܘܗܝ ܕܝܢ ܕܡܪܢ:
ܬܡܢ ܗܘܘ ܒܒܝܬܗ. ܘܩܪܝܢ ܗܘܘ ܕܢܚܙܘܢܗ ܠܗ̇. ܘܟܕ
ܢܦܩܘ ܘܢܬܪܘ ܒܥܒܕܝܢ. ܫܪܝ ܕܟܘܢ ܒܥܕܬܐ ܦܪܐ* ܬܪܥܘܠܝܐ.
ܘܪܦܠ ܗܘܐ ܕܝܢܐ ܢܦܠ ܥܠ ܬܠܡܝܕܘܗܝ ܕܫ̈ܠܝܚܐ ܘܐܡܪ
ܠܗܘܢ. ܫܠܡܐ ܒܟܠܟܘܢ. ܬܒܥܝܢ ܕܒܥܝܢ ܡܢ ܡܕܡ ܬܫܡܫܬܗ
ܕܥܠܡܐ. ܘܠܡܪܢ ܕܟܠܟܘܢ ܕܬܗܘܘܢ ܠܗ ܒܙ̈ܘܓܐ.
ܐܡܪܝܢ ܫ̈ܠܝܚܐ. ܥܒܕܝܢ ܡܕܡ ܕܥܒܕܬ ܠܬܪܥܘܬܐ ܘܦܬܚ
ܢܦܝܫ ܒܠܒܝ.܀ ܐܡܪ ܐܝܟܢܐ. ܦܩܕ ܠܗܘܢ ܒܗܝܡܢܘܬܐ
ܕܗܘܐ ܡܕܡ ܐܠܗܐ ܘܡܕܡ ܒܒܢܝܢܫܐ. ܐܡܪܝܢ ܫ̈ܠܝܚܐ. ܘܡܟܢܐ
ܒܟܕ ܕܠܐ ܗܘܐ ܠܒܗܬܬܗܘܢ.܀ ܗܫܐ ܕܝܢ ܡܫܬܕܪܝܢ
ܠܝ. ܕܗܐ ܚܙܝ ܥܒܬܒܗܘܪܐ ܫ̈ܢܝܐ. ܕܢܥܡܝܢ ܢܟܪܝ ܡܒܪܬܗ

* MS. ܦܪܐ, with red spots on the ܐ.

ܐܡܪܝܢ ܠܗ ܦܩܘܕ ܡܪܢ، ܘܢܦܩܘܢ ܬܠܡܝܕܐ ܗܠܝܢ. ܘܬܠܡܝܕܗ
ܕܡܪܝ ܢܬܬܦܩܘܢ ܒܗܝܟܠܗ ܕܐܘܪܫܠܡ. ܘܢܣܬܟܪ ܡܢ
ܟܠܗܝܢ ܒܢܝܬܐ. ܐܡܪ ܐܒܓܪܘܣ. ܠܐ ܦܩܕ ܐܢܐ ܡܢ
ܫܠܝܚܐ ܫܡܥܘܢ ܗܕܐ. ܐܠܐ ܚܕܐ ܐܢܐ ܠܟܘܢ ܒܥܘܬܐ
ܡܛܠ ܟܠܗܘܢ ܒܢܝ̈ܢܫܐ. ܢܠܒܫܘܢ ܐܢܘܢ ܕܡܫܝܚܐ ܠܐ ܦܪܥ
ܐܢܐ ܠܗ. ܐܘ ܟܢܫ ܕܐܬܓܠܝ ܥܠܘ: ܗܘ ܕܩܡ ܠܗ ܡܢ
ܐܪܥܐ ܕܦܠܣܛܝܢܐ ܥܡ. ܘܦܩܕ ܘܐܢܬ، ܟܗܢܐ ܪܘܪ̈ܒܐ.
ܘܦܩܕ ܥܠ ܕܘܟܬܐ ܕܒܗ ܦܠܝܛܝܢ ܗܘܘ ܡܫܝܚܐ ܗܠܝܢ. ܐܝܟ
ܡ̈ܠܟܐ ܒܗܪ̈ܐ. ܕܠܐ ܬܘܒ ܢܦܩܘܢ ܡܢܗ ܕܟܘܬܐ[v] ܒܗܕ̈ܪܐ
ܠܒܪ̈ ܐܘܪܫܠܡ. ܘܐܡܪܘ ܗܠܝܢ ܕܡܫܝܚܐ ܠܐܒܓܪܘܣ.
ܦܩܘܕ ܡܪܝ، ܘܢܐܬܘܢ ܬܠܬܝܢ ܡܢ ܪ̈ܫܝܢ ܕܡܕܝܢܬܐ
ܐܘܪܫܠܡ. ܘܢܐܙܠ ܐܢܘܢ ܡܛܠ ܝܫܘܥ ܕܡܪܝ ܘܥܠ
ܕܬܐܘܡ ܠܫܠܝܚܘܬܐ ܡܫܝܚܝܢ ܒܫܡܗ. ܘܐܬܘ ܕܢܐܙܠ
ܘܠܐ ܦܝܪ ܦܬܟܪܐ. ܘܚܙܐ ܗܘܘܐ. ܘܟܠ ܕܢܐܙܠ
ܒܦܪܨܘܦܗ ܒܫܡܬܐ. ܘܦܪܣܐ ܬܪܘܨܬܐ. ܘܢܦܩ
ܐܒܓܪܘܣ ܗܘ ܘܬܠܬܝܢ ܫܠܝܚܐ. ܘܒܪܘܗ ܒܗܘ. ܘܐܬܐ
ܗܘܐ ܠܒܪܗ ܒܐܒܗܐ ܕܡܕܢ̈ܚܐ ܕܫܡܝܐ.[w] ܘܐܙܠ ܢܦܩ
ܒܬܪܗ ܕܡܪܗ، ܡܪܝܐ. ܘܢܦܩܬ ܡܫܡܫܢܘܬܐ ܕܝܠܗ.
ܘܐܡܪ ܠܗ: ܒܝܠ ܐܡܪ، ܠܡܪܬܝ. ܐܒܓܪܘܣ
ܕܡܫܝܚܬܐ ܗܕܐ ܚܕܐ ܕܢܦܩܘܕ ܠܝ. ܘܦܩܕܬ ܘܟܠ
ܘܫܩܠ ܡܕܡ ܘܢܦܩ ܥܠ ܬܪ̈ܥܝܗ: ܘܦܩܐ ܘܐܡܪ. ܥܠܡ
ܠܟ ܢܠܒܫ ܐܠܗܐ ܒܗܘ. ܘܥܠܡ ܠܒܠܒܐ ܕܐܬܓܠܝ ܡܢܟ. ܥܠܡ
ܠܗܘܢ ܠܫܡܫܐ ܕܠܚܝܡ ܠܟܘܪܣܝܐ ܡܕܝܢܐ ܕܟܪܟ.
ܕܡܕܒܪܢܐ ܒܗ ܐܠܗܘܬܗ. ܘܦܩܕ ܦܘܡܐ ܐܦ ܠܫܢܐ

[v] MS. ܕܟܗ̈ܢܘܢ ܒܪܡ.   [w] Read ܘܕܩ̈ܕܫܐ?

ܠܐܢܫ ܒܟܠܗ ܟܢܫܬܗ: ܘܫܩܠ ܡܢ ܗܘ ܥܦܪܐ ܘܫܕܐ ܠܐܪܥܐ
ܒܠܘܗܝ ܡܬܛܒܠܝܢ. ܘܟܠ ܡܢ ܕܡܬܛܒܠܝܢ ܗܘܘ ܐܬܐܣܝܘ ܚܠܝܡ
ܗܘܘ ܡܢܗ. ܘܡܬܦܩܕ ܠܗ. ܕܟܠ ܕܢܦܠܐ ܠܐܪܥܐ ܗܢܝ. ܢܬܦܨܐ
ܡܢ ܒܝܫܬܐ ܒܡ ܒܠܗ ܒܪܓܙܗ. ܘܗܘ ܕܢܦܠܐ ܢܬܦܨܠ.
ܘܐܡܦܪܢ ܒܝܫܬܐ ܕܐܢܐ ܐܢܫ ܡܫܬܐܠ: ܢܫܡܥ ܕܐܝܬ ܠܝ
ܒܗ̇ ܕܗܘܬ ܡܣܟܠܐ ܕܟܢܫܐ. ܘܡܚܐ ܕܒܘܣܪܢܐ. ܘܥܒܕܗ̇
ܕܐܬܦܪܘ: ܘܗܘܝܘ ܢܗܘܘܢ ܒܥܘܕܪܢܐ ܠܟܠ ܕܫܐܠ ܠܗܘܢ. ܀
ܐܘ ܕܢܝܚܐ ܢܦܫܐ. ܐܝܬܐ ܠܡܥܒܕ ܘܢܨܕܝܢ. ܡܛܠ ܕܚܕ
ܟܪܝܐ ܐܝܬ ܠܗ ܒܟܢܫܬܗ ܡܢ ܗܠܝܢ ܕܡܟܝܟܝܢ ܒܡܟܝܟܘܬ
ܘܡܟܬܒ ܠܗ. ܘܐܬܪ ܡܢ ܚܟܡܬܐ ܘܫܡܥܝܢ ܢܦܩܬܐ ܓܪܡ
ܒܗ ܡܢ ܢܦܫܬܐ. ܘܓܒܪ ܠܗ ܙܒܢ ܒܙܒܢܐ ܕܠܐ ܢܕܥ ܡܢܐ
ܦܝܐ. ܐܝܢܐ ܒܪ ܡܢ ܕܢܟܐ (fol. 450) ܘܡܢ ܐܟܡܬܐ ܒܟܕ
ܫܠܝܐ ܘܐܟܦ ܘܐܬܝܐ ܘܓܪܡ ܡܢ ܢܦܫܬܐ:[u] ܐܝܟ ܡܫܗ
ܕܡܟܝܟܐ. ܐܘ ܐܝܟ ܚܕ ܟܪܝܐ ܕܡܟܝܟܝܢ ܒܐܬܪܘܬܗܘܢ. ܒܟܠܐ
ܬܪܐܝܬ ܗܘ ܡܥܒܕ ܕܐܬܓܠܝ ܒܠܒ ܢܛܠ ܒܥܘܕܪܢܐ ܠܟܠ
ܕܡܬܟܪܝܢ ܒܗ. ܐܦ ܢܣܒ ܛܠܝܘܬܗ ܡܢ ܥܦܪܐ ܕܪܓܠܝ ܒܗ.
ܘܡܢ ܦܘܣܩܢ ܠܦܘܩܕܢ ܕܐܡܪܬܐ ܢܛܪܘܢ ܒܟܬܒܐ ܘܠܫܢܐ
ܘܢܣܒܘܗܝ ܛܠܝܘܬܗ ܕܒܪ ܐܠܗܐ. ܕܢܣܒ ܚܝܐ ܠܟܠܗ
ܒܪܝܬܐ ܕܡܗܝܡܢܐ ܒܗ. ܀ ܐܡܪ ܕܢܝܚܐ. ܪܒ ܗܘ ܡܕܡ
ܕܡܟܬܒ ܗܘܐ ܒܟܬܒܘܗܝ. ܘܕܚܝܠܬܐ ܠܟܘܢ ܥܠ ܫܪܪܐ
ܗܘܐ ܒܬܫܒܘܚܬܗ. ܐܝܟ ܥܡܕ ܟܠܗܝ ܡܬܥܗܕܬܐ ܕܥܠܝܗ̇
ܫܩܠ. ܐܦ ܢܚܘܐ ܠܝ ܐܝܟܢܐ ܦܩܕܗ ܗܠܝܢ ܟܪܝܐ. ܘܐܝܟܢܐ
ܒܓܙܪܐ ܠܟܘܢ ܗ̇ܝ ܒܗܬܐ ܥܠ ܪܫ. ܣܢܣܗ ܕܡܢܝܢ ܘܐܝܟ
ܘܢܦܩܘ ܠܗ. ܀ ܐܡܪ ܠܗܘܢ. ܡܚܝܐ ܐܢܫ ܠܟܘܢ ܗܢܐ.

[u] MS. ܦܬܘܬܐ ܡܢ.

ܒܠܒܘܫ ܕܢܘܟܪܝܝܢ ܐܝܬܝܗܘܢ ܡܛܠ ܡܥܫܢܐ. ܗܢܘܢ ܡܟܝܠ ܕܙ̈ܢܝܢ
ܠܡܥܫܢܘ ܘܐܡܪܘ ܡܢ ܚܕ ܦܘܡܐ. ܕܢܒܐ ܫܚܝܡܝ̈ܢ. ܘܕܠܐ ܡܢ
ܕܒܝܬ ܕܡܥܫܢܘܬܐ ܡܟܐ ܕܐܬܝܬܐ ܕܢܒܘܢ ܠܚܠܡܐ. ܘܕܠܐ ܡܢ
ܐܒ̈ܗܝܢ ܒܪ ܡܢܘܡ ܕܡܥܠܝܢ. ܘܕܠܐ ܒܡܟܐ ܡܥܠܝܢ. ܘܠܘ
ܠܢ ܒܠܚܘܕ ܡܥܠܝܢ. ܐܠܐ ܐܦ ܠܐܒܐ ܕܥܕܪܢ ܠܚܠܡܐ.
ܐܡܪ ܐܝܡܡܘܢܐ. ܓܠܘ ܠܢ. ܐܝܟܘ ܝܠܕܐ ܕܐܬܝܠܠ
ܒܠܘܗܝ. ܘܓܠܝܠܐ ܕܚܘ̈ܒܐ ܘܠܘܚܫܬܐ ܕܟܠܒ ܒܗ: ܘܢܬܫܐ
ܕܠܒܫ ܗܘܐ ܀ ܐܡܪ̈ܝܢ. ܡܪܢ ܫ̈ܐܠܢ ܗܠܝܢ ܕܠܒܫ ܗܘܬ.
ܓ̈ܠܐ ܐܪ̈ܓܝܢ ܒܠܒܗܘܢ. ܘܡܓܠܘ ܠܒܪ. ܘܫܩܠ ܐܢܘܢ
ܘܚ̈ܡܐ ܐܢܘܢ ܘܦܬܚ ܐܢܘܢ ܝܬܪ ܝܠܕܗ. ܘܫܕܪ ܐܢܘܢ ܐܪܒܥܐ
ܕܡܫܡܫ ܐܝܟ ܬ̈ܠܬܝܢ ܐܡ̈ܝܢ. ܘܟܬܒܝܢ ܒܠ ܝܠܕܐ
ܕܡܫܢܐ. ܘܐܪܫܝܡܘܗܝ ܘܠܐ ܡܢ ܐܦܩܐ ܕܢ̈ܟܣܐ. ܘܗܘܝܢ
ܒܐܦܐ ܐܟܘܪܬܐ ܒܫܬܗܘܢ ܘܟܒܝܢ ܒܠܒܗܘܢ ܦܓܪܐ
ܘܟܐ̈ܦܐ. ܘܐܬܦܠܓܪ[1] ܠܓܐܝܬ. ܘܠܘܡܒܠ ܪܫ ܡܢܗܘܢ
ܕܫܘܒ ܚܓܝܢ ܒܗܘܬܐ ܣܠܝܠܬܐ ܟܕܘ ܐܪܒܥ. ܐܝܟ
ܕܢܓܠܐ ܐܝܟܢ ܕܐܢܫ ܠܪܫ ܡܢܗܘܢ ܕܡܪ̈ܝܢ ܘܡܟܐ ܕܗܘܐ
ܐܘܠܨܢܐ ܠܐܢܫ ܡܢܢ. ܟܕ ܫܡܥ ܪܫ ܝܠܕܗ ܕܗܘ ܕܓܪܝܗ:
ܘܐܦ ܟܠܢܐ ܠܗ ܐܬܝܠܠ. ܀ ܐܠܗܐ ܢ̈ܦܪܐ ܡ̈ܥܬܝܢ
ܐܝܡܡܘܢܐ ܢܣܝܢܐ. ܗܘ ܐܪܘܪܐ ܬ̈ܠܬܝܢ ܘܡܫܬ̈ܟܚܢܐ
ܘܬ̈ܪܬܝܢ ܢܦ̈ܩܬܐ ܕܢܘܟܪܝܝܢ ܒܫ̈ܢܝܢ: ܘܟܬܒܝܢ ܫܡ̈ܗܝܗܘܢ.
ܕܟܢ̈ܫܐ ܘܢ̈ܫܐ ܘܛ̈ܠܝܐ. ܕܐܝܟ ܡܢܗܘܢ ܕܟܕ ܡܢܘܡ ܘܦܪܘܫ
ܡܢ ܦܘܬܐ. ܗܠܝܢ ܕܐܬܝܢܘܗܝ ܡܢ ܫܪܒܬܐ ܕܐܘܪܫܠܡ.
ܘܡܟܐ ܕܢܫܝܢ ܐܝܟ ܕܟܬܝܒ: ܐܘܠܝܢ ܠܬܘܡ ܒܥܡܗ ܘܦܘܫܩ
ܐܒܗܘܢ ܒܗ ܒܗܘܬܐ ܘܡܬܒܝܠܢ. ܀ ܘܐܦ ܐܝܟ ܒܪܝܫܐ

[1] Better ܘܐܬܦܠܓܪܘ.

ܘܗܒܠܐ ܡܗܕܝܢ ܘܦܚܡܝܢ ܘܩ̈ܢܝܢ ܘܒܢ̈ܝܢ ܡܢ ܡܕ̈ܝܪܐ ܒܗܡ
ܦܗܕܝܢ ܒܥܕܢܐ ܗܢܐ. ܕܡܫܝܚܐ ܕܡܢ ܡܪܝܡ. ܗܘ̣ ܒܠܚܘܕ
ܕܝܠܝܬܐ. ܘܠܗ ܡܫܒܚܝܢ ܗܘܘ̈ ܒܢ̈ܬܐ ܕܥܡܗ ܕܝܠܕ ܠܝ ܢܘܗܪܐ.
ܘܡܫܝܚܐ ܕܐܬܝܠܕ ܡܢ ܡܪܝܡ ܚܠܦ ܫܘܠܛܢܗ ܕܣܛܢܐ.
ܘܠܐ ܐܝܟ ܚܝܠܐ ܘܠܐ ܐܝܟ ܫܘ̈ܠܛܢܐ ܘܠܐ ܐܝܟ
ܫܘ̈ܠܛܢܐ ܘܐܩܘܦܬܐ ܕܒܕܘ: ܠܐ ܡܫܡܫ ܠܒܢܐ ܕܢܚܠܠ.
ܘܠܐ ܦܘܡܐ ܕܢܘܪܚܡ. ܘܠܐ ܚܠܠܐ ܘܠܐ ܬܫ̈ܬܝܬܐ ܡܕܡ
ܕܒܕܘ ܡܫܝܚܐ ܒܪܐ ܕܐܠܗܐ ܒܚܠܡܝ. ܡܢܝܢ ܕܐܡܪܘܗܝ
ܘܚܙܝܢ ܒܓܘ ܕܢܝܚ. ܘܐܬܢܓܕܘ ܡܢ ܒܒܘܪܐ ܐܚܬܐ ܒܒ̈ܙܝܢ:
ܢܓܕܐ ܡܫܢܐ ܀ ܘܡܢ ܒܬܪ ܕܐܬܢܓܕܘ: ܐܡܪܘ ܬܫܡܫ
ܠܡܫܝܚܐ. ܡܛܠ ܕܬܐܘܡܗ ܚܒܝܢ ܐܢܬܘܢ. ܡܫܘܚܝܢ ܠܟܘܢ
ܡܢܘܢ ܚܒܝܒܝܢ. ܚܠܝܢ ܠܚܠܡܝܢ ܬ̈ܠܬܐ ܕܗܘ̣ܝ ܒܐܘܪܫܠܡ.
ܡܢܘ ܗܢܐ ܐܣܟܡܐ ܕܗܘܐ ܕܡܪܢ ܒܥܘܪܗ ܕܐܬܝܠܕ ܡܢ
ܐܒ̈ܗܝܢ ܒܪܘܚܐ ܕܢܫܡܐ ܕܝܘܩܢܐ. ܀ ܐܡܪ ܕܢܝܐ ܠܬܫܒܚܬ
ܠܡܫܝܚܐ. ܒܠܒܕ ܕܚܒܝܒ ܐܢܬܘܢ ܐܡܪܘ ܘܠܐ ܬܕܝܠܘܢ. ܀
ܐܡܪܝܢ ܗܘܢ. ܐܝܟܐ ܡܠܟ ܡܫܝܚܐ ܕܟܠܗܘܢ ܐܘܕܥ.
ܘܐܝܟܐ ܐܝܬܝ ܦܘܠܐ ܗܠܝܢ ܕܐܬܦܬܚ ܒܐܝܕܘܗܝ.
ܘܐܗܦܟܐ ܕܦܪܚܝܢ ܠܗ ܒܗ ܚܝܠܐ. ܘܗܝ ܠܗܘܢܬܐ ܕܟܠܒ
ܒܗ. ܘܒܠܝܠܐ ܕܒܩܒܐ ܗܘ ܕܗܦܟܝܢ ܠܗ ܒܪܝܫܗ. ܘܬܟܐܢܐ
ܗܢܘܢ ܕܒܢܝܐ ܕܐܠܦܫܗ. ܐܝܟܐ ܡܠܟܝܢ. ܀ ܐܡܪ
ܐܣܟܡܐ ܠܚܒܘܪܐ. ܐܡܪܘ ܘܦܠܘ ܡܕܡ ܕܐܡܪܝܢ
ܠܗܘܢ. ܐܡܪܝܢ. ܘܗܢܘܢ ܡܢܝ ܢܕܚܝܢ ܐܝܟܐ ܐܢܘܢ ܕܢܝܐ
ܕܝܢ ܒܗ ܝܘܡܐ ܡܢ ܚܠ ܒܐܝܟ ܕܠܗ: ܘܐܗܦܟ ܠܗܘܢ
ܕܐܦܪܘܗ ܒܡܪܝ ܘܐܡܪ. ܒܡܫܝܚܐ ܕܐܬܝܠܕ ܡܢ ܡܪܝܡ
ܘܗܝܡܢܘܬܗ ܒܗ: ܐܦ ܗܢܐ ܡܫܝܚ ܐܝܟܐ ܒܗ. ܐܡܪܘ

ܘܗܘܐ ܢܦܩ ܡܢ ܡܕܝܢܬܐ ܕܐܒܘܗܝ. ܘܟܠܗܝܢ ܒܬܘ̈ܠܬܐ ܕܠܟܠ
ܘܕܠܬܚܬ: ܡܢܐܒܝܢ ܕ̈ܝܠܗܘܢ ܘܫܒܩܝܢ ܠܗ ܘܡܬܒܥܝܢ ܠܗ
ܒܕܡܘܬܐ ܠܟܠܗ. ܐܝܟ ܒܪ ܠܡܕܝܢܬܐ ܠܐ ܥܠܠ. ܐܠܐ ܗܘ
ܕܢܝܚ ܡܢܗ: ܕܐܬܚܙܝ ܡܕܝܢܬܐ ܒܪܗ ܕܐܠܗܐ ܕܐܬܒܠܝ
ܡܢ ܡܕܒܪܐ. ܀ ܐܡܪܝܢ ܣ̈ܒܐ. ܢܐܬܐ ܡܘܫܐ ܢܒܝܐ
ܘܬ̈ܬܬܚܙܝ ܕܢܦܩ ܒܗܘܢ[s] ܠܦܪܥܘܢ: ܘܦܩܕ ܒܢ̈ܝ
ܠܐܝܣܪܐܝܠ. ܘܕܒܪܐ ܦܪܥܘܢ ܕܢܦܠܐ ܠܐܝܣܪܐܝܠ. ܡܢܐ
ܕܡܦܠܐ ܠܢܒܝܐ ܘܡܦ ܡܘܫܐ ܠܣܘܦܪܐ ܡܢܝܢܐ ܘܦܠܐ
ܐܢܘܢ ܠܬ̈ܠܠܗܘܢ ܕܢܒܝܐ ܬ̈ܠܠܝܢ: ܀ ܐܡܪܝܢ ܣ̈ܒܐ
ܠܡܕܝܢܬܐ. ܘܫܡܥ ܕܐܬܒܠܝ ܡܢ ܡܕܒܪ. ܕܗܘܐ ܒܥ̈ܕܢܐ
ܘܐܬܦܢܝܘ ܡܢ ܦܪܕܝܣܐ. ܘܠܐܦܪܘܣܐ ܒܗ ܟܠܗ ܠܗ ܢܒܝܐ
ܐܘܫܛ ܠܗ ܐܝܕܗ ܘܐܣܩܗ. ܘܐܠܘ ܒܠ ܢܒܝܐ ܘܟܠ ܡܕܝܢܬܐ
ܠܐ ܫܠܝܛ ܗܘܐ: ܡܢ ܐܝܟܐ ܡܫܬܡܥܝܢ ܗܘܘ ܠܗ ܗܠܝܢ
ܟܠܗܘܢ ܀ ܐܡܪܝܢ ܣ̈ܒܐ. ܠܐ ܡܬܟܣܝܢ ܕܝܕܘܥ
ܒܡܕܒܪܐ: ܡܛܠ ܕܡܢ ܡܠܟܘܬܗ ܕܒܪ ܡܢܝܢ ܠܓܒܪܘܬܢ
ܘܒܗ ܡܫܠܡܐ ܐܢ ܕܬܫܡ ܐܢܬܘܢ ܘܐܦ ܐܢܬܘܢ ܠܗ. ܀
ܐܡܪܝܢ ܣ̈ܒܐ ܠܡܕܒܪܐ. ܘܠܐ ܚܙܐ ܕܐܢܬ ܒܗ ܢܦܫܐ
ܐܬܪܝܬܘܢ: ܘܠܐ ܕܗܘܬܐ ܫܠܝܡ ܐܢܬܘܢ ܀ ܐܡܪܝܢ
ܣ̈ܒܐ. ܘܠܐ ܕܗܘܐ ܒܪ ܐܢܫ. ܘܠܐ ܐܠܝܨ ܒܪ ܫܦܠ
ܕܐܝܟ ܡܫܬܐ ܡܢ ܕܐܟܚܕ ܒܝܬ ܠܗܘܢ ܡܕܒܪܐ. ܘܠܐ ܫܒܩ
ܕܐܫܬܪܝ ܘܡܘܬܐ ܠܐ ܚܙܐ. ܠܗܘ ܕܡܫܬܪܐ ܐܢܫ ܫܒܩ. ܒܪ
ܡܕܒܪ. ܀ ܐܡܪܝܢ ܣ̈ܒܐ ܠܡܕܒܪܐ. ܠܐ ܒܫܡܝܐ ܘܠܐ
ܒܐܪܥܐ: ܠܗܘ ܕܡܫܬܪܐ ܡܢ ܫܡܥ ܕܐܬܒܠܝ ܡܢ ܡܕܒܪ.
ܘܐܒܘܗܝ ܡܫܒܚܝܢ ܕܫܠܝܚܘܗܝ ܠܡܘܪܝܢ ܘܪܘܚܗ ܩܕܝܫܐ.

[s] Read ܒܗ̈ܝܢ.

ܢܗܝܪ ܐܝܬܘܗܝ ܡܢܗܪ. ܕܢܚ ܕܢܘܗܪܗ، ܕܡܫܝܚܐ ܚܝ.
ܢܗܝܪ ܕܡܫܝܚܐ ܒܪ ܡܪܝܐ. ܗܘ ܒܪܗ، ܠܐܒܘܗܝ. ܕܒܠܐ
ܫܘܬܦܢ ܒܒܪܝܬܐ ܕܐܒܘܗܝ. ∴ ܐܡܪܝܢ ܒܒܘܪܐ. ܠܡܢܐ
ܡܛܠ ܕܡܫܝܚܐ ܕܒܗ ܫܘܬܦܝܢ ܐܝܬܘܗܝ. ܡܢ ܐܢܫܘܬ ܕܗܘܐ
ܦܘܪܩܢܐ ܘܦܠܛ ܙܢܐ ܕܦܘܪܩܢܗ ܘܒܣܘܥܪܗ ܒܗ ܥܕܬܐ
ܘܐܘܪܚܐ. ∴ ܐܡܪܝܢ ܬ̈ܘܒ ܠܡܫܝܚܐ. ܟܠܗ ܕܠܐ ܐܬܦܠܓ
ܐܢܫܘܬ ܒܟܠܬܗ. ܟܠ ܕܒܦܓܪ: ܗܘܐ ܕܡܫܝܚܐ ܕܡܢ ܡܪܝܡ
ܗܘ ܝܐܬܐ ܘܢܓܕܬ ܚܠܦ ܟܠ. ܘܦܪܩܗ ܠܥܠܡܐ ܡܢ
ܛܥܝܘܬܐ. ܐܢܫܘܬ ܒܪ ܐܠܗ ܓܒܠܬ: ܚܕ ܦܘܪܩܢܐ ܡܬܬܦܪܫ
ܗܘܐ. ܡܫܝܚܐ ܗܝ ܕܡܟܝܬ: ܦܘ̈ܪܩܢܐ ܕܟܠ ܒ̈ܢܝܢ ܒܗ
ܐܬܦܪܫ[1] ܠܐܠܗܐ. ∴ ܐܡܪܝܢ ܒܒܘܪܐ. ܠܡܢܐ ܡܛܠ
ܡܫܝܚܐ ܡܢ ܢܒܝܘܬ: ܕܐܝܟ ܚܘܝܐ ܕܚܝ̈ܐ ܠܐ ܚܝܘ
ܒܡܕܒܪܐ. ܕܟܠ ܕܚܙܐ ܠܗ ܚܠܡ. ܘܦܩܕ ܐܠܗܐ ܥܕܬܐ
ܘܡܠܠ ܥܡܗ. ܘܦܩܕ ܘܫܠܚܗ ܡܢ ܥܕܬܐ ܠܐܘܪܚܐ. ܕܐܝܟ
ܟܕ ܒܗ ܩܛܠ ܗܘܐ. ܘܢܝܬܘ ܒ̈ܢܝܐ ܠܥܠܡܗ. ∴ ܐܡܪܝܢ
ܬ̈ܘܒ ܠܡܫܝܚܐ. ܘܡܥܡܕ ܘܫܒܠܬܐ ܘܡ̈ܠܐܟܐ ܕܢܚܬܐ:
ܟܠ ܡܐܬܝܬܗ ܕܡܫܝܚܐ ܘܟܠ ܪܐܙܐ ܕܦܓܪܘܬܗ ܢܦܪܩ
ܗܘܘ. ∴ ܐܡܪܝܢ ܒܒܘܪܐ ܠܬ̈ܘܒ ܠܡܫܝܚܐ. ܦܘܪ ܠܒܘܢ
ܦܘܠܘܣ ܕܐܠܗܐ ܠܥܒܕܐ. ܕܟܠ ܕܐܡܪ: ܒܥܒܕܐ ܡܫܬܒܚ.
ܘܟܠ ܕܟܬܒ ܒܐܘܪܚܐ ܡܦܬܟܪ. ∴ ܐܡܪܝܢ ܬ̈ܘܒ
ܠܡܫܝܚܐ. ܐܠܗܐ ܗܘܐ ܒܟܠܟܠܐ ܠܥܒܕܐ ܗܕܐ ܕܡܟܝܢ.
ܟܕ ܥܒܕܐ ܘܗܘܪܐ. ܘܠܐ ܐܝܟ ܗܟܢ ܠܗ ܒܚܘܫܒܗ
ܐܠܐ ܐܠܗܝ ܐܬܠܒܫܗ. ܡܫܝܚܐ ܕܝܢ ܕܩܛܠ ܠܗ ܟܠܗܘܢ
ܠܚܝܐ ܥܒܕܐ ܩܛܠ. ܐܠܐ ܠܟܠ ܡܢ ܟܠܗܘܢ ܥܒܕܝ ܩܛܠ.

[1] Better ܐܬܦܪܫܘ.

ܐܠܐ ܡܬܒܬܒܐܝܬ ܡܢ ܦܘܪ̈ܫܢܘܗܝ. ܕܐܦ ܐܢܫܐ ܐ̇ܚܕ ܒܥܒܐ
ܐܒܝܐ. ܕܐܡܪܢ ܐܠܗܘܬܗ ܢܚܙܘܢܝܗ. ✣ ܐܬܟܢܫܘ ܬ̈ܢܝܢ
ܠܡܫܝܚܐ. ܐܡܪ ܒܗ ܬܟܐܬ ܓܡܪ ܒܕܐܝܬܘܗܝ ܕܠܐ ܠܫܒܬ ܒܢ̈ܝ
ܘܐܡܪ ܠܗ. ܒܪܝ, ܫܒܬ: ܗܐ ܩܘܪ̈ܒܢܐ ܦܝܫܝܢ ܒܥܕ̈ܬܐ
ܐܚܪ̈ܢܐ. ܕܗܟܢܐ ܐܦ ܡܗܘܢܐ ܘܠܒܘܫܬܐ. ܘܒܬܪ ܡܫܝܚܐ
ܕܐܬܬܐ ܘܐܬܒܝܢ ܡܢ ܬ̈ܢܫܐ ܚܝ̈ܠܐ ܘܢܦܩܬ. ܘܒܬܘܬܗ
ܢܫܟܚܐ ܠܚܠܡܘܗܝ ܒܫܢܬܐ. ܘܢܩܘܡ ܠܬ̈ܠܬܐ ܝܘ̈ܡܝܢ. ܘܢܩܘܡ
ܠܦܓܪܗ, ܒܗܘ ܠܫܡܝܐ. ܘܗܘܐ ܐܝܟ ܡܠܝܚܐ ܡܢ ܦܘܡܗ.
ܘܫܠܡ ܠܕܐܝܬܝܗܝ ܗܕܐ. ܘܩܘܪܒܢܐ ܗܠܝܢ ܘܐܬܕܠܝ
ܠܒܝܬ ܠܚܡܐ ܕܝܘܕܐ. ܘܦܠܚܝܢ ܠܗ ܠܡܫܝܚܐ ܕܐܬܝܠܕ ܡܢ
ܒܬܘܠܬܐ. ܘܗܟܢܐ ܦܘܩ. ܘܐܬܐ ܡܫܒ̈ܚܐ ܘܐܬܝܘ
ܩܘܪ̈ܒܢܐ ܗܠܝܢ ܕܐܬܝܗܒ ܒܟܗܢܘܬܗܘܢ. ܘܡܢ ܕܐܝܬܘܗܝ ܕܐܬܐ
ܬܠܓ ܒܪ̈ܝܬܐ ܕܢܓܕܘܢ ܕܡܬܩܪܐ. ܘܡܢ ܡܫܝܚܐ ܕܐܬܝܠܕ
ܡܢ ܡܪܝܡ. ܢܘܪܐ ܒܪ̈ܝܬܐ* ܕܫܒ̈ܩܝܢ ܗ̈ܘܘ, ܡܢ ܐܕܡ ܠܫܢܬ.
ܐܬܒܪ̈ܬܒ ܒܬܦܪ̈ܬܐ. ܘܒܠܗܘܢ ܒܪ̈ܝܬܐ[p] ܘܐܢ̈ܫܐ ܢܣܒܘ[q]
ܠܒ̈ܢܝ ܘܒ̈ܢܝܐ ܢܣܒܘ ܠܒܢ̈ܝ ܒܢ̈ܝܢ ܕܒܝܬܐ ܠܐܒܪܗܡ. ܒܗ
ܕ̈ܝܢ ܒܠܗܘܢ ܒܪ̈ܝܬܐ ܘܐܡܡ̈ܐ: ܕܐܬܐ ܡܫܝܚܐ ܘܡܬܝܠܕ
ܒܒܝܬܠܚܡ. ܚܙܝ ܕܝܢ ܠܐ ܫܡܥܬܘܢ ܒܟܠܗ̇ ܕܐܬܟܬܒܬ. ✣
ܐܬܟܬܒ ܒܦܘܪ̈ܩܐ. ܕܠܡܢܐ ܠܒܪ ܗܘ ܡܢ ܐܒܪܗܡ ܒܪ ܡܪܝܡ.
ܕܓܒܪܐ ܠܐܠܗܐ ܘܓܒܠܗ ܥܡܡܐ ܘܡܠܠ ܒܗܘܢ: ܐܝܟ ܕܡܡܠܠܝܢ
ܥܡ ܚܕ. ✣ ܐܬܟܬܒ ܬ̈ܢܝܢ ܠܡܫܝܚܐ. ܒܝܘܡܗ̇ ܕܠܐ

[p] We should probably read ܫܒ̈ܩܝܢ ܗ̈ܘܘ. ܡܢ ܐܕܡ ܠܫܢܬ ܠܐܬܒܪ̈ܬܒ ܒܬܦܪ̈ܬܐ, and omit the words ܘܒܠܗܘܢ ܒܪ̈ܝܬܐ, which occur again immediately below.

[q] The MS. has ܢܣܒܘ ܘܐܢ̈ܫܐ.

ܕܪܒܘܢ ܕܢܦܩܐ ܡܢ ܥܠܡܐ. ܘܫܐܠܬܐ ܕܬܫܪܒܘܢ. ܘܒܕ
ܒܡܫܝܚܘܬܐ ܦܓܪܢܝܬܐ ܡܫܟܚ ܗܘܐ: ܕܐܝܟܢܐ ܢܐܙܠ
ܠܒܝܬܠܚܡ: ܟܠ ܚܕ ܡܢܗܘܢ ܡܢ ܐܝܟܐ ܕܐܝܬܘܗܝ ܗܘܐ.
ܡܛܠ ܫܕܪܠܗ ܦܘܩܕܢܐ ܩܠܝܠܐ ܘܟܬܒܐ ܕܢܘܗܪܐ. ܘܐܬܕܒܪܘ
ܡܢ ܪܘܫܐ ܕܡܘܕܥܢܐ ܘܐܬܝܢ ܠܒܝܬܠܚܡ. ܡܪܝܡ ܕܝܢ ܒܗ
ܝܥܕܬ ܕܡܠܝܢ ܠܗܬܝ: ܦܘܫܬ ܠܐܘܪܚܝ ܡܢ ܒܪܘܫܐ ܕܒܗ
ܪܡܫܐ ܗܘܬ. ܘܐܡܪܬܐ ܠܝ. ܒܪܝܟ ܗܘ ܡܪܝܐ ܕܫܒܠ
ܪܚܡܬ، ܘܫܘܪܒܘܢ ܠܝ ܕܐܬܝܠܕܘܢ ܘܐܬܝܠܕ ܒܓܠܐ ܐܝܟܢܘܬ.
ܗܫܐ ܢܚܬܬ ܕܐܬܘܬܐ ܪܒܬܐ ܘܫܒܚܐ ܐܝܟܐ ܠܗ ܘܡܢ ܡܢܬܐ
ܐܢܐ. ܐܠܐ ܒܗܢܐ ܐܢܐ ܕܐܬܡܪܢܘܢ ܠܝ ܒܪܗ ܫܘܒܚܗܘܢ
ܕܡܢܬܐ ܐܢܐ. ܘܐܡܪܢܐ ܐܢܬܘܢ ܕܗܒܢܐ ܘܠܝܠܐܝܬ
ܡܠܝܬܘܢ. ܐܡܪܝܢ ܟܠ ܠܒܢܝ. ܐܝܟ ܐܡܝܪ ܡܕܡܢܐܝܬ
ܡܠܠ ܕܡܕܡܢܐ ܐܝܬܝܟ ÷ ܐܡܪܝ ܒܢܝ. ܐܢܐ ܠܗܬ ܡܕܒܚܗ
ܕܡܪܝܐ ܕܒܕܬܐ ܕܐܦܘܗܝ. ܘܐܡܪ ܗܘܬ. ܒܗ ܦܪܘܬܢ
ܪܘܫܐ ܕܡܘܕܥܢܐ ܕܐܡܗܘܗ ܕܪܒܝܢ ܡܢܒ ܠܗ ܡܪܝܐ ܕܬܕܦܪ ܡܢ
ܥܠܡܐ. ܐܠܐ ܦܪܗܒ ܠܐ ܠܗܬܝ ܠܒܝܬܠܚܡ. ܘܡܫܒܚܬܗ

÷ ÷ ÷ ÷ ÷

÷ ÷ ÷ ÷

÷ ÷ ÷ ÷ ÷

÷ ÷ ÷ ÷

ܕܦܓܥܝܢ ܡܢ ܕܥܠܡܘܢ.° ÷ ܐܡܪܝܢ ܒܣܘܪ̈ܐ ܡܢ ܐܝܟܐ
ܡܫܘܝܢ ܐܢܬܘܢ ܠܝ ܕܒܪ ܡܢܫܡ ܐܢܬܘ ܡܫܝܚܐ. ÷ ܐܡܪܝܢ
ܪ̈ܘܚܡ ܠܡܫܝܚܐ. ܣܝܡ ܡܫܘܝܢ. ܐܡܪ ܕܢܒܝܐ. ܠܐ ܒܥܠܡܬܐ
ܘܠܐ ܒܛܘܫܝܐ. ܬܐܡܪܘܢ ܫ̈ܠܝܡܘܢ ܚܕ ܠܗܘܟܠ ܚܕ.

° Add. 12,174, fol. 449 rect.

ܒܗܪܟܫܗ: ܘܐܡܪ ܫܠܡ ܠܗ ܡܠܟܬ ܐܠܗܐ: ܘܫܠܡ ܠܗ
ܠܡܫܝܚܐ ܕܐܬܓܠܝ ܡܢܗ. ܕܐܫܡܥ ܠܫܠܝܚܘܗܝ. ܠܐ ܬܬܒܥܐ
ܠܗ. ܡܛܠ ܕܒܫܘܒܚܐ ܪܒܐ ܢܦܩܐ ܐܢܬܝ، ܡܢ ܥܠܡܐ
ܗܢܐ. ܘܟܕ ܗܠܝܢ ܫܡܥܬ ܚܕܘܬܐ ܪܒܬܐ ܐܬܡܠܝܬ. ܘܒܥܬ
ܘܐܡܪܬ ܠܝܘܚܢ. ܒܪܝ ܡܩ̈ܕܫܐ ܢܦܫܐ ܠܗܘܢ ܡܘ̈ܗܒܬܐ
ܕܒܗ ܕܡܫܝܚܘܬܐ ܐܝܟ ܢܘܗܪܐ ܒܢܘܗܪܐ. ܐܡܪ ܠܗ ܝܘܚܢ.
ܘܐܡܪ ܗܘ ܠܗ ܡܪܝ ܫܡܥ ܡܫܝܚܐ ܒܪܗ. ܘܫܡܥܢ ܗ̈ܘܝ
ܕܡ̈ܠܐ ܕܬܪ̈ܝܗܘܢ ܡܢ ܒܪܬܐ. ܐܦ ܗܠܝܢ ܬܠܬ ܒܬ̈ܘܠܬܐ
ܠܗܦܟܢ ܡܢܟܝܢ ܗ̈ܘܝ، ܘܒ̈ܟܝܢ. ܐܡܪ ܠܗ ܝܘܚܢ. ܐܢ ܐܢܬܝ
ܕܡܠܟܬ ܐܠܗܐ ܐܢܬܝ، ܗܟܢܐ ܒܥܝܐ ܠܗ ܕܬܦܩܐ ܐܢܬܝ، ܡܢ
ܥܠܡܟܝ ܗܢܐ ܢܟܪ̈ܝܢ ܫܪ̈ܟܢܐ ܘܐܝܠܝܢ ܕܠܐ ܝܕܥܘ
ܦܘܩ̈ܕܢܘܗܝ، ܕܐܠܗܐ. ܗܕܝܢ ܐܘܕܝܬ ܠܝ ܪܘܚܐ (fol. 9)
ܕܩܘܕܫܐ ܒܟܠ ܦܬܝܢ. ܕܒܗܝܢ ܐܝܬܝܢ ܗܘܝܢ. ܘܐܡܪܬ ܠܝ.
ܐܡܗ ܕܪ̈ܒܝܢ. ܦܩܕ ܠܗ ܕܢܥܐ ܕܬܦܩ ܡܢ ܥܠܡܐ
ܗܢܐ. ܐܠܐ ܡܘܡܐ ܝܠܗ ܠܗܬܢ. ܠܟܠܬܝܗܝܢ. ܠܥܡܡܐ
ܐܘܕܥܬ ܒܝܗܘܕ. ܘܠܦܠܚܘ ܟܦܪ̈ܝܗܘܢ. ܘܠܬܘܡܐ
ܒܗܢܘ. ܘܠܡܬܝ، ܒܟܢܝܘܗܝ. ܘܠܒܪܬܘܠܡܝ ܒܐܪܡܢܝܐ
ܘܠܐܕܝ، ܒܠܕܝܢܬܐ ܘܠܝܗܘܒ ܒܡܕܝܢܬܐ ܕܝܗܘܢ.[m]
ܐܝܟܢܐ ܕܝܢ ܐܝܟ ܝܗܘܕܐ ܕܡܫܝܚܐ ܘܡܘܗܒܬ ܐܝܟ ܝܗܘܕܐ
ܕܝܬܝܢ ܘܦܠܚܘ ܘܡܫܡܫܢ ܡܫܝܚܐ ܘܡܬܠܡܕ ܕܗܘܐ
ܥܠܡܐ ܟܠܗ ܝܘܡܢܐ ܒܪ̈ܘܚܐ. ܗܠܝܢ ܝܗܒܢܐ ܡܫܝܚܐ
ܗܘܘ: ܪܘܚܐ ܕܩܘܕܫܐ ܐܡܪܬ ܐܝܟ.[n] ܘܐܡܪܬ
ܠܗܘܢ. ܘܡܘܡܐ ܘܠܐ ܬܦܩܘܢ ܕܢܘܟܪܝܐ ܡܛܠ. ܐܠܐ
ܡܛܠ ܗܕܐ ܡܠܟܘܢ: ܕܬܐܠܝܢ ܠܟܠܬܝܗܝܢ ܠܘܬ ܐܡܗܘܢ

[m] Read ܕܝܗܘܢ?.

[n] The MS. has ܠܗܘܢ twice.

ܗ̈ܘܘ ܫܡ̈ܥܝܢ ܕܒܨ̈ܠܘܬܐ ܕܒܡܪܝ̱ ܗ̈ܘܘ܂ ܒܗ ܡܢܝܢ
ܐܡܗ ܕܡܪܝ̱. ܒܨܠܘܬܐ ܘܒܥܘܬܐ ܘܦܠܚܘܬܐ. ܘܒܟܠ ܬܠܬܝܗܘܢ:
ܘܐܡܪܝ̱ ܠܗ̇. ܢܒܥܐ ܐܢܬ[k] ܡܪܬܝ܆ ܕܬܫܠܛܝܢ ܥܒܕܝܢ
ܐܒܗ̈ܝܢ ܘܐܢܫ̈ܝܢ ܘܟܠ ܡܕܡ ܕܐܢܬ ܠܝ. ܘܒܥܒܕ ܟܒܝܢ
ܕܢܐܬܐ. ܘܠܐ ܥܒܕܝܢ ܠܗ ܒܗܕܐ ܕܒܥܬܝܢ. ܗܢܝܢ ܒܥ̈ܠܬ
ܐܚܕ̈ܝܗ ܠܥܡܢ̈ܝ ܘܩܪܝܬ ܐܢ̈ܝ ܘܐܡܪܬ ܠܗܝܢ. ܬܬܘܒܠ
ܝܠܗܬ، ܡܕܡ ܙܒܢܐ ܕܐܢܬ ܠܝ ܒܥܡܟܐ. ܕܡܢ ܠܒܗܝܢ ܫܪܒܬܐ
ܕܐܘܪܓܠ ܐܢܬܝܢ ܠܒܘܙ ܒܕܪܬܝܢ ܠܗ ܝܒܫܐ. ܘܗܡܝܢ
ܒܟܠ ܘܢܦܩܝܢ ܠܒܝܬ ܠܚܡ. ܘܬܡܢ ܝܠܕܬ ܘܗܒܢܐ ܐܡܪܬ.
ܙܒܠ ܡܥܝܢܐ ܥܒܕ ܒܟܠܗ ܕܠܕܬܟܝ. ܘܬܐ ܠܘܬܝ، ܐܢܬ
ܘܬ̈ܠܝܢܐ ܬܠܡܝ̈ܕܝܟܝ. ܕܐܚܪܢܘ̱ ܒܕܠܐ ܐܢܝܗܘܢ. ܘܒܗܘܕܐ
ܢܫܐ ܐܢܬܝ ܕܫܒܩܒ ܐܢܬ ܠܝ܆ ܒܟܠ ܡܐ ܕܒܒܢܐ ܐܢܐ
ܠܟܝ. ܒܕ ܫܠܡܬ ܝܠܕܬܗ̇: ܗܘܝܢ ܒܐܦܣܘܣ ܐܢܬܘܢ،
ܗܘܐ. ܘܪܘܚܐ ܕܩܘܕܫܐ ܐܘܕܒܬܗ ܒܕ ܒܥܠ ܕܢܠ̈ܝܐ
ܒܪܬܐ ܕܐܦܣܘܣ ܘܐܡܪܬ ܠܗ. ܐܡܪܗ̇ ܕܪܒܝܢ ܦܪܒ ܠܗ
ܘܒܢܐ ܕܬܦܠܐ ܡܢ ܒܠܥܡܐ ܗܢܐ. ܘܗܟܢ ܐܠܦܐ ܪܘܚܐ ܕܬܫܝܢ
ܐܠܐ ܗܘܪܒ ܘܠܠ ܠܝ ܠܗܬ ܠܒܝܬ ܠܚܡ. ܘܗܘܐ ܡܫܪܪ
ܐܢܐ ܠܗܬܢ ܠܒܠܗܘܢ ܬ̈ܠܝܢܐ ܫܒܝ̈ܚܝ. ܗܢܝܢ ܝܠ ܗܘܝܢ
ܘܐܡܪܝ̱. ܡܪܝ̱ ܫܘܒ ܡܫܝܚܐ: ܒܪܗ ܕܐܠܗܐ[l] ܡܒܪܟܐ.
ܗܒ ܒܬ̈ܦܠ ܣܠܩܐ ܕܐܙܠ ܠܗܬ ܐܡܟܝ ܠܒܝܬ ܠܚܡ. ܘܐܣܝܐ
ܕܐܠܐ ܬܗܘܝܬ. ܘܒܕܐܠܐ ܒܕܚܠ ܫܠܡ ܝܠܕܬܗ: ܘܪܘܚܐ
ܕܩܘܕܫܐ ܐܟܠܬܗ ܒܒܢܝܢܐ ܕܢܗܘܪܐ. ܘܠܒܝܬ ܠܚܡ
ܠܠܬܐܝܬ ܡܠܝܐ. ܘܒܕ ܡܠ ܠܒܠܝܬܐ ܕܒܗ ܐܢܬܝܗ ܗܘܬ
ܡܪܝܡ. ܐܫܟܚܗ̇ ܒܕ ܙܥܘܪܐ ܒܪܘܚܐ. ܘܩܪܒ ܢܫܩܗ̇ ܒܠ

[k] Better ܐܢܬܝ.

[l] The MS. has ܕܐܠܗܐ twice.

ܢܦܫܗ ܘܒܥܝܐ. ܘܐܢ ܗܘܝܢ ܠܐ ܡܫܟܚܐ ܐܢܬܝ. ܦܘܩ ܡܢ
ܐܘܪܫܠܡ. ܘܠܐ ܬܐܬܝܢ[h] ܬܘܒ ܠܘܬ ܡܪܢܐ ܘܠܡܠܟܘܬܗ.
ܡܛܠ ܕܡܠܟܘܬܐ ܦܩܕ ܗܟܢܐ. ܐܡܪܐ ܠܗܘܢ ܡܪܝܡ.
ܠܐ ܙܕܩ ܗܘܐ ܕܬܐܬܘܢ ܠܘܬܝ, ܒܗܠܝܢ ܡ̈ܠܐ. ܡܛܠ
ܕܐܢܐ ܡ̈ܠܟܘܗܝ ܠܐ ܫܡܥܬ ܐܢܐ. ܘܦܘܩܕܢܘܗܝ ܠܐ
ܡܩܒܠܐ ܐܢܐ. ܐܠܐ ܗܕܐ ܡܢ ܢܦܫܝ ܥܒܕܐ ܐܢܐ.
ܕܡܫܝܚܘܬܗܘܢ ܕܐܚܒܢܝ ܗܘܐ ܪ̈ܚܡܬܐ ܠܝܬ ܠܝ. ܘܗܦܟܘ
ܫܗ̈ܕܐ ܠܒܬܘ̈ܠܬܗܝܢ ܡܛܠ ܕܫ̈ܒܝܢ ܠܗ ܪ̈ܚܡܬܐ. ܗܢܝܢ ܓܝܪ
ܠܒ̈ܢܐ ܕܡܫܡܫܢܘܬܗ ܘܐܡܪܝܢ ܠܗܘܢ. ܫܘܕܐ ܐܡܪܝܢ ܠܝ
ܕܠܐ ܫܒܩܝܢ ܠܝ ܕܐܬܦܢܐ ܠܐܘܪܫܠܡ. ܘܡܛܠ ܢܦܫܐ ܐܢܐ
ܠܝ ܠܡܬܠܚܡܘ ܠܡܠܬܐ ܕܠܟ. ܐܠܐ ܐܢ ܐܝܬ ܒܟܝܢ ܕܒܥܝܐ
ܕܬܐܙܠ ܥܡܝ ܬܐܬܐ. ܬܠܬ ܒܢ̈ܝ ܒܬܘ̈ܠܬܐ ܒܒܢܬܗ ܒܟܪܝ
ܗ̇ܘ, ܐܡܝܢܐܝܬ. ܕܐܬܚܙܝܢ ܩ̈ܕܡܝܗ ܙ̈ܢܝܐ ܘܡܕܒܪ̈ܢܝܐ
ܕܐܘܪܫܠܡ. ܕܫܕܐ ܡܢܗܘܢ ܐܬܬܗ̇ ܗܘܬ ܒܪܬܗ ܕܢܝܩܕܡܘܣ
ܪܫܡܗ ܕܡܫܝܚܐ. ܘܥܡܗ̇ ܒܠܬܐ. ܕܒܥܡܗ̇ ܪ̈ܫܡܐ ܒܪܬܐ
ܡܚܝܬܗ ܕܒܪ ܐܠܗܐ. ܘܐܚܪܬܐ ܐܬܬܗ̇ ܗܘܬ ܒܪܬܗ
ܕܓܡܠܐܝܠ ܪܫ ܒܢܘܫܬܐ ܘܡܠܟ ܢܩܘܫܐ. ܘܥܡܗ̇ ܢܘܪܐ.
ܕܒܕܡܘܬ[i] ܢܘܪܐ ܡܬܠ ܫ̈ܠܒܐ ܡܫܝܚܐ. ܕܟܠ ܠܦ̈ܘܡܗ,
ܘܫܡܗ̇ ܠܕܬܗ ܡܕܝܢܬܐ. ܗ̇ܝ ܕܡ ܐܚܪܬܐ ܐܬܬܗ̇ ܗܘܬ
ܒܪܬܗ ܕܡܫܠܡܢܐ: ܡܢ ܠܘܩܐ ܕܒܝܬ ܐܪ̈ܡܠܘܬ. ܘܥܡܗ̇
ܦܬܚܬܐ. ܕܡܬܐܡܪܐ ܦܬܚܬܐ ܪܘܚܐ ܡܕܝܢܐ: ܕܡܢܗ̇
ܡܬܗܡܝܢ ܫ̈ܢܝܐ ܠܫ̈ܘܢܝܐ ܘܟܠ ܡܗ̈ܝܡܢܬܐ ܦܬ̈ܚܬܐ: ܗܠܝܢ

[h] Better ܬܐܙܠܝܢ.

[i] Before ܕܒܕܡܘܬ the MS. has ܕܒܡܫܝܚܐ, but with marks over it, indicating that it should be deleted.

ܘܬܫܡܫܬܐ ܗܢܐ ܐܝܟ ܕܠܡܠܐܟ̈ܐ ܕܢܘܗܪܝܢ ܗܘܘ ܠܗܦܟܝ
ܘܣܓܕܝܢ. ܕܢܐܡܪܘܢ ܒܗܘܢ ܡܢܐ ܠܗ* ܡܫܒܚܝܢ ܐܫܒܘܚ.[c]
ܐܠܐ ܟܕ ܗܦܟܬ ܠܒܝܬܗ. ܠܐܘܪܫܠܡ ܟܠܗ ܥܡܗ ܘܐܡܪܝܢ
ܠܒܢܝܢܐ. ܡܪܝܡ ܐܡܬܐ ܘܡܫܝܚܐ ܢܦܩܬ ܠܟ ܡܪܢ ܡܠܟܐ.
ܘܠܬܠܡܝܕܐ ܕܡܪܝܐ ܢܘܗܪܐ ܒܝܘܡ ܕܡܬܒܠܠ ܒܥܒܘܗ.
ܘܟܠ ܗܕܐ ܐܝܟ ܐܠܗܐ ܕܢܣܠܠ ܒܥܒܘܗ ܐܫܒܚܘܢ. ܘܗܫܐ
ܡܕܡ ܕܫܦܝܪ ܒܟܘܢܫܗܘܢ ܒܕܢܚܐ. ܘܗܕ ܫܡܥܘ ܡܘܗܒܬܐ
ܗܕܐ. ܐܡܪܘ[d] ܠܡܠܟܘܬܐ ܕܫܡܝܐ ܘܫܡܥܘ ܗܟܢܐ ܘܐܬܘ
ܐܢܫܐ ܕܗܘܢܐ ܬܡܢ ܠܟܪܝܘܗ ܬܠܬܐ ܕܐܘܪܫܠܡ.
ܘܐܡܪܝܢ ܒܒܝܬܐ ܡܢܝܢ ܡܠܟܘܬܐ ܫܡܥ ܦܘܪܩܢܗ
ܠܡܪܝܡ ܕܠܐ ܬܦܘܩ ܬܪܥܐ ܓܝܪ ܡܪܝܐ ܘܡܠܟܘܬܐ.
ܦܘܩ ܠܗ ܕܟܠܝܐ ܕܠܘܬ ܐܬܬܘܕܝܬ ܥܠܗ ܐܘܪܫܠܡ. ܕܠܐ
ܬܗܘܐ ܚܙܝܐ ܘܡܫܬܐ ܒܝܬܗ ܒܡܕܝܢܬܗ ܡܬܠܬܗ:
ܐܬܬ̈ܝܗ ܡܠܟܘܬܐ. ܘܠܐ ܐܝܬܝܗ ܘܦܘܪܩܢܗ. ܡܕܡ ܕܒܝܬܗ.
ܘܦܬܚܘ ܟܕ ܐܘܠܦ ܠܗܬܗ: ܐܡܪܝܢ ܠܗ. ܡܪܝܡ ܐܬܬܕܟܪ[e]
ܬܫܒܘܚܬܐ ܕܒܢܝܢ ܠܟ ܡܢܝܢ ܐܠܗܐ. ܘܠܐ ܬܫܒܚܝܢ ܠܒܢܝܢܐ
ܘܬܡܪܢ: ܕܗܘ[f] ܕܐܬܬܠܕ ܡܢܟܝ ܒܪܗ ܗܘ ܕܐܠܗܐ. ܡܛܠ
ܕܗܘܕܝܢ ܐܝܟ ܫܡܝܐ ܘܐܪܥܐ ܕܟܪܝܗ ܗܘ ܕܢܘܗܪ.
ܚܙܬܐ. ܐܠܐ ܟܘܠ ܠܟܢܫ ܫܡܥܬܐ ܘܫܡܥܢ ܢܗܘܐ
ܕܡܫܝܚܐ. ܘܡܘܬܒܝܢ ܠܟܢܝ ܐܘܪܚܬܐ ܘܡܬܩܢܝܢ ܠܟ
ܬܫܒܘܚܬܐ. ܘܦܬܚܝܢ ܫܘܒܚܐ ܒܐܪ̈ܥܬܐ ܘܡܬܬܩܢܐ[g] ܐܝܟܢ، ܡܢ

[c] So the MS., with two marks over each word, showing that the scribe saw there was something wrong. Perhaps we should read ܠܐ ܡܫܒܚܝܢ ܐܫܒܘܚ.   [d] Better ܐܡܪܘ.

[e] Better ܐܬܕܟܪܝ.   [f] Better ܘܬܬܡܪܝܢ.   [g] Better ܘܡܬܬܩܢܐ.

ܕܢܬܓܠܐ ܠܥܡܐ. ܕܐܠܘ ܬܠܡܝܕܘ ܘܐܒܗܬܗ ܠܟܠܗܘܢ
ܒܡܫܬܥܝ. ܒܝܘܡ ܐܚܕ ܘܒܙܢܐ ܕܗܘܕܝܐ. ܐܦ
ܡܗܝܡܢܘܬܐ ܕܒܙܢܐ ܕܗܘܕܝܐ ܐܚܪܢܐ ܕܐܫܬܘܕܝ، ܟܕ ܦܠܓ
ܫܪܝ ܠܝ. ܘܟܠܠ ܐܬܬܪܘ ܐܘܕܪܝܢ ܡܢ ܗܕܡܝ: ܠܡܒܪܝܘ
ܦܪܝܬܐ ܕܡܠܟܘܬܗ. ܡܛܘܠ ܕܝܢ ܐܝܟܢ ܟܬܪ ܗܠܝܢ ܟܠܗܝܢ:
ܒܬܪܘܬܐ ܪܟܬܐ ܦܫܝܛܐ ܗܘܬ. ܘܥܕ ܡܒܙܐ ܘܓܙܓܠܬܐ
ܠܥܒܕ ܒܝܓܠܘܬܐ ܐܡܝܢܐ ܗܘܬ. ܘܡܢ ܒܝܬܐ ܕܓܠܘܒܐ ܦܓ
ܡܬܚܫܒܢܐ ܗܘܬ. ܘܕܠܝܢ ܦܓܥܐ ܐܦ ܠܡܦܠܛܗ ܒܟ[ܝܢ]
ܗܘܘ. ܘܢܘܠܘܐ ܥܕ ܡܒܙܐ ܦܫܝܢ ܗܘܘ ܠܗܘܢ ܘܐܡܪܝܢ.
ܒܫܦܝܘܬܐ ܦܓܥܐܬܐ. ܕܐܝܟܘ ܕܬܦܘܩ ܠܬܡܢ ܠܡܓܠܘ
ܒܚܐܦܐ ܬܬܘܒܘܢ ܡܢܒܘܢ ܒܠ ܕܗܦܟܬ ܡܒܙܝܢܘܬܐ
ܠܐܘܪܚܠ. ܒܪܬܗ ܗܘܬ ܕܝܢܘܩܐ. ܐܝܟܐ ܕܐܝܬܘܗܝ،
ܗܘܐ ܘܪܒܗ ܕܢܬ ܒܪ ܕܘܝܕ ܡܢ ܫܒܛܐ ܕܝܗܘܕܐ.
ܐܡܗ ܕܝܢ ܚܢܢ ܡܬܦܪܢܐ ܗܘܬ. ܠܗ ܕܝܢ ܥܒܕܐ ܐܝܬܘܗܝ،
ܗܦܟ ܡܛܠܡ. ܘܒܝܘܡ ܡܢ ܝܘܡܝܢ ܕܒܪܘܟܬܐ: ܦܢܝܬܐ
ܘܒܦܘܡܐ ܥܦܠܬ. ܘܥܕ ܡܒܙܐ ܒܒܪܝܘܬܐ ܒܦܬܬ. ܘܟܕ
ܕܒܝܐ ܦܓܥܐܐ ܐܓܪܬ ܒܒܟܘܬܗ. ܡܒܙܐ ܐܡܪܐ ܗܘܬ.
ܪܒܘܠ ܡܚܫܝܐ ܕܐܝܬ ܠܝ ܒܡܒܝܢ ܫܪܝ ܕܒܪܝܢ ܡܢ ܟܠܒܐ
ܗܢܐ ܕܗܘܐ ܡܩܕܡܐ ܒܟܡ ܠܡܪܓܡܝܢ. ܘܒܪܫܒܗ ܕܓܠܘܬܗ
ܦܠܘܬ ܠܥܡܐ: ܡܠܐܟܗ ܕܡܪܝܐ ܢܚܬ ܠܘܬܗ ܘܗܒܢܐ
ܐܡܪ ܠܗ. ܫܠܡ ܠܟ ܡܠܝܬ ܛܝܒܘܬܐ. (fol. 8) ܐܫܬܡܥܬ
ܒܪܝ ܠܓܠܘܬܟ ܒܥܡܟܐ ܡܢܡ ܒܪܟ ܫܡܟ ܡܫܝܚܐ. ܘܡܢ
ܗܫܐ ܠܢܗܪܘܬܐ ܕܡܘܪܐ. ܢܗܘܐ ܐܢܫ[b] ܡܢ ܟܠܡܐ ܗܢܐ.
ܐܚܪܢܐ ܕܫܐܠܬ. ܘܟܕ ܗܠܝܢ ܐܡܪ ܠܗ ܐܙܠ ܡܢ ܠܘܬܗ

[b] Better ܐܢܫܐ, and afterwards ܕܫܐܠܬ.

ܬܫܥܝܬܐ ܕܩܕܝܫܬܐ ܝܠܕܬ ܐܠܗܐ ܒܬܘܠܬܐ.[a]

ܠܐܚ̈ܝ ܚܒܝ̈ܒܐ ܘܡ̈ܗܝܡܢܐ ܕܒܟܠܗ̇ ܬܒܝܠ: ܐܝܠܝܢ ܕܣܦܝܩܝܢ ܒܠ ܡܫܬܪ̈ܝܘܬܐ ܘܒܟܝܢ ܡܠܬܐ ܕܫܢܝܐ: ܘܒܟܠܝܢ ܠܫܘܒܚܗ ܕܐܠܗܐ ܢܣܦܩܝܢ. ܘܒܪܘܚܬܗ ܐܫܬܪܝܢ: ܫܠܡܐ ܘܛܝܒܘܬܐ ܒܡܫܒܚܢ: ܡܢ ܐܠܗܐ ܐܒܘܢ ܘܡܢ ܡܪܢ ܝܫܘܥ ܡܫܝܚܐ. ܘܪܘܚܗ ܩܕܝܫܐ ܐܡܝܢ. ܡܗ ܕܒܥܝܢ ܕܡܢ ܠܒ̈ܢܝ ܐܪ̈ܥܐ ܕܡܫܝܚܝܘܬܐ: ܕܡܠܬܐ ܕܫܢܝܐ ܗܘ̇ ܕܐܝܬܘܗܝ ܗܘܐ ܘܐܬܬܠܝ ܠܘܬ ܐܒܐ. ܫܪܪܐ ܬܘܒ ܐܝܬܝܗ ܠܡܠܟܐ ܘܐܬܬܠܝܢ ܡܢ ܐܝܬܝܬܐ ܒܡܕܝܢܬܐ ܪܒܬܐ. ܘܫܦܝܪ ܒܗ ܫܘ̈ܩܐ ܐܝܟ ܫܪܪܐ ܠܫܘܪܪܐ ܕܡܬܒܣܡܢܘܬܗ. ܘܡܛܠ ܬܪܝܨܘܬܐ ܕܗܝܡܢܘܬܐ. ܒܐܘܡܢܘܬܐ ܕܠܗܘܢ ܩ̈ܕܝܫܐ. ܘܕܪܫ ܐܘܪܚܐ ܕܡܗܝܡܢܘܬܐ ܘܕܫܘܒܚܐ ܘܕܥܘܬܪܗ ܫܠܝܐ. ܠܟܠܗܘܢ ܬܠܡ̈ܝܕܐ ܫܪ̈ܝܪܐ: ܘܦܠܛܝܢ ܓܒܝܐܝܬ ܫܟܚܐ ܘܡܬܐ ܘܡܒܘܪܬܐ ܕܠܐ ܡܬܒܪܝܬܐ ܡܕܡ ܐܘ ܦܠܚܘܬܐ. ܘܡܢ ܒܬܫܒܘܚܬܐ ܡܢ ܒܗ ܡ̈ܠܬܐ. ܟܕ ܠܐ ܚܙܐ ܫܒܠܐ ܟܠܗ ܥܘܠ. ܘܡܛܠ ܟܠܗܘܢ ܡܐ̈ܬܐ ܕܟܠܗ̇ ܕܢܦܩ ܠܝ ܠܘܬ ܐܒܘܗܝ. ܘܗܠܝܢ ܒܝܘܡܬܐ ܠܥܡܐ ܒܡ ܥܘܡܩܐ ܪܒܐ ܘܣܠܩ ܦܓܪܐ ܕܬܠܡܝܕܐ. ܘܒܗܠܝܢ ܟܠܗܝܢ ܗܘ̈ܕܐ ܐܝܬܝ. ܘܡܕܒܪܝܢ ܕܗܘܕܘܬܢ ܫܪܪܬܐ ܐܝܬܝܗ̇. ܡܛܠ ܕܣܝܡ ܒܟܬܒܐ. ܘܦܬܚ ܒܐܝ̈ܕܝ. ܘܟܠ ܕܒܗܠܝܢ ܡܗܝܡܢ ܐܝܬ ܠܗ ܚܝܐ ܕܠܥܠܡ ܒܡܫܝܚܐ. ܡܛܠ ܕܗܢܘ ܚܝܐ ܐܝܬܘܗܝ ܡܫܪܪܐ ܘܡܗܝܡܢܐ. ܘܗܢ ܗܟܢܐ ܐܬܦܫܛܢ ܡܟܝܠ ܡܢܝܢ

ᵃ Add. 14,484, fol. 7 vers.

THE HISTORY

OF THE LAST DAYS AND DEATH

OF THE

VIRGIN MARY,

THE HOLY MOTHER OF GOD;

WHICH IS ALSO CALLED

The *Transitus, Assumptio,* or Κοίμησις *Beatæ Virginis.*

ܡܢ ܬܒܪ ܦܠܛܘܣܝܢܐ. ܟܠ ܕܒܐܝܕܘܬ ܢܦܫ ܗܘܘ ܠܗ ܠܗܕܐ
ܩܕܡܐܝܬ. ܐܝܟ ܠܟܬܒܐ ܠܐ ܫܠܛܬ ܗܘܬ ܠܒܐܝܫܘܬܗܘܢ
ܘܟܠ ܠܗ ܒܐܝܕܘܬ ܢܦܫ ܗܘܘ ܠܗ ܠܗܕܐ. ܐܘܕܥܐ ܟܬܒܬ
ܢܟܘܬܐ ܘܩܡܨܬ ܡܛܠ ܕܢܦܫ ܡܢ ܒܐܝܕܘܬܐ. ܥܠܝܗ ܠܗ
ܦܝܠܛܘܣ: ܕܡܛܠ ܕܒܝܬ ܗܘܐ ܐܬܬܐܬ. ܠܐ ܢܟܪܐ ܗܘܐ ܗܘܬ
ܕܐܘܓܣܛܘܣ. ܘܕܐܡܪܝܢ ܡܠܟܘܬܗ ܕܩܠܛܐ ܦܪܐ ܢܦܫܗ
ܘܡܫܬܗ.. ܗܘܐܦܘܬ ܐܡܪ. ܐܓܪܬܗ ܕܩܠܛܐ. ܟܕ
ܠܟܠ ܗܘܐ ܐܝܟܠܐ ܕܡܠܟܐ ܒܗܝܡܢܘܬܐ: ܘܫܪܐ ܗܘܐ
ܫܪܝܐ ܒܐܬܐܓܪܘܢ ܕܡܫܝܚܐ: ܟܕ ܚܙܐ ܒܟܠܐ ܕܡܬܪܝܡ
ܠܒܫܬܗ ܐܡܪ ܠܗ. ܒܕܡܐ ܠܡܫܬܐ ܐܝܟ ܕܡܢ ܟܪ
ܐܢܫܐ ܕܫܠܡ ܗܘܐ ܡܢܝ. ܡܚܕܐ ܡܚܕܐ ܐܝܬ ܗܘ ܡܢ
ܒܝܬܐ ܕܡܬܩܢܬܐ. ܘܚܙܐ ܗܘܐ ܡܠܟܐ ܕܐܡܪ ܠܟܠ
ܡܢܗ: ܘܡܫܬܟܚ ܗܘܐ ܐܝܟ ܕܠܡܫܬܐ. ܀ ܫܠܡܬ
ܐܓܪܬܐ ܕܦܝܠܛܘܣ ܕܠܘܬ ܛܝܒܪܝܘܣ. ܀

[ܘܗܘܐ] ܝܕܥܬ ܕܐܢܬ ܐܢܬ. [ܐܠ]ܗܐ ܒܪ ܐܠܗܐ. ܘܐܢܐ
[ܠܐ]ܢܫܘܬܟ ܫܪܪܬ ܘܠܐ [ܠܐܠܗܘ]ܬܟ. ܐܠܐ ܗܪܘܕܣ
ܡܢ ܒܢ̈ܝ ܐܝܣܪܝܠ ܐܠܝܨܘܢ ܕܐܟܒܫ[d] ܟܝ ܒܡܠܟܐ. ܗܘܐ
ܗܟܝܠ ܟܠ ܐܠܗܗ ܕܐܝܣܪܝܠ. ܐܢܬܬ ܕܝܢ ܒܒܥܘܬܐ ܪܒܬܐ
ܐܡܪܬ ܐܠܗܐ ܕܫܡܝܐ ܘܐܪܥܐ ܕܠܟ. ܐܠܗܗ ܕܐܝܣܪܝܠ:
ܠܐ ܐܝܟ ܒܢ̈ܘܗܝ ܕܦܠܚܘܗ ܦܠܚܘܗ: ܘܠܐ ܐܝܟ
ܙܒܢܘܗܝ ܕܒ̈ܢܝ ܐܝܣܪܝܠ: ܘܠܐ ܐܝܟ ܗܘܫܥܐ ܕܒ̈ܢܝ
ܒܡ̈ܢܝܐ ܬܦܪܘܒܝܢ. ܐܠܐ ܐܬܕܒܪ ܠܒܟܠ ܡܬܚܫܒܢܘܬܟ.
ܡܪܝ ܕܝܢ ܩܕܡ ܘܐܘܫܒܢ ܠܝ ܘܠܐܢܬܬܝ ܘܠܬ̈ܘܗܘܒܐ. ܘܫܪܬ
ܒܗ ܘܫܪܬ. ܒܪ ܐܢܬ ܗܘ ܫܘ̈ܒܚܬܐ ܕܝܠܗܘܢ. ܘܐܡܪܬ.
ܗ̇ܘ ܡܢܕܡ ܕܥܒܕܘ ܕܢܦܠܘܢ ܥܠܝܗܘܢ ܐܟܡ̈ܘܬܐ ܒܐ̈ܢܫܐ
ܘܠܐ ܚܙܘ. ܒܟܠܝܢ ܕܐܠܝܢ ܡܢܘ ܗܢܐ: ܒܪܗ ܕܐܢܫܐ
ܒܪܗ ܕܡܒ̈ܪܟܬܐ ܕܐܬܚܙܝ، ܡܟܝܠ ܬܘܒ. ܡܢܘ ܗܘ ܒܪܗ ܡܫܬܐ:
ܘܡܫܬܒܚ ܒܪܘܚܐ ܡܢ ܟܠ ܕܒܪܐ ܘܐܬܬܩܢ ܠܥܠܡ ܥܠܡܝܢ.܀.
ܘܩܠܝܦܘܣ ܚܕ ܡܢ ܡܬܠܡ̈ܕܢܐ ܕܗܘܘ ܒܢ̈ܘܗܝ ܐܓܪܘܦܘܣ
ܘܦܝܠܝܦܘܣ ܘܓܐܝܘܣ. ܗܢܘܢ ܟܠܗܘܢ ܗܘܘ ܒܐܘܪܫܠܡ
(fol. 122) ܕܬܠܬܐ ܕܝܠܗ. ܕܡܬܩܪܝܢ ܠܗ ܒܠܠܝܬܐ: ܗ̇ܝ
ܕܠܗܬ ܠܡܫܝܚܐ ܗ̇ܘ ܕܐܙܕܩܦ ܒܐܘܪܫܠܡ. ܠܐ ܗܘܬ
ܗܘܬ ܠܥܕܪܐ. ܘܠܐ ܫܒܩܘܗ̇ ܗܘܐ ܢܗܘܐ. ܐܠܐ ܗܘ،
ܗܘܐ ܢܗܘܐ ܒܡܫܩܘܬܐ ܕܠܐ ܐܢܬܬܐ. ܗܘ ܘܫܒܥܐ
ܒܢ̈ܘܗܝ ܕܡܢ ܐܢܬܬܐ ܡܫܒܚܬܐ. ܘܡܬܕܪܝܢ ܦܘܩ ܕܠܐ
ܒܪܢܫܐ.܀ ܬܐܕܘܪܘܣ ܥܒܕ ܠܦܝܠܛܘܣ ܗܓܡܘܢܐ. ܡܢܗ
ܒܪܢܫܐ ܕܗܘܐ ܥܠܘܗܝ ܒܡܠܟܐ ܡܫܝܚܢ. ܕܫܡܥ ܗܘܐ

[d] The MS. has ܕܐܟܒܫ ܐܠܨܘܢ.

ܕܡܒܪܟܝܢ ܐܠܗܐ ܠܒܘܪܟܬܗ. ܒܗ̇ ܐܬܐܡܪܬ̈. ܕܥܠ ܓܒܪܐ
ܕܐܒܘܗ̇ ܗܘܬ. ܢܚܙܐ ܟܝܬ ܡܢܘ ܕܠܗ. ܗ̇ܘ ܐܝܟܢܐ ܕܐܬܒܪܟܘܢ.
ܘܗܟܢܐ ܢܬܚܙܘܢ ܕܡܢ ܐܘܠܐ. ܗ̇ܘ ܐܝܟܢܐ ܕܐܬܦܬܚܘܢ.
ܘܠܗܘܢܬܐ ܘܦܬܚܘܢ. ܒܡܢܐ ܕܐܬܒܪܟ ܐܒܪܗܡ. ܗܘܐ
ܕܐܝܟ ܥܒܕܘܗܝ. ܘܗܝܡܢܘ ܒܐܝܕܝ ܐܠܗܐ ܕܒܗ ܗܘ.
ܐܝܟ ܓܒܪ ܦܠܝܛ ܠܫܒܠܐ ܕܒܗܘܬܐ. ܘܬܒܪܬ ܬܪ̈ܒܐ
ܕܚܝܠ. ܘܡܐܬܝܬܐ ܕܠܝܗ̇، ܕܟܬܒܐ ܕܬܘܗܐ. ܘܒܗ ܥܡܕܬ
ܗܠܝܢ ܦܘܪܩܢܐ ܐܝܬܝܗ̇، ܘܪ̈ܘܗܡܝܢ. ܐܬܘ ܐܘܕܝܘܢ ܒܗ
ܚܟܡ. ܡܛܠ ܕܐܟܦ ܗܢܘ ܠܡܬܠܝܗ ܗܘܘ. ܒܗ ܡܬܬܚܝܡܝܢ
ܗܘܘ ܒܝܫܬܐ ܕܦܓܪܘ ܗܘܘ ܒܗ. ܐܝܟ ܕܐܦ ܐܢܐ
ܒܡܫܡܫܢܐ ܕܒܪܗ، ܐܬܗܘܐ ܒܐܘܠܨܢܐ. ܘܐܠܨܢ ܠܒܘܫܐ
ܕܒܪܘܢ[ܬܐ.] ܘܐܕܒܪ ܠܗ ܪ̈ܘܚܐ[ܡܫܝܚܐ] ܣܡܝܟܝܢ ܒܗܝ ܐܝܟ[ܬܬܝ،]
ܘܐܙܠ ܠܓܠܝܠܐ. [ܘܒܗ] ܐܙܠ ܗܘܝܬ ܒܐܘܪܚܐ ܗܠܝܢ ܡܫܘܚܕ
ܗܦܟܬ. ܕܗܠܝܢ ܗܘܢܘܗ ܗܦܟ ܗܘܐ ܐܝܟ ܒܗ. ܕܐܬܐܡܪ
ܗܘܐ ܒܟܢ ܘܐܠܝܬ. ܕܐܝܟ ܐܬܘ، ܒܠܗܘܢ. ܘܐܕܘܢ ܠܗܘܢ
ܒܗ. ܘܐܠܦܐ ܠܒܪܢܫܐ ܡܪܝܐ ܕܒܢܝܢܫܐ. ܘܒܗ ܡܬܦܪܢܣܝܢ
ܗܘܘ ܠܗܘܢ ܐܘ ܗܪܘܕܣ. ܘܠܐ ܪܒܐ ܐܝܬܘܗܝ ܡܢ
ܫܘܒܚܐ. ܘܪܒܘܬܐ ܕܣܘܠܐ. ܘܐܬܬܪܒܝܬ ܐܪܒܥܐ. ܘܗܦܟܬ
ܪܘܚܐ ܒܫܘܒܚܐ ܕܐܝܟ ܗܘ. ܘܠܐ ܒܫܘܠܛܢܐ ܕܐܘܪܫܠܡ
ܐܬܝܢ، ܡܬܒܬܘܢ. ܒܗ ܕܝܢ ܦܫܬ ܒܗ ܒܐܘܪܚܐ. ܫܢܝ ܗܘܐ
ܡܢ ܒܗ ܦܐܝܡ ܘܡܬܒܠܠ ܒܗܘ ܬܠܬܝܢܐ. ܐܝܟܐ ܕܝܢ ܬܠܝܬ
ܟܠܗ ܕܫܡܥܬ. ܕܗܘܘ ܗ̇ܘ ܐܝܟܐ ܕܐܫܬܠܡܬܘܢ ܠܗ. ܕܗܘܘ
ܡܢܐ ܕܒܪܝܬܐ ܘܡܢܐ ܟܠ. ܫܡ ܕܝܢ ܒܗ ܫܘܚܠܦܗ، ܒܟܠ
ܢܦܠ ܒܠ ܦ̈ܠܓܝ ܦܘܡ ܬ̈ܠܡܝܗ، ܘܒܟܠܗ ܪܘܚܐ ܐܚܪܢ ܗܦܟܬ.
ܐܦܠܬ ܡܢܝ، ܕܐܬܦܬ ܘܕܢܬ ܠܝ ܬܪܥ ܒܠ ܒܡܫܝܚܐ.

ܬܫܥܝܬܐ ܕܦܝܠܝܦܘܣ ܕܠܘܬ ܗܪܘܕܘܣ ܀

ܦܝܠܝܦܘܣ: ܠܗܪܘܕܘܣ ܦܦܪܟܐ ܫܠܡ. ܀.
ܗܕܐ ܘܚܝ. ܕܟܡܐ ܝܘܡܐ ܕܐܫܬܠܡܬ ܠܝ ܠܡܫܘܕܥܘ. ܐܝܟ
ܥܢܝܬ ܗܘܬ ܥܠ ܢܦܫܝ ܘܐܫܬܘܕܝܬ ܗܘܬ ܒܥܝܢܬ ܐܝܢܐ.
ܡܢ ܗܘ ܐܝܢܐ ܕܐܡܪ ܡܢ ܒܬܪ ܡܝܬܘܬܐ ܠܬܠܬܐ ܝܘܡܝܢ ܘܩܝܡ.
ܘܣܬܪܬ ܗܘܬ ܒܗ ܓܒܪܝܢ. ܟܕ ܓܒܪܐ ܗܘܝܬ ܕܐܝܢܐ
ܐܫܬܘܕܝܬ ܠܟ ܒܓܠܝܢܘܬܗ. ܠܦܬ ܕܝܢ ܗܢܐ: ܡܢ
ܡܫܠܡܢܐ ܘܡܢ ܐܣܛܪܛܝܓܐ ܕܢܛܪܝܢ ܗܘܘ ܠܩܒܪܗ.
ܕܐܡܪ ܠܗ ܡܢ ܒܬܪ ܡܝܬܘܬܐ. (fol. 121) ܫܪܝܬ ܕܝܢ ܐܫܐܠܬ
ܕܐܬܐܡܪ ܠܝ. ܕܥܠܠܐ ܐܝܟܢܐ ܦܪܝܫܬ. ܒܗ ܒܓܘܪܬܐ
ܘܒܗ ܒܡܠܐ. ܘܒܗ ܒܡܠܘܬܐ ܘܒܗܘܢ ܒܬܠܡܝܕܘܗܝ.
ܟܕ ܠܐ ܡܟܝܠ ܚܙܝܬ. ܐܠܐ ܒܦܪܘܣܐ ܠܡܫܝܚܐ ܡܟܪܙ.
ܘܠܬܠܡܝܕܘܗܝ ܕܠܒܬܪ. ܘܗܘܐ ܫܡܥܐ ܘܐܪܒܥܐ ܫܢܝܢ. ܘܗܘܐ
ܦܘܠܘܣ ܐܝܟ. ܟܕ ܡܫܡܫܢܐ ܒܗܘܢ ܚܙܘܐ ܕܐܬܓܠܝ
ܠܗ: ܟܕ ܡܥܕܪ ܗܘܝܬ ܕܐܫܬܠܡܘܗܝ ܠܡܫܘܕܥܘ ܠܚܒܪܐ
ܕܐܘܪܫܠܡ: ܡܛܠ ܓܒܪܐ ܚܕܐ ܕܗܘܐ ܗܘܐ ܠܗܘܢ.
ܘܗܢܐ ܟܕ ܫܡܥܬ ܡܢ ܦܘܠܐ ܐܝܬܝܗ[b] ܕܐܡܪ ܗܘ ܡܫܘܕ
ܘܐܬܝܬ ܕܥܠܠܐ ܕܓܒܪܬ ܒܗܢ ܠܠܓܝܘܢ[c] ܡܬܦܪܘܫܐ
ܘܠܐܘܣܛܪܛܝܓܐ* ܕܒܣܢܝ: ܗܢܘܢ ܕܢܛܪܝܢ ܗܘܘ ܠܗ
ܠܩܒܪܗ. ܘܐܡܪܬ ܕܠܡܢܐ ܪܒܐ. ܐܝܠܝܢ ܕܚܒܫܘ ܠܦܪܘܩܢ
ܕܡܫܝܚܐ. ܘܢܬܚܙܐ ܒܗ ܬܠܡܝܕܘܗܝ. ܟܕ ܕܝܢ ܡܫܡܫܝܢ ܗܘܘ
ܘܬܚܘܡ ܘܡܢܛܪ ܗܘܘ ܒܗ. ܢܚ ܒܗܘܢ ܘܐܡܪ ܠܗܘܢ
ܫܠܡ ܠܟ ܡܫܡܫܢܐ ܐܝܬܝܗ ܦܘܠܐ. ܗܟܢ. ܗܘ ܕܐܬܐ

[b] Read ܐܠܢܫܝ.

[c] Read ܠܠܓܝܘܢܘܣ.

ܕܡܢ̈ܗܘܢ ܕܐܠܗܐ. ܘܐܢܬܬ ܬܘܒ. ܒܗܘ ܟܠܗ ܐܟܠܐ
ܕܒܪܬܝ. ܐܬܓܒܪܬ ܒܚܝܠܗ ܕܫܘܡܠܐ. ܡܛܠ ܕܙܕܝܩ ܕܢܚܘܪ
ܠܚܝܠܐ ܕܐܠܗܘܬܐ. ܠܝܬ ܠܚܕܪ, ܒܝ̈ܘܡܬܐ ܚܝܠܐ ܐܚܪܢ
ܡܪܢܐ. ܗܢ ܗܟܢܐ ܓܝܪ: ܐܘܠܝܢܐ ܪܒܐ ܐܝܬܐ ܒܟ ܠܚܘ̈ܫܒܐ
ܘܟܠ ܥ̈ܬܝܕ ܢܗܘܐ. ܡܛܠ ܕܐܫܠܡܘ ܠܝ ܠܕܝܢܐ. ܗܘܐ
ܓܝܪ ܫܘܡܠܝܐ ܕܟܠܗܝܢ ܕܫܠܡܘ ܕܢܗܘܘܢ ܒܥ̈ܡܡܐ ܪ̈ܬܐ.
ܒܢ̈ܘܗܝ ܓܝܪ ܕܢܘܗܪܐ ܢܥܒܕܘܢ ܠܒܪ. ܠܐ ܓܝܪ ܢܛܪܘ ܐܠܝܢ
ܕܡܟܪܙܝܢ ܗ̇ܘ, ܒܟܠ ܡܕܝܢܐ ܘܒܟܠ ܒܝܬ. ܡܛܠ ܗܢܐ ܐܗܘܪ
ܫܪ̈ܝܢ ܘܦܩܕ ܒܐܢܘܬܐ. ܕܒ ܟܠܠܝܐ ܘܟܐܡܟܐ
ܡܬܕܒܪ ܐܢܬ ܠܫܘܒ ܒܡ ܐܢܬܬܟ. ܘܕܠܟܘܢ ܒܢ̈ܝܟܐ
ܬܗܘܐ ܡܠܟܘܬܐ. ܫܠܝܡ ܓܝܪ] ܒܟܠܐ ܒܝܬܝ [ܒܟܐܒܐ].
ܟܝ ܕܝܢ ܐܢܬ ܐܬܪܐ ܠܟܠܗܝܢ ܐܘ ܦܝܠܛܐ. ܡܛܠ ܕܒܢܐ
ܙܒܢܐ ܗܘܝܢ ܒܫܘܠܛܢܐ. ܡܟܘܪܗ, ܠܒܢܬܝ ܒܫܠܝܐܝܬ.
ܒܐܢܐ ܗ, ܓܝܪ ܕܡܒܝܢ ܢܬܦܒܪ: ܠܒܪ ܡܢ ܕܡܢ ܒܚܘ̈ܫܒܐ.
ܫܘܐ ܕܒܬܪ ܙܒܢܐ ܙܒܘܪܐ ܐܝܟ ܕܐܡܪܝܢ ܒܬ̈ܝܒܐ.
ܒܟܐܬܬܗ ܕܫܘܒ ܡܟܝܢܐ ܡܙܪܟܐ ܠܗܘܢ ܬܟܒܬܐ.
ܗܦܘܟ ܫܠܝܛ ܒܡ ܦܘܠܚܢܐ ܐܢܬܬܟ. ܫܪܪ ܠܝ ܘܕܝܢܐ
ܕܒܪܬ ܘܒܝܘܡܬܐ ܕܠܐ. ܕܢܗܘܘܢ ܠܐ ܝܕܥܝܢ ܒܡܗܕܢܐ
ܕܦܘܪܫܢܐ. ܡܢ ܒܬܘ ܓܝܪ ܥܪ, ܬܩܠܬܐ ܕܢܦܩ ܡܢ ܦܓܪܝ.
ܘܕܝܢܐ ܒܠܒܢܐ ܗܘ ܡܦܟܠ ܐܢܐ. ܘܡܢ ܕܢܝܐ ܕܒܬܘܢ
ܕܫܠ ܐܢܐ. ܒܬܪ̈ܝܢ ܓܝܪ ܝܘܡܝܢ ܚܝ ܘܝܡ ܒܟ̈ܢܘܬܗ, ܕܐܠܗܐ
ܚܝܐ. ܗܢܐ ܕܝܢ ܕܢܝܐ ܕܒܠܟܘܢ ܕܙܒܢܐ ܗܘܘ. ܗ̇ܘ ܕܝܢ
ܕܒܬܘܢ ܕܢܝܐ ܗܘ ܕܠܟܠܢ . ܀ .

ܫܠܡܬ ܐܓܪܬܐ ܕܠܘܬ ܦܝܠܛܘܣ ܗܓܡܘܢܐ.

ܐܓܪܬܐ ܕܗܪܘܕܘܣ ܕܠܘܬ ܦܝܠܛܘܣ ܗܓܡܘܢܐ[a] ܀

ܗܪܘܕܘܣ: ܠܦܘܢܛܝܘܣ ܦܝܠܛܘܣ ܗܓܡܘܢܐ ܕܐܘܪܫܠܡ ܫܠܡ.܀.
ܒܣܘܓܐܐ ܪܒܐ ܐܝܬܝ. ܟܬܒ ܐܢܐ ܠܟ ܗܠܝܢ. ܕܗܟܢܐ
ܕܬܫܡܥ ܐܝܟ ܢܟܐܒ ܠܟ ܥܠܝ. ܒܪܬܝ ܓܝܪ ܗ̇ܝ ܕܚܒܝܒܐ
ܗܘܬ ܠܝ ܗܪܘܕܝܐ. ܟܕ ܡܫܬܥܝܐ ܒܢܗܪܐ ܕܡ̈ܝܐ ܕܐܚܝܕ.
ܒܗܘܢ ܟܠܗ̇. ܐܬܦܬܚܬ ܬܚܘܬܝܗ̇. ܘܢܚܬܬ ܠܘܥܕܡܗ̇
ܟܠܗ̇ ܠܬܚܬ. ܘܐܬܦܣܩ ܪܫܗ̇. ܘܦܫ ܠܥܠ ܡܢ ܐܓܠܝܕܐ.
ܘܗܐ ܐܡܗ̇ ܫܩܝܠܐ ܠܗ ܠܪܫܗ̇ ܥܠ ܒܘܪ̈ܟܝܗ̇ ܒܚܝܢܗ̇.
ܘܐܝܬܘܗ̇، ܟܠܗ̇ ܒܝܬܝ ܒܐܒܠܐ ܪܒܐ. ܐܢܐ ܓܝܪ ܟܕ ܫܡܥܬ
ܥܠ ܗ̇ܘ ܓܒܪܐ ܝܫܘܥ. ܪ̈ܚܫܬ ܗܘܝܬ ܕܐܬܐ ܠܘܬܟ.
ܘܐܚܙܝܘܗܝ ܒܠܚܘܕ. ܘܐܫܡܥ ܡܠܬܗ : ܐܢ ܕܕܡܐ ܠܒܢ̈ܝ
ܐܢܫܐ. ܘܥܕܡܝ. ܕܟܠ ܒܢܝ̈ܫܬܐ ܗܦܟ̈ܬܐ ܕܗܘ̈ܝܢ
ܠܝ ܒܝܘܡܝ ܡܛܠܬܗ ܕܐܢܫܐ. ܘܕܒܪܢܬ ܒܚܛܝ̈ܬܝ. ܗܐ ܡܩܒܠ
ܐܢܐ ܦܘܪܥܢܐ ܕܒܐܝܫܘܬܐ. ܕܗܟܢܐ ܓܝܪ ܦܝܠܝܦܐ ܕܐܚܝ
ܢܟ̈ܬܝܐ ܥܒܕܬ ܥܠ ܐܢܬܬܐ. ܡܛܠ ܗܢܐ ܒܐܝ̈ܕܝ ܐܢܘܢ
ܕܒܢ̈ܘܗܝ ܕܐܠܗܐ. ܕܒܗܠ ܐܒܕ ܐܢܝ ܣܘܥܪܢܗ ܡܦܩܠ.
ܐܝܬ ܕܝܢ ܕܫܦܝܬ ܕܬܒܝܪܐ ܠܗܘ ܐܠܗܐ ܒܪ ܐܒܐ. ܡܛܠ ܗܕܐ
ܠܟܘܢ ܗܘ ܦܠܐ ܕܬܪܥܠܘܢ ܥܠ. ܐܪܒܥܝܢ ܕܝܢ ܒܢܝ.
ܒܐܘܠܨܢܐ ܕܫܒܬܐ ܕܡܩܦܠܢܐ ܗܘܝܢ. ܘܗܢܐ ܬܘܒ ܐܝܬ،
ܒܐܘ̈ܠܨܢܝ ܘܒܘܣܘܢܝܐ ܪܒܐ. ܒܥܬ ܓܝܪ ܟ̈ܬܒܝ. ܘܐܝܬ،
ܒܒܝܪܘܬܐ ܪܒܬܐ. ܡܛܠ ܕܪܕܦܬ ܠܫܘܬܦܐ ܕܡܟܝܟܘܬܐ
ܕܟ̈ܝܐ : ܕܐܝܬܘܗܝ، ܢܘܚܐ. ܡܛܠ ܗܠܝܢ ܐܚܝ. ܒܟ̈ܝܢ ܐܢܘܢ

[a] Add. 14,609, fol. 120 rect.

THE LETTERS

OF

HEROD AND PILATE.

ܡܕܡ ܕܣܒܪ (fol. 16) ܠܐ ܚܙܐ ܠܗ. ܐܠܐ ܕܢܦܩ ܠܗ ܐܝܕܗ ܘܢܓܕ ܒܗ̇. ܘܢܦܠܬ ܘܐܬܦܠܓܬ ܀ ܀ (XIX.) ܘܟܕ ܗ̇ܘܐ ܫܡܥܘܢ. ܟܕ ܬܪܬܥܣܪܐ ܫܢܝܢ ܐܝܬܘܗܝ ܗܘܐ ܠܐܘܪܫܠܡ ܐܝܟ ܕܐܝܬ ܗܘܐ ܥܝܕܐ ܠܝܘܣܦ. ܘܠܡܪܝܡ ܠܡܐܙܠ ܠܥܐܕܗܘܢ. ܘܟܕ ܥܒܪܘ ܦܨܚܐ. ܗܦܟܘ ܠܒܝܬܗܘܢ. ܘܟܕ ܦܫ ܠܡܐܬܐ ܗ̇ܘ ܫܡܥܘܢ ܒܐܘܪܫܠܡ. ܘܠܐ ܝܕܥܘ ܝܘܣܦ ܘܠܐ ܡܪܝܡ ܐܡܗ ܐܠܐ ܕܣܒܪܘ ܕܥܡ ܒ̈ܢܝ ܫܪܒܬܗܘܢ ܗܘ. ܘܟܕ ܐܬܘ ܠܐܘܪܚܐ ܕܝܘܡ ܚܕ. ܒܥܘ ܗܘܘ ܠܗ ܠܘܬ ܒ̈ܢܝ ܚܝܢܗܘܢ ܘܠܘܬ ܟܠ ܕܝܕܥ ܠܗܘܢ. ܘܟܕ ܠܐ ܐܫܟܚܘܗܝ. ܠܡܒܥܝܗ. ܗܦܟܘ ܠܗܘܢ ܠܐܘܪܫܠܡ. ܘܒܥܘ ܗܘܘ ܠܗ. ܘܒܬܪ ܬܠܬܐ ܝܘܡܝܢ ܐܫܟܚܘܗܝ، ܟܕ ܝܬܒ ܒܝܬ ܡ̈ܠܦܢܐ ܘܫܐܠ ܠܗܘܢ ܘܡܫܬܐܠ ܠܗܘܢ. ܘܡܬܕܡܪܝܢ ܗܘܘ ܟܠ ܕܫܡܥܝܢ ܗܘܘ. ܡܛܠ ܕܡܫܬܐܠ ܗܘܐ ܠܗܘܢ ܠܗܠܝܢ ܡ̈ܠܦܢܐ. ܘܡܦܢܐ ܗܘܐ ܠܗܘܢ ܦܬ̈ܓܡܐ ܕܚ̈ܟܡܐ ܘܕܪ̈ܐ ܘܡ̈ܠܬܐ ܕܚܟܡܬܐ. ܘܐܡܪܐ ܠܗ ܐܡܗ. ܒܪܝ. ܠܡܢܐ ܥܒܕܬ ܠܢ ܗܟܢ ܕܐܒܘܟ ܗܘܝܢ ܘܡܬܦܠܓܝܢ ܘܒܥܝܢ ܠܟ. ܒܟܝܐ ܫܡܥܐ ܘܐܡܪ. ܡܢܐ ܒܥܝܢ ܗܘܝܬܘܢ ܠܝ. ܠܐ ܝܕܥܝܢ ܐܢܬܘܢ: ܕܒܝܬ ܐܒܝ ܘܠܐ ܠܝ ܠܡܗܘܐ. ܚܒܘ ܫܦܝܪܐ ܘܐܡ̈ܪܐ ܠܡܪܝܡ. ܐܝܬܝܗ̇ ܐܡܗ ܕܝܘܢܐ ܫܠܝܐ. ܒܪܚܡ ܡܪܝܐ. ܕܐܝܟ ܗܘܕܐ ܒܪܐ ܬܫܒܘܚܬܐ ܕܡܫܒܚܬܐ ܕܟ̈ܠܗܘܢ ܠܐ ܣܦܩܝܢ ܘܠܐ ܫܒܩܢ ܕܐܡܪ ܡܠܠ. ܘܡܢ ܐܝܟ ܗܢ ܐܡܗ. ܘܡܬܕܡܪܐ ܗܘܐ ܠܗܘܢ ܐܡܗ ܕܡܢ ܢܦܫܗ ܗܘܬ ܒܠܗܝܢ ܡ̈ܠܐ ܗܠܝܢ. ܫܡܥܘܢ ܕܝܢ ܡܬܪܒܐ ܗܘܐ ܘܪܒܐ ܒܚܟܡܬܐ ܘܒܩܘܡܬܐ ܠܘܬ ܐܠܗܐ ܘܠܘܬ ܒ̈ܢܝ ܐܢܫܐ ܐܡܝܢ. ܀ .

ܫܠܡܬ ܬܫܥܝܬܗ ܕܡܪܝ ܫܡܥܘܢ ܀

ܒܡܠܬܐ ܗ̇ܝ، ܕܡܚܦܘ، ܗܘܐ ܘܡܟܝܠ ܘܐܒܝܬ، ܐܝܠܝܢ ܠܛܠܝܐ
ܗܠܝܢ. ܐܡܗ ܕܝܢ ܡܪܝܡ ܡܬܕܡܪܐ ܗܘܬ ܒܟܠ ܕܚܙܝܐ
ܗܘܬ. (XII.) ܘܬܘܒ ܒܙܒܢ ܡܫܬܒܚܐ ܗܘܐ ܝܫܘܥ. ܘܙܪܥ
ܦܐܬܐ ܚܕܐ ܕܚܛܐ ܘܚܨܕ ܡܐܐ ܟܘܪ̈ܝܢ ܘܝܗܒ ܐܢܘܢ
ܠܟ̈ܠ ܦܪ̈ܝܬܐ ÷ . . ÷ (XIII.) ܐܒܘܗܝ، ܗܘܐ ܓܝܪ ܝܫܘܥ
ܟܕ ܬܩ̈ܢܐ ܢܝ̈ܪܝܢ. ܘܝܘܣܦ ܢܓܪܐ ܗܘܐ ܘܡܬܒܥ ܐܢܫܝܢ
ܠܗ ܚܕ ܗܘܐ. ܐܠܐ ܐܦ ܩܝܣܐ ܘܢܝܪ̈ܐ. ܘܐܘܚܕ ܗܘܐ
ܐܢܫ ܠܘܬܗ ܥܪܣܐ ܕܢܥܒܕ ܐܚܝܢ. ܘܠܝܬ ܗܘܐ ܡܫܘܚܬܐ
ܒܫܘܐ ܕܩܝܣܐ ܕܚܕ ܓܒܐ. ܐܠܐ ܟܪܝܐ ܗܘܬ ܡܢ ܚܒܪܬܗ̇.
ܘܐܡܪ ܛܠܝܐ ܝܫܘܥ ܡܫܘܚܬܐ ܗ̇ܝ ܕܩܝܣܐ ܘܐܬܬܚܠ
ܘܡܬܘܚܗ̇ ܘܐܫܘܝܗ̇ ܠܚܒܪܬܗ̇. ܘܐܡܪ ܠܝܘܣܦ ܐܒܘܗܝ.
ܚܙܝ ܥܠ ܡܕܡ ܕܪܓܝܬ ܐܢܬ. (XIV.) ܝܘܣܦ ܕܝܢ ܟܕ ܚܙܝܗ،
ܕܗܟܢܬ: ܨܒܐ ܕܢܠܦܝܘܗܝ، ܣܦܪܐ. ܘܐܫܠܡܗ ܠܚܕ
ܣܦܪܐ. ܘܐܡܪ ܠܗ ܣܦܪܐ. ܐܡܪ ܐܠܦ. ܘܐܡܪ ܝܫܘܥ.
ܘܐܘܣܦ ܬܘܒ ܣܦܪܐ ܕܢܐܡܪ ܒܝܬ. ܘܐܡܪ ܠܗ ܝܫܘܥ.
ܐܡܪ ܠܝ ܠܘܩܕܡ ܡܢܘ ܗܘ، ܐܠܦ. ܘܗ̇ܝܕܝܢ ܥܠ ܒܝܬ ܐܡܪ
ܠܝ. ܘܫܩܠ ܣܦܪܐ ܘܡܚܝܗܝ، ܘܒܪܫܥܬܗ ܢܦ̣ܠ ܘܡܝܬ.
ܘܝܫܘܥ ܐܙܠ ܠܒܝܬ ܐܒܘܗܝ، ܘܦܩܕ ܝܘܣܦ ܠܡܪܝܡ ܐܡܗ
ܘܐܡܪ ܠܗ̇. ܘܦܩܕܗ̇ ܕܠܐ ܬܦܩܝܘܗܝ، ܕܢܦܘܩ ܠܒܪ ܡܢ ܒܝܬܐ.
ܕܠܐ ܢܗܘܘܢ ܡܬܠܝܢ ܐܝܠܝܢ ܕܩܛܠܝܢ ܠܗ. (XV.) ܣܦܪܐ ܕܝܢ
ܚܕ ܐܡܪ ܠܝܘܣܦ. ܐܫܠܡܝܘܗܝ، ܠܝ ܘܐܢܐ ܡܠܦ ܐܢܐ ܠܗ.
ܥܠ ܕܝܢ ܝܫܘܥ ܠܒܝܬ ܣܦܪܐ. ܘܫܩܠ ܟܬܒܐ ܘܩܪܐ ܗܘܐ.
ܠܐ ܗܠܝܢ ܕܟܬܝܒܢ. ܐܠܐ ܬܕܡܪ̈ܬܐ ܪ̈ܘܪܒܬܐ. (XVI.) ܘܬܘܒ
ܫܕܪ ܗܘܐ ܝܘܣܦ ܠܝܥܩܘܒ ܒܪܗ ܕܢܠܩܘܛ ܩܝܣܐ. ܘܐܙܠ
ܗܘܐ ܝܫܘܥ ܥܡܗ. ܟܕ ܕܝܢ ܠܩܛܝܢ ܗܘܘ ܩܝ̈ܣܐ. ܐܟܕܢܐ
ܚܕܐ ܢܟܬܬ ܠܝܥܩܘܒ ܒܐܝܕܗ. ܘܟܕ ܐܬܩܪܒ ܠܗ ܝܫܘܥ:

ܦܠܛ ܐܢܫ ܠܗ ܡܢܗܘܢ ܕܦܠܐ ܠܗ ܠܡܐܙܠܘ. ܘܒܬܠܬܗ
ܠܐܘܪܚܐ. ܗ̇ܘ ܕܝܢ ܟܕ ܚܙܐ ܥܬܝܕ ܗܘܐ. ܘܟܕ ܕܝܢ
ܦܩܕܐ ܓܒܪ̈ܐ ܠܡܥܒܪ ܠܗ ܡܢ ܐܠܦ. ܘܒܬܪ̈ܬܐ ܩܠܝܬܐ
ܛܠܝܐ ܗܘܐ ܠܗ ܒܠ ܗ̇ܝ ܒܠܥܒܕܬܐ. ܘܐܡܪ ܠܗ ܕܐܒܘܢܐ
ܘܠܡܥܒܪ ܒܠܚܘܕ. ܗ̇ܘ ܕܝܢ ܥܬܝܕ ܗܘܐ. ܦܩܕܝܢ ܓܝܪ ܗ̇ܘ
ܦܩܕܐ ܘܡܫܡܫܢܐ ܒܐܝܕܗ ܥܠ ܪܫܗ. ܘܐܡܪ ܝܫܘܥ. ܫܕܪܐ
ܕܡܬܝܒܐ ܟܕ ܫܠܚ ܡܕܝܪܐ ܪ̈ܕܐ. ܘܗ̇ܘ ܠܐ ܡܕܪܟ. ܐܢܫ
ܕܝܢ ܡܚܒܒ ܐܢܫ ܕܢܗܘܐ ܠܐܠܗܐ ܕܡܢܝܢ ܡܬܬܠܠ ܒܗܕܡܬܐ
ܘܒܫܘܠܛܢܐ. ܚܕܐ ܗ̇ܘ ܦܩܕܐ ܘܐܡܪ. ܗܢܐ ܡܕܝܢ ܗܘ
ܪܒܐ. ܐܦ ܐܠܗܐ ܗ̇ܘ ܐܦ ܡܠܟܐ ܗܘ. ܐܘ ܡܢܐ
ܐܡܪ ܠܗ ܢܕܒ ܐܢܫ. ܦܩܕܝܢ ܚܒܝܫ̈ܐ ܛܠܝܐ ܝܫܘܥ ܘܐܡܪ.
ܢܒܕܘܢ ܦܐܪ̈ܐ ܐܠܝܢ ܕܠܝܬ ܒܗܘܢ ܦܐܪ̈ܐ ܘܢܣܒܘܢ
ܡܟܘܪ̈ܐ ܦܐܪ̈ܐ ܕܫܢܐ ܕܕܢܚܐ. (IX.) ܬܘܒ ܕܝܢ ܒܝܘܡ
ܒܘܡܟܐ ܕܫܒܬܐ ܡܫܒܬܚܐ ܗܘܐ ܝܫܘܥ ܒܠ ܐܪ̈ܥܐ.
ܘܢܦܠ ܣܕ ܡܢ ܛܠܝܐ ܘܡܝܬ. ܘܟܕ ܣܗܘ ܗܠܝܢ ܣܓܝ̈ܐ ܦ̈ܓܪܘ.
ܘܦܓܥ ܝܫܘܥ ܒܠܒܘܕܘܗܝ. (fol. 15) ܘܐܣܝܕܘܗܝ ܘ̈ܒܥܝܘܗܝ
ܕܗ̇ܘ ܕܡܚܒ ܘܐܬܩܪܝ ܠܗ. ܕܐܝܟ ܥܕܬܐ، ܠܛܠܝܐ.
ܘܝܫܘܥ ܐܡܪ. ܕܠܐ ܓܕܫܬܗ. ܡܕܝܢ ܕܝܢ ܓܥܬܝܢ ܗܘܐ ܠܗ.
ܦܩܕܝܢ ܢܒܫܬ ܝܨܕ ܡܫܬܐ ܘܐܡܪ ܠܗ. ܘܠܘܝ: ܡܟܢܐ ܟܢ
ܥܡܗ ܗܘܐ. ܐܢܫ ܓܕܫܬܝ. ܗ̇ܘ ܕܝܢ ܒܣܪ ܩܡ ܒܪܫܬܗ
ܘܐܡܪ ܠܗ ܠܐ ܡܕܪ. ܘܡܬܒܥܘ ܒܠܚܘܕ ܐܦ ܐܬܪܥܝܗ،
ܕܛܠܝܐ ܗ̇ܘ ܡܬܓܒܝܢ ܗܘܘ ܠܐܠܗܐ ܒܠ ܬܕܡܪ̈ܬܐ
ܗܠܝܢ. (XI.) ܬܘܒ ܕܝܢ ܒܝܘܡ ܒܬܪ ܕܗܘܐ ܝܫܘܥ ܟܕ ܫ̈ܒܥ
ܫ̈ܢܝܢ ܥܣܪ̈ܬܗ ܐܡܢܗ ܠܡܚܠܝܐ ܫ̈ܢܝܐ. ܘܟܣܝܐ ܕܒܥܝܐ
ܦܓܥܐ: ܢܦܩܬ ܡܠܬܗ ܘܐܬܬܦܪܬ. ܦܪܘܫ ܕܝܢ ܝܫܘܥ

ܕܢܣܝܘܢܐ ܢܣܝܒ ܠܟܠ̈ܗ ܓ̈ܢܣܗ. ܘܕܢܣܝܘܢܐ ܡܥܒܪ ܠܫܘܒܚܬܐ.
ܐܝܟ ܝܘܣܦ ܘܐܡܪ. ܘܐܝܟ ܡܫܝܚܐ ܠܫܠܝܚܐ ܕܐܡܪ ܗܘܐ
ܠܡܪܢܐ. ܠܡܢܐ ܠܝ ܠܝܠܝܐ ܪܘܓܙܐ ܗܢܐ ܕܢܣܝܘܢܐ. ܐܝܟ
ܝܘܣܦ[e] ܘܐܡܪ ܠܗܘܢ (fol. 14) ܡܠܦܢܐ. ܗܠܝܢ ܟܠܗܝܢ ܕܡܠܦܬ
ܘܗܠܝܢ ܥܡ̈ܠܝܗ ܢܣܝܘܢܐ ܐܝܟ ܠܗܘܢ. ܠܒܪ ܡܢܗܘܢ
ܐܢܬ، ܠܒܪ ܘܡܢܗ ܐܝܟ ܠܗ ܡܢܗܘܢ. ܐܡܪܐ ܒܥܘܪ
ܠܝܬ ܠܝ. ܐܢܬ ܒܢܣܝܘܢܐ ܐܢܬ ܘܒܢܣܝܘܢܐ ܗܘ ܡܫܒܚܬ.
ܒܪ ܠܒܪ ܐܢܬ ܡܬܦܠܓ. ܐܢܬ ܐܢܬ، ܗܘܝܬ. ܐܢܬ ܕܝܢ ܣܦܪܬ
ܕܐܬܝܬ ܐܒܐ. ܬܪܥܐ ܡܢ ܡܪܘܬܐ ܕܐܝܟ ܐܚܝܕ ܠܐ
ܢܛܪ ܠܝ ܘܠܐ ܡܫܟܚ ܢܐܠܨܢܝ. ܘܢܝܠܢܐ ܗܘ ܕܐܡܪܬ
ܟܠܗܘ: ܢܛܠܘܗܝ، ܡܢ ܕܥܠܝܗ ܗܘ. ܕܟܠܐ ܕܐܬܬܪܡܝܬ
ܘܪܒܐܝܬ ܐܚܝܢܐ ܡܢܢ ܕܐܬܬܠܝܬ ܒܢܣܝܘܢܐ. ܠܐ ܠܒܪ
ܢܛܪ ܐܢܬ ܡܢ ܐܝܟܢܐ ܐܢܬ. ܐܢܐ ܠܒܪ ܒܠܥܘܕܝ، ܢܛܪ
ܐܢܐ ܫܪܝܪܐܝܬ ܕܐܡܪܬ، ܐܬܬܠܝܬܘܢ. ܘܕܒܢܝܐ ܕܟܢܐ
ܐܢܬ ܠܗܘܢ ܕܐܬܟܬܪܘ ܬܢܢ. ܗܢܘܢ ܕܝܢ ܒܪ ܫܡܥܘܢ
ܬܡܗܘ. ܘܩܡܘ ܘܐܡܪܝܢ. ܐܘ ܚܝܠܐ ܘܢܨܝܚܘܬܐ ܕܬܕܡܘܪܬܐ.
ܕܐܝܟ ܗܠܝܢ ܟܠܗܝܢ ܠܐ ܫܡܥܢܢ ܡܢܡܬܘܡ ܕܐܝܟ ܗܠܝܢ. ܠܐ
ܒܥܝܢܐ. ܠܐ ܫܦܝܪܐ ܘܠܐ ܦܪܝܫܐ. ܗܝܕܝܢ ܡܢ ܐܝܟܢܐ
ܐܬܦܠܓ ܕܒܪ ܣܡ̈ܝܟ ܝܘ̈ܡܝܢ ܐܝܬܘܗܝ. ܘܐܝܠܝܢ ܟܠܗܝܢ ܡܬܦܠܓ.
ܐܝܟ ܗܢܘܢ ܠܐ ܚܙܐ ܐܢܫ ܡܬܟܬܘܡ.. ܐܝܟ ܫܡܥܘܢ
ܘܐܡܪ ܠܗܘܢ. ܬܬܕܡܪܘܢ ܐܢܬܘܢ ܒܡܕܡ ܕܐܡܪܬ ܠܟܘܢ
ܕܢܛܪ ܐܢܐ ܕܐܡܪܬ، ܗܘܝܬܘܢ. ܘܬܘܒ ܡܕܡ ܚܕܪ ܐܢܬ
ܠܝ ܕܐܡܪ ܠܟܘܢ. ܗܢܘܢ ܕܝܢ ܒܪ ܫܡܥܘܢ ܢܬܘܒ ܘܠܐ
ܐܫܟܚܘ ܠܡܡܠܠܘ. ܘܐܡܪ ܠܗ ܡܠܦܢܐ ܠܝܘܣܦ. ܐܢܐ

[e] Read ܝܘܣܦ.

ܦܘܠܘܣ. ܐܦ ܠܡܫ̈ܡܫܬܗܘܢ ܐܘܟܝܬ. ܘܟܕ ܚܙܐ ܦܘܠܘܣ ܡܕܡ
ܕܚܙܐ ܐܡܪ ܠܗ. ܕܠܐ ܒܡܪܐ ܬܗܘܐ ܒܡܡܠܠܘܬܟ. ܘܦܐܪ̈ܝܟ
ܢܐܟܠܘܢ. ܐܝܟ ܗܘܠܟܬܐ ܕܒܟܠܐ ܕܐܬܦܫܛܬ ܡܢ ܙܘܢܐ
ܘܬܘܒ ܠܝܬܝܗ̇. ܘܡܚܐ ܓܠܝܢܐ ܗܘ ܡܢ ܓܠܝܢܐ. (IV.) ܘܬܘܒ
ܐܙܠ ܗܘܐ ܦܘܠܘܣ ܥܡ ܐܒܘܗܝ. ܘܓܠܝܢܐ ܚܕ ܟܕ ܙܗܝܪ
ܓܪܡܗ ܒܟܬܦܗ. ܐܡܪ ܠܗ ܦܘܠܘܣ. ܠܐ ܬܐܙܠ ܐܘܪܚܟ.
ܘܡܢ ܓܠܝܢܐ ܢܦܠ ܘܡܚܬ. ܘܡܚܐ ܟܠ ܕܚܙܐܘܗܝ. ܘܐܡܪܝܢ.
ܐܝܟܢܐ ܐܬܡܠܝ ܓܠܝܢܐ ܗܢܐ ܕܟܠܗܝܢ ܡ̈ܠܘܗܝ. ܟܕܒܐ ܐ̈ܢܫ.
ܘܐܬܦܪܥ ܐܢܫܘܗܝ. ܕܗܘ ܕܡܚܬ ܠܗܬ ܝܘܣܦ ܘܐܡܪ̈ܝܢ
ܠܗ. ܗܢܐ ܓܠܝܢܐ ܐܝܬ ܠܢ ܠܐ ܡܫܟܚ ܐܢܬ ܠܡܚܡܪ ܒܗܢ
ܒܗܕܐ ܦܪܫܬܐ. ܐܠܐ ܐܠܦܘܗܝ ܕܢܗܘܐ ܡܟܝܟ̈.
(V.) ܦܬܚ ܕܝܢ ܠܗܬ ܓܠܝܢܐ ܘܢܦܠ ܗܘܐ ܠܗ ܘܐܡܪ. ܠܡܢܐ
ܗܠܝܢ ܒܟܪ ܐܢܬ. ܘܡܛܠ ܡܢܐ ܡܬܠܠ ܐܢܬ ܗܠܝܢ.
ܘܫܡܥܝܢ[d] ܗܠܝܢ ܘܦܫܝܢ ܠܝ. ܐܡܪ ܦܘܠܘܣ. ܐܠܘ ܠܐ
ܫ̈ܡܝܢ ܗ̈ܘ ܡ̈ܠܘܗܝ ܕܐܟܢ: ܠܐ ܗܘܐ ܠܡܢܐ ܢܒܥ ܗܘܐ
ܠܡܪܕܐ. ܘܬܘܒ ܐܡܪ. ܕܐܠܘ ܩܕܡ ܒܗܘܢܐ ܗܘܘ ܗܠܝܢ.
ܠܘܬܐ ܠܐ ܡܬܟܠܝܢ ܗܘܘ. ܗܠܝܢ ܠܐ ܢܣܒܘ ܬܫܡܫܬܐ.
ܘܒܪܬܒܬܗ ܐܬܟܪܙܘ ܗܠܝܢ ܕܪܥܝܢ ܗܘܘ ܠܗ. ܘܩܫܦ ܕܝܢ
ܢܓܕ ܘܐܦܫ ܒܐܘܪܚܐ ܘܐܬܬܠܠ ܒܗ. ܚܙܝܢ ܒܒܐ ܦܘܠܘܣ
ܘܐܡܪ ܠܗ. ܦܬܚܐ ܠܝ ܕܬܗܘܐ ܒܦܪ ܠܝ ܘܡܫܟܚ ܠܝ.
ܐܢܬ ܒܪ ܕܠܐ ܒܡܫܘܚܬܐ ܒܒܝܬ. (VI.—VIII.) ܡܠܦܢܐ ܕܝܢ
ܚܙ ܕܫܡܥܗ ܗܘܐ ܠܗ. ܫܡܥܗ ܟܕ ܡܬܠܠ ܥܡ ܐܒܘܗܝ،
ܘܐܡܪ. ܐ̈ܘ ܓܠܝܢܐ ܒܝܫܐ. ܘܐܡܪ ܠܝܘܣܦ ܐܒܘܗܝ.
ܒܕܡܟܐ ܠܐܡܗ، ܠܐ ܢܪܒܝܬ ܬܓܠܐ ܠܓܠܝܢܐ ܗܢܐ ܕܢܐܠܦ

[d] Perhaps ܘܚܫܝܢ. Gr. *καὶ πάσχουσιν οὗτοι.*

ܛܠܝܘܬܗ ܕܡܪܢ ܝܫܘܥ[a] ܀

(II.) ܛܠܝܐ ܕܝܢ ܝܫܘܥ ܡܫܝܚܐ: ܟܕ ܗܘܐ ܒܪ ܚܡܫ ܫܢܝܢ ܡܫܬܥܐ ܗܘܐ ܥܠ ܡܥܒܪܬܐ ܕܢܗܪܐ ܕܡܝܐ ܘܡܟܢܫ ܗܘܐ ܘܡܦܠܓ ܠܗܘܢ ܠܡܝܐ. ܘܦܩܕ ܠܗܘܢ ܒܡܠܬܐ ܘܡܟܢܫ ܠܗܘܢ ܠܡܫܘܬܐ ܘܥܒܕ ܠܗܘܢ ܢܗܘܘܢ ܕܟܝܢ ܘܫܦܝܪܝܢ. ܘܓܒܠ ܡܢ ܐܪܥܐ ܛܝܢܐ ܪܛܝܒܐ. ܘܥܒܕ ܦܪ̈ܚܬܐ ܬܪܬܥܣܪܐ. ܐܝܬܝܗ̇ ܗܘܬ ܕܝܢ ܫܒܬܐ ܘܛܠܝ̈ܐ ܣܓܝ̈ܐܐ ܐܝܬ (fol. 13) ܗܘܐ ܥܡܗ. ܚܙܝܗ ܕܝܢ ܐܢܫ ܡܢ ܝܗܘܕܝܐ ܟܕ ܛܠܝܐ ܗܢܘܢ ܥܒܕ ܐܙܠ ܐܡܪ ܠܝܘܣܦ ܐܒܘܗܝ. ܘܐܟܠܗ ܥܠ ܝܫܘܥ ܘܐܡܪ ܠܗ. ܕܒܫܒܬܐ ܓܒܠ ܛܝܢܐ ܘܥܒܕ ܦܪ̈ܚܬܐ. ܡܕܡ ܕܠܐ ܫܠܝܛ ܒܫܒܬܐ. ܘܐܙܠ ܝܘܣܦ ܘܟܐܐ ܒܗ ܘܐܡܪ ܠܗ. ܠܡܢܐ ܥܒܕ ܐܢܬ ܗܠܝܢ ܒܫܒܬܐ. ܦܫܛ ܝܫܘܥ ܐܝܕܗ ܒܟܦܐ[b] ܕܐܝܕܘܗܝ ܘܐܦܪܚ ܐܢܝܢ ܠܦܪ̈ܚܬܐ ܩܕܡ ܐܢܫܝܢ ܕܐܡܪܘ.[c] ܘܐܡܪ ܐܙܠܝ ܦܪ̈ܚܝܢ ܘܥܗܕܝܢ ܒܚܝܝܟܝ ܠܝ ܐܢܫܝܢ ܕܚܝܝܢ. ܐܙܠ ܕܝܢ ܦܪ̈ܚܬܐ ܗܠܝܢ ܟܕ ܡܨܦܪ̈ܢ. ܟܕ ܕܝܢ ܚܙܐ ܦܪܘܫܐ ܗ̇ܘ ܬܕܡܘܪܬܐ ܗܕܐ. ܘܫܪܝ ܐܡܪ ܠܪ̈ܚܡܘܗܝ. (III.) ܒܪܗ ܕܝܢ ܕܚܢܢ ܣܦܪܐ ܐܦ ܗܘ ܐܝܬܘܗܝ ܗܘܐ ܥܡ ܝܫܘܥ. ܘܫܩܠ ܫܒܘܛܐ ܡܢ ܪܘܚܬܐ ܘܫܕܐ ܘܦܬܚ ܠܡܥܒܪܬܐ ܘܐܪܕܝ ܐܢܘܢ ܠܡܝܐ ܗܠܝܢ ܕܟܢܫ ܗܘܐ

[a] Add 14, 484, fol. 12, vers.

[b] The MS. has ܒܟܦܐ, but the points ̈ indicate the transposition of the letters.

[c] Read ܡܚܕܐ ܐܡܠܬܗ ܕܐܡܪ? expressing the ἅμα τῷ λόγῳ of Tischendorf's text B, p. 151.

THE GOSPEL

OF

THOMAS THE ISRAELITE,

OR

OF THE INFANCY OF OUR LORD.

ܘܐܬܦܢܝ ܠܕܝܪܐ. ܢܦܫܗ ܕܡܪܝܐ ܕܐܬܦܢܝܬ ܕܡܐ. ܗܘܐ ܕܝܢ
ܡܪܝܐ ܢܛܪ ܠܗ. ܕܗܟܢܐ ܘܒܗ ܐܬܪ ܐܢܬ. ܕܠܐ ܦܘܠܚܢܐ.
ܟܕ ܗܢܐ ܕܝܢ ܕܠܐܝܬ ܡܬܚܙܐ ܐܬܦܢܝ ܠܕܝܪܐ ܘܠܐ ܚܙܝܘ
ܒܢܝ ܐܢܫܐ ܐܝܟ ܐܬܦܢܝ. (XXIV.) ܐܠܐ ܟܕ ܗܢܐ
ܕܫܠܡܬ. ܐܙܠܘ ܐܢܫ ܒܝܬܐ. ܘܠܐ ܐܫܟܚܘܗܝ
ܒܡܕܒܪܐ ܕܡܪܝܐ. ܦܢܝܢ ܗܘܘ ܕܝܢ ܒܬܪܗ ܘܒܥܘ ܠܗ
ܠܕܝܪܐ ܕܢܫܐܠܘܢ ܗܘܘ ܒܫܠܡܗ ܥܠܘܗܝ. ܘܢܫܩܘܢ
ܠܐܠܗܐ. ܘܟܕ ܐܘܕܥ ܠܗ. ܕܢܫܠܡ ܒܫܠܡܘܢ ܘܐܡܪܝܢ ܫܪ
ܗܢܘܢ ܘܥܠ ܠܒܝܬ ܡܫܟܢܐ. ܘܫܪܐ ܥܠ ܐܪܥܐ ܡܫܟܢܗ
ܕܡܪܝܐ ܕܗܟܢܐ ܕܐܫܬܪܝ ܘܡܫܬܒܩ ܐܝܟ ܕܐܦܐ. ܘܠܐ ܗܘܐ
ܕܐܬܦܢܝ. ܠܕܝܪܐ ܐܬܦܢܝ. ܘܠܐ ܢܬܦܢܐ ܕܗܢܐ ܕܒܝܬܐ
ܕܫܐܬ ܬܫܡܫܬܐ. ܘܢܦܩܘ ܐܘܪܚܐ ܕܠܕܝܪܐ ܐܬܦܢܝ.
ܘܟܕ ܢܦܩܘ ܒܬܪܗ ܕܗܟܢܐ ܐܬܦܢܝ ܘܢܦܩܘ ܬܠܬܐ
ܝܘܡܝܢ. ܘܟܬܒ ܡܫܡܗܬܐ ܦܠܓܗ ܐܬܬܥܝܪܘ ܒܫܡܐ ܕܠܒܝܬܐ
ܢܦܩܘܢ ܒܫܡܐ ܕܡܘܢܐ ܕܕܝܪܐ. ܘܫܠܡܬ ܦܓܪܐ
ܠܥܠܡܐ. ܫܒܘ ܕܐܬܩܛܠ ܠܗ ܡܢ ܥܘܬܪܐ ܕܦܘܪܣܐ ܕܠܐ
ܢܦܩܘ ܡܟܬܒܐ ܕܗܟܢܐ ܕܚܙܐ ܠܡܪܝܐ ܡܫܝܚܐ ܒܦܓܪ.
(XXV.) ܐܢܐ ܗܢܐ ܒܥܠ ܝܘܡܝ ܒܬܪܬ ܬܪܬܝܢ ܗܘܐ ܕܝ ܗܦܟܐ
ܥܠܘܒܝܬ ܒܐܘܪܫܠܡ. ܟܕ ܡܢ ܗܘܪܘܕܣ ܡܦܩܬܐ ܡܪܝܐ.
ܢܦܩܬ ܢܦܫ ܠܐܬܪܐ ܚܘܪܒܐ ܕܒܝܬܐ ܕܫܒܩ ܥܠܘܒܝܬܐ
ܡܢ ܐܘܪܫܠܡ. ܡܫܝܚܐ ܐܢܐ ܕܝܢ ܠܐܠܗܐ ܕܝܗܒ ܠܝ ܫܘܠܡܐ
ܕܐܬܟܬܒ ܒܬܪܬܝܢ ܗܘܐ ∴ ○ ○ ∴

ܫܠܡ ܣܘܠܦܗ ܕܬܪܝܢ ܐܩܠܝܣܝܣܛܝܩܝ ܕܝܘܚܢܢ ܕܐܣܝܐ ∴ ○ ∴

ܘܠܒܘܢܬܐ. ܘܐܬܒܚܠ ܠܗܘܢ ܡܢ ܡܠܐܟܐ ܕܠܐ ܢܗܦܘܢ[e]
ܠܗܪܘܕ. ܘܗܦܟܘ ܒܐܘܪܚܐ ܐܚܪܬܐ ܐܙܠܘ ܠܐܬܪܗܘܢ ܀
(XXII.) ܟܕ ܕܝܢ ܚܙܐ ܗܘܐ ܗܪܘܕܣ ܕܒܙܚܘ ܒܗ ܡܓܘܫ̈ܐ
ܪܓܙ. ܘܫܕܪ ܠܩܛ̈ܘܠܐ ܘܦܩܕ ܠܗܘܢ ܠܡܩܛܠܘ ܛܠ̈ܝܐ. ܡܢ ܒܪ
ܬܪ̈ܬܝܢ ܫܢ̈ܝܢ ܘܠܬܚܬ. ܐܝܟ ܙܒܢܐ ܕܒܥܐ ܡܢ ܡܓܘܫ̈ܐ.
ܟܕ ܫܡܥܬ ܡܪܝܡ ܕܛ̈ܠܝܐ ܡܬܩܛܠܝܢ ܕܢܩܛܠ. ܘܫܩܠܬܗ
ܠܝܫܘܥ ܘܟܪܟܬܗ ܒܥܙܘܪ̈ܐ. ܘܐܪܟܒܬܗ ܒܚܡܪܐ
ܕܬܘܪܐ. ܐܦ ܐܠܝܫܒܥ ܟܕ ܫܡܥܬ ܕܡܬܒܥܐ ܝܘܚܢܢ ܫܩܠܬܗ
ܘܣܠܩܬ ܠܛܘܪܐ. ܘܚܝܪܐ ܗܘܬ ܕܐܝܟܐ ܬܛܫܝܘܗܝ. ܘܠܝܬ
ܗܘܐ ܐܬܪܐ. ܗܝܕܝܢ ܐܬܬܢܚܬ ܐܠܝܫܒܥ ܘܐܡܪܐ ܠܛܘܪܐ.
ܛܘܪܐ ܕܐܠܗܐ ܩܒܠ ܠܐܡܐ ܥܡ ܒܪܗ̇. ܘܡܢ ܫܠܝ
ܐܬܦܬܚ ܛܘܪܐ ܗ̇ܘ ܘܩܒܠܗ̇. ܘܢܘܗܪܐ ܪܒܐ ܡܢܗܪ
ܗܘܐ ܠܗܘܢ ܛܘܪܐ ܗ̇ܘ. ܡܛܠ (fol. 12) ܕܡܠܐܟܗ
ܕܡܪܝܐ ܐܝܬ ܗܘܐ ܥܡܗܘܢ. ܘܗܘ ܡܢܛܪ ܗܘܐ ܠܗܘܢ.
(XXIII.) ܗܪܘܕܣ ܕܝܢ ܒܥܐ ܗܘܐ ܠܝܘܚܢܢ. ܘܫܕܪ ܕܫ̈ܡܫܐ ܠܘܬ
ܙܟܪܝܐ ܠܗܝܟܠܐ ܘܐܡܪܘ ܠܗ. ܐܝܟܐ ܡܛܫܝܬܗ̇[f] ܠܒܪܟ.
ܟܕ ܥܢܐ ܙܟܪܝܐ ܘܐܡܪ ܠܗܘܢ. ܐܢܐ ܡܫܡܫܢܐ ܐܢܐ ܕܐܠܗܐ
ܘܒܗܝܟܠܗ ܕܡܪܝܐ ܐܡܝܢ ܐܢܐ. ܘܠܐ ܝܕܥ ܐܢܐ ܕܐܝܟܐ
ܒܪܝ. ܘܐܙܠܘ ܕܫ̈ܡܫܐ ܘܐܡܪܘ ܠܗ. ܘܐܡܪ ܗܪܘܕܣ. ܒܪܟ
ܕܗܘܐ ܥܬܝܕ ܕܢܡܠܟ ܥܠ ܐܝܣܪܐܝܠ. ܘܫܕܪ ܕܫ̈ܡܫܐ ܘܐܡܪܘ
ܠܗ. ܐܡܪ ܫܪܝܪܐܝܬ ܐܝܟܘ ܒܪܟ. ܐܘ ܠܐ ܝܕܥ ܐܢܬ:
ܕܕܡܟ ܬܫܘܕ ܐܢܐ ܗܘ ܕܝܠܝ. ܘܐܙܠܘ ܕܫ̈ܡܫܐ ܘܐܡܪܘ ܠܗ.

[e] Such seems to be the reading of the MS.; or it may perhaps be ܢܐܬܘܢ, as the word is not quite distinct. I would read ܢܐܙܠܘܢ.

[f] Read ܡܛܫܝܬܝܗܝ.

ܠܗ ܘܐܡܪܬ. ܦܪܘܩܐ ܐܢܐ ܡܛܠ ܕܡܠܟܘܬܐ ܩܘܬ ܠ
ܟܠܟܝ ܕܐܬܗܘܟܬ ܠܫܠܝܐ. ܘܐܡܦܪܬ ܡܠܟܬܐ ܐܬܐܠܗ
ܠܐܝܣܪܝܠ. ܘܐܬܐܣܝܬ ܘܢܦܩܬ ܡܢ ܡܥܪܬܐ ܒܗ ܡܢ ܕܦܐ.
ܘܐܫܬܡܥ ܩܠܐ ܕܐܡܪ ܠܫܠܘܡ ܠܐ ܬܚܘܝܢ ܬܕܡܪ̈ܬܐ
ܗܠܝܢ ܠܐܢܫ ܕܚܙܝܬܝ ܥܕܡܐ ܕܐܬܐ ܠܐܘܪܫܠܡ. (xxi.) ܘܗܐ ܝܘܣܦ
ܐܬܛܝܒ ܢܦܘܩ ܠܝܗܘܕ. ܘܗܘܐ ܫܓܘܫܝܐ ܪܒܐ ܒܐܘܪܫܠܡ[c]
ܕܝܗܘܕ. ܐܬܘ ܓܝܪ ܡܓܘ̈ܫܐ ܘܐܡܪܝܢ ܐܝܟܘ ܡܠܟܐ
ܕܐܬܝܠܕ ܒܝܗܘܕ. ܟܘܟܒܗ ܓܝܪ ܚܙܝܢ ܒܡܕܢܚܐ ܘܐܬܝܢ
ܠܡܣܓܕ ܠܗ. ܘܟܕ ܫܡܥ ܗܪܘܕܣ ܐܬܕܠܚ. ܘܫܕܪ ܕܫ̈ܢܐ
ܠܘܬ ܡܓܘ̈ܫܐ ܘܩܪܐ ܠܪ̈ܒܝ ܟܗ̈ܢܐ. ܘܫܐܠ ܐܢܘܢ ܘܐܡܪ
ܠܗܘܢ ܐܝܟܐ ܟܬܝܒ ܕܡܬܝܠܕ ܡܫܝܚܐ. ܘܐܡܪܝܢ ܥܬܝܕ
ܠܗܘܢ ܟܠܗܘܢ. ܐܡܪܝܢ ܠܗ. ܒܒܝܬ ܠܚܡ ܕܝܗܘܕܐ. ܘܫܐܠ
ܐܢܘܢ ܠܡܓܘ̈ܫܐ ܘܐܡܪ ܠܗܘܢ ܡܢܐ ܐܬܐ ܚܙܝܬܘܢ
ܡܛܠ ܗܢܐ ܡܠܟܐ ܕܐܬܝܠܕ. ܐܡܪܝܢ ܡܓܘ̈ܫܐ. ܚܙܝܢ
ܟܘܟܒܐ ܕܢܗܝܪ ܛܒ ܒܢܘܗܪܗ ܕܢܚ ܩܕܡ ܟܘܟ̈ܒܐ
ܐܚܪ̈ܢܐ. ܘܐܬܚܫܟܘ ܟܘܟ̈ܒܐ ܡܢ ܢܘܗܪܗ ܕܗܢܐ
ܕܐܦ ܠܐ ܡܬܚܙܝܢ ܗܘܘ. ܘܝܕܥܢ ܕܡܠܟܐ ܐܬܝܠܕ
ܠܐܝܣܪܐܝܠ. ܘܐܬܝܢ ܠܡܣܓܕ ܠܗ. ⁘ ⁘ ܘܐܡܪ ܠܗܘܢ
ܗܪܘܕܣ. ܙܠܘ ܒܥܘ ܥܠ ܛܠܝܐ. ܘܐܢ ܕܐܫܟܚܬܘܢܗܝ[d]
ܬܘ ܚܘܐܘܢܝ. ܕܐܦ ܐܢܐ ܐܐܙܠ ܘܐܣܓܘܕ ܠܗ. ܘܟܕ
ܢܦܩܘ ܡܓܘ̈ܫܐ. ܘܗܐ ܟܘܟܒܐ ܗܘ ܕܚܙܘ ܒܡܕܢܚܐ
ܐܙܠ ܗܘܐ ܩܕܡܝܗܘܢ ܥܕܡܐ ܕܐܬܐ ܘܩܡ ܠܥܠ ܡܢ
ܛܠܝܐ. ܘܟܕ ܚܙܐܘܗܝ ܠܛܠܝܐ ܥܡ ܡܪܝܡ ܐܡܗ: ܢܦܠܘ
ܣܓܕܘ ܠܗ. ܘܩܪܒܘ ܠܗ ܩܘܪ̈ܒܢܐ ܕܗܒܐ ܘܡܘܪܐ

[c] Read ܒܒܝܬܠܚܡ.

[d] Read ܕܐܫܟܚܬܘܢܝܗܝ.

ܒܝܬ ܡܘܬܒܝܐ. ܘܡܛܠ ܕܠܐ ܦܘܫܐ ܐܢܬܬܐ. ܘܠܐ ܦܘܫܬ
ܐܢܬܬܝ. ܐܠܐ ܡܢ ܪܘܚܐ ܕܩܘܕܫܐ ܒܛܢܐ. ܘܐܡܪܬ
ܐܘܣܬܐ ܗܕܐ ܥܒܪܬܐ ܗ̇. ܐܡܪ ܠܗ̇ ܝܘܣܦ. ܬ̇ܝ
ܘܬܒܝܢܝ. ܘܐܙܠܬ̇ ܒܚܒܗ ܘܡܛܠ ܒܗ̇ ܒܡܕܒܪܬܐ. ܒܒܢܝܐ ܕܝܢ
ܕܢܗܘܪܐ ܦ̈ܠܠܐ ܗܘܬ ܒܡܕܒܪܬܐ ܒܒܢܝܐ ܕܐܬܝܢ، ܒܦܠܐ
ܘܐܬܦܬܐ ܢܦܩ ܛܕܐ ܡܢ ܡܕܢܚ ܐܡܗ. ܘܡܛܠ ܐܘܣܬܐ
ܘܐܡܛܪܬ. ܡܘܡܐ ܗܘ ܠܗ ܪܒܐ ܕܫܪܝܬ ܫܘܐ ܗܘܝܐ ܒܝܕܬܐ.
ܘܟܕ ܢܩܦܬ ܡܢ ܡܕܒܪܬܐ ܐܪܒܥܬܗ̇ ܥܠܡ ܘܐܡܪܬܐ. ܒܠܡ
ܠܒ. ܫܘܐ ܒܝܕܬܐ ܐܝܬ ܠܝ ܕܐܬܥܬܒܐ ܡܕܡܒܪ. ܒܬܘܠܬܐ
ܡܠܕܬ. ܡܕܡ ܕܗܘܐ ܚܒܢܐ ܠܐ ܦܩܘ ܠܗ. ܐܡܪܬܐ ܥܠܡ
ܫ ܗܘ ܡܪܝܐ ܐܠܗܐ ܕܠܐ ܡܗܝܡܢܐ ܐܢܐ. ܐܠܐ ܫܪܝܬ
ܕܒܬܘܠܬܐ ܗ̇. (xx.) ܘܡܠܬ ܐܘܣܬܐ ܠܡܕܒܪܬܐ ܘܐܡܪܬܐ.
ܡܪܝܡ ܗܘ ܢܦܩܝ. ܠܐ ܗܘܐ ܓܒܪ ܕܥܕܪ ܐܝܟܢܐ ܕܐܢܬ
ܠܡܚܝ. ܐܠܐ ܗܘ ܢܦܩܝ ܕܐܢ ܒܬܘܠܬܐ ܐܢܬܝ. ܘܡܢܘܬ
ܘܫܪܬ ܕܒܬܘܠܬܐ ܗ̇. ܘܐܡܠܠܬ ܘܐܡܪܬܐ. ܦ̇ ܠܒܬܘܠܬܝ
ܘܠܡܣܪܘܬ ܡܗܝܡܢܘܬܝ. ܕܢܦܩܬ ܠܐܠܗܐ ܫܢܐ. ܘܗܘܐ ܐܡܝ
ܢܩܕܐ ܘܢܦܠܐ ܡܚܝ. ܘܡܛܠ ܥܠܡ ܒܘܪܟܐ ܦܪܩ ܡܪܝܐ
ܘܐܡܪܬܐ. ܐܠܗܐ ܐܢܬ. ܐܬܪܚܡܝ. ܡܛܠ ܕܪܘܒܐ ܐܢܐ
ܕܐܒܪܗܡ ܘܕܐܝܣܚܩ ܘܕܝܥܩܘܒ. ܘܠܐ ܬܦܪܘܫ ܦܪܩ
ܒ̈ܢܝ ܐܢܫܐ. ܡܪܝܐ ܐܢܬ ܢܛܪ ܐܢܬ. ܕܒܥܡܟ ܐܘܣܬܐ
ܚܒܪܐ ܗܘܝܬ. ܘܐܡܪܬܐ ܡܚܝܟ (fol. 11) ܢܦܩܢܐ ܗܘܝܬ.
ܚܒܪܐ ܡܠܐܟܐ ܘܐܡܪ. ܥܠܡ ܥܒܕ ܡܪܝܐ ܒܒܘܬܝ.
ܘܠܐ ܦܩܕ ܐܬܪܚܡܝ ܠܛܠܝܐ. ܘܬܗܘܐ ܠܝ ܐܘܣܬܐ.
ܘܐܬܡܛܠܬ ܡܪܝܡ[b] ܫܪܘܬܐ. ܘܡܛܠ ܠܘܬ ܛܠܝܐ ܦܓܪܗ

[b] Read ܫܠܘܡ.

ܒܪܗ̇[a] ܕܝܢ ܝܘܣܦ ܕܡܕܒܪܐ ܢܦܩ ܐܝܟ ܕܢܠܩܛ. ܘܩܫܐ ܟܠ
ܣܡܝܪܗ: ܘܐܘܬܒܗ̇ ܘܢܟܬܗ ܒܪܗ. ܘܟܕ ܢܦܠ ܡܝܬܐ
ܕܬܠܬܐ: ܫܪܝ ܝܫܘܥ ܠܡܪܝܡ ܕܡܟܪܝܐ. ܘܐܡܪ ܝܫܘܥ.
ܒܒܪ ܗܘ ܕܐܝܬ ܒܗ ܟܕܒܐ ܕܢܦܩ. ܘܬܘܒ ܫܪܝ ܒܗ
ܠܝܠܕܐ. ܘܐܡܪ ܠܗ. ܡܪܝܡ: ܡܢܘ ܗܢܐ ܕܗܐ ܒܪܗ ܫܪܐ
ܐܢܐ ܦܪܘܫܝܐ ܒܗ ܫܪܐ. ܘܒܪܗ ܒܡܪܝ. ܐܡܪܝܢ ܠܝܫܘܥ.
ܬܪܝܢ ܒܢܝܢܫܝܢ ܫܪܐ ܐܢܐ ܒܚܕܐ. ܫܒ ܒܠܚܘܕ ܒܗ ܟܕܒܐ
ܘܡܪܝܡ ܘܫܪܐ ܕܫܪܐ ܘܕܒܪ. ܘܟܕ ܢܦܠ ܦܠܓܗ̇ ܕܐܘܪܚܐ:
ܐܡܪܝܢ ܠܗ ܠܝܫܘܥ. ܐܫܬܡܥ ܡܢ ܡܪܝܐ. ܡܛܠ ܕܗܢܐ
ܕܐܝܬ ܒܗ ܡܫܪܝܢܐ ܕܢܦܩ. (xviii.) ܘܐܫܟܚ ܡܕܝܢܬܐ
ܫܒܝܩ. ܘܡܫܠܡܗ̇ ܠܠܘܬܝ. ܘܐܚܝܕ ܒܠ ܒܚܕܗ̇ ܠܒܢܘܗܝ. ܘܢܦܩ
ܒܚܕܐ ܐܘܟܬܐ ܒܒܝܬ ܠܫܡ. ܐܢܐ ܕܝܢ ܝܫܘܥ ܡܫܝܚ
ܗܘܘܬ: ܘܚܙܝܬ ܒܠ ܡܕܡ ܒܗ ܬܫܒܚܬܗ. ܘܡܢ ܟܠ ܐܬܪܘܬ،
ܘܪܗܛ ܒܠ ܡܕܡ ܒܠܒܫܗ. (xix.) ܗܘܝܢ ܫܢܝܢ ܐܬܬܐ
ܕܫܢܬܐ ܡܢ ܠܦܘܪܐ. ܘܐܡܪܬ ܠܗ. ܠܐܡܟܐ ܐܙܠ ܐܢܬ
ܒܒܪܐ. ܘܐܡܪܬ ܠܗ ܐܘܟܬܐ ܒܒܪܬܐ ܟܠܒܐ ܐܢܐ.
ܘܐܡܪܬ ܠܗ. ܡܢ ܐܝܟܢܐ ܐܢܬ: ܘܐܡܪܬ ܠܗ. ܐܡܝܢ.
ܘܐܡܪܬ ܠܗ. ܡܢ ܗܘ ܗܘܐ ܕܝܠܕܐ ܒܗܕܐ ܡܕܝܢܬܐ.
ܘܐܡܪܬ ܠܗ. ܡܕܝܢܬܝ ܗܝ. ܘܐܡܪܬ ܠܗ. ܠܐ ܠܐ ܗܘܬ
ܐܝܬܝܟ ܗܕܐ. ܘܐܡܪܬ ܠܗ. ܡܪܝܡ ܗܝ ܗܝ ܕܐܬܪܒܝܬ

[a] Add. 14,484, fol. 10 rect.

THE
PROTEVANGELIUM JACOBI,
OR THE HISTORY OF
THE BIRTH OF OUR LORD
AND OF
THE VIRGIN MARY.

October, 1865.

EDINBURGH,
20, South Frederick Street.

LONDON,
14, Henrietta Street,
Covent Garden, W.C.

WILLIAMS AND NORGATE'S

PUBLICATIONS.

Contributions to the Apocryphal Literature of the New Testament, collected from Syriac MSS. in the British Museum, and edited with an English Translation and Notes, by W. Wright, LL.D., Assistant in the Department of MSS., British Museum. 8vo. cloth, 7*s* 6*d*

A Light thrown upon Thucydides, to illustrate the Prophecy of Daniel as to the coming of the Messiah; in remarks on Dr. Pusey's "Daniel the Prophet;" and in reply to Dr. Hincks on the Metonic Cycle and the Calippic Period. To which is added a review of Dr. Temple's Essay on the Education of the World. By Franke Parker, M.A., Trin. Coll. Cambridge, and Rector of Luffingcott, Devon. 1 vol. 8vo. [*nearly ready.*]

Dr. Strauss' New "Life of Jesus." The authorized English translation. 2 vols. 8vo. cloth. (To be published in October), 24*s*

Dr. Davidson's Fuerst's Hebrew Lexicon. Hebrew and Chaldee Lexicon to the Old Testament, with an Introduction, giving a short History of Hebrew Lexicography. By Dr. Julius Fuerst. Third Edition, improved and enlarged, containing a Grammatical and Analytical Appendix. Translated from the German by Samuel Davidson, D.D., LL.D. Parts I-VI. Royal 8vo. double columns. Price One Shilling each (to be completed in 20 parts)

An Introduction to the Old Testament, critical, historical and theological, containing a discussion of the most important questions belonging to the several Books. By Samuel Davidson, D.D., LL.D. 3 vols. 8vo. cloth, 42*s*

Daniel; or, the Apocalypse of the Old Testament. By Philip S. Desprez, B.D., Incumbent of Alvedistone. With an Introduction by Rowland Williams, D.D., Vicar of Broadchalke. 8vo. cloth, 10*s* 6*d*

Prehistoric Times, as illustrated by Ancient Remains and the Manners and Customs of Modern Savages. By Sir John Lubbock, Bart., F.R.S., etc., President of the Ethnological Society. 8vo. with 156 woodcut illustrations and 4 plates, 8vo. cloth, 15*s*

Ancient Syriac Documents relative to the earliest Establishment of Christianity in Edessa and the neighbouring Countries, from the year after our Lord's Ascension to the beginning of the Fourth Century. Discovered, edited, translated, and annotated by W. Cureton, D.D. Canon of Westminster. With a Preface by W. Wright, Ph. D., LL.D. 4to. Cloth, 31*s* 6*d*

Dante Allighieri. Critical, Historical, and Philosophical Contributions to the Study of the Divina Commedia. By H. C. Barlow, M.D. Royal 8vo. with facsimiles of MSS. Cloth boards, 25*s*

Orthodoxy, Scripture and Reason: an Examination of some of the principal Articles of the Creed of Christendom. By the Rev. W. Kirkus, LL.B. Post 8vo. cloth, 10*s* 6*d*

Christianity versus Theology. In Ten Letters addressed to his Brother Laymen. By William Parry, an Octogenarian Layman of the Church of England. Crown 8vo. 2*s*

An Introduction to the Philosophy of Primary Beliefs. By Richard Lowndes. Crown 8vo. cloth, 7*s* 6*d*

Æthiopic Liturgies and Prayers, translated from MSS. in the Library of the British Museum, and of the British and Foreign Bible Society, and from the Edition printed at Rome in 1548. By the Rev. J. M. Rodwell, M.A., Rector of St. Ethelburga, Bishopsgate. Part I. (reprinted from the "Journal of Sacred Literature.") 8vo. Sewed, 2*s*

H. De Rheims' First Practical Lines in Geometrical Drawing, containing a copious Series of Examples and Problems in Practical Geometry, use of Mathematical Instruments, Construction of Scales, Descriptive Geometry, Orthographic and Horizontal Projections, Theory of Shadows, Isometrical Drawing and Perspective. The whole founded on Questions given at the Military and other Competitive Examinations. Illustrated with upwards of 300 Diagrams. By J. F. H. De Rheims. 69 plates, 8vo. cloth, 9*s*

Late, but not Too Late. A Tale, by Ann Barnett. Post 8vo. cloth, 7s 6d

Endless Torments. An Answer to the Archbishop of York on the subject of Endless Torments, by a Bachelor of Divinity. 12mo. sewed, 2s

Scholia on Passages of the Old Testament. By Mar Jacob, Bp. of Edessa, now first Edited in the original Syriac, with an English Translation and Notes by the Rev. G. Phillips, D.D., President of Queen's College, Cambridge. 8vo. Cloth, 5s

The Book of Job, translated from the original Hebrew, with Notes by the Rev. J. M. Rodwell, M.A., Rector of St. Ethelburga, Bishopsgate. Post 8vo. cloth, 3s 6d

Offices from the Service Books of the Holy Eastern Church, with a Translation, Notes, and Glossary, by Richard F. Littledale, LL.D. Crown 8vo. cloth, 6s

On the Inspiration of the Scriptures, shewing the Testimony which they themselves bear as to their own Inspiration. By James Stark, M.D., F.R.S.E., Author of the "Westminster Confession of Faith critically compared with the Holy Scriptures," &c. Crown 8vo. cloth, 3s 6d

Herbert Spencer's Principles of Biology. Vol. I. Being the Second Vol. of "A System of Philosophy." 8vo. cloth, 1864, 16s

Herbert Spencer. A System of Philosophy. Vol. I. First Principles. 8vo. cloth, 1862, 16s

Herbert Spencer. Education: Intellectual, Moral, and Physical. 8vo. cloth, 1861, 6s

Herbert Spencer. Essays: Scientific, Political, and Speculative. 8vo. cloth, 1858, 12s

Herbert Spencer. Second Series of Essays: Scientific, Political, and Speculative. 8vo. cloth, 1863, 10s

Herbert Spencer. Principles of Psychology. 8vo. cloth, 1855, 16s

Herbert Spencer's Classification of the Sciences, to which are added Reasons for dissenting from the Philosophy of M. Comte. 8vo. sewed, 1864, 2s 6d

The Analogy of Thought and Nature investigated. By E. Vansittart Neale, M.A. Post 8vo. cloth, 7s 6d

The Odes of Horace. Books I. and II. Translated into English Verse, to which are added the Carmen Seculare, and Appendix. By Hugo Nicholas Jones. Crown 8vo. half bound, Roxburgh style, gilt top, 4s 6d

Bengelii Gnomon novi Testamenti in quo ex nativa verborum vi simplicitas, profunditas, concinnitas, salubritas sensuum coelestium indicatur. Edit. III. per filium superstitem E. Bengel quondam curata Quinto recusa adjuvante J. Steudel. Royal 8vo. printed on Writing Paper, 1862, cloth bds. 12s

Anselm (Archiep. Cantuar.) Cur Deus Homo? libri II. Foolscap 8vo. cloth, 2s; sewed, 1s 6d

Platonis Phaedo. Edited, with Introduction and Notes, by W. D. Geddes, M.A. Professor of Greek in the University of Aberdeen. 8vo. cloth, 8s

The Teutonic Name-System applied to the Family Names of France, England, and Germany. By Robert Ferguson. 621 pp. 8vo. cloth, 14s

The River-Names of Europe. By Robert Ferguson. Post 8vo. cloth, 4s 6d

Baedeker's Traveller's Guides in English.

1. PARIS, including Routes from London to Paris, and from Paris to the Rhine and Switzerland. With Map and Plans, 1865, 4s 6d
2. SWITZERLAND, with the Lakes of Northern Italy, Savoy, and the adjacent Districts of Piedmont, Lombardy, and the Tyrol. With general Travelling Maps, special Maps, and Plans, Panoramas and Views. 12mo. cloth, 5s 6d
3. THE RHINE, from Switzerland to Holland, the Black Forest, Vosges, Haardt, Odenwald, Taunus, Eifel, Seven Mountains, Nahe, Lahn, Moselle, Ahr, Wupper, and Ruhr. With Views, Maps, and Plans of Towns, &c. 12mo. cloth, 4s
4. THE TRAVELLER'S MANUAL of Conversation in English, German, French, and Italian; together with a copious Vocabulary and short Questions in those Languages. 17th Edition, 1864, 3s

I Poeti Italiani Moderni. A Selection of Extracts from Modern Italian Poets (from Alfieri to the present time). With explanatory notes and short biographical notice of each author, by Louisa A. Merivale. Post 8vo. cloth, 5s

Uhland's Poems, translated from the German by the Rev. W. W. Skeat, M.A. late Fellow of Christ's College, Cambridge. Post 8vo. cloth, 7s

Principles of Hindu and Mohammedan Law. Republished from the Principles and Precedents of the same. By Sir William Macnaghten. Edited, with an Introduction, by the late Dr. H. H. Wilson, Boden Professor of Sanskrit in the University of Oxford. Second edition, 8vo. cloth, 6s

Indian Epic Poetry, being the Substance of Lectures recently given at Oxford: with a full Analysis of the Ramayana, and the leading Story of the Maha Bharata. By M. WILLIAMS, Boden Professor of Sanskrit. 8vo. cloth, 5*s*

The Study of Sanskrit in Relation to Missionary Work in India. By Professor MONIER WILLIAMS. An inaugural Lecture delivered before the University of Oxford, with Notes and Additions. 8vo. 1861, 2*s*

Bopp's Comparative Grammar of the Sanskrit, Zend, Greek, Latin, Lithuanian, Gothic, German and Slavonic Languages. Translated by Professor EASTWICK, and Edited by Professor H. H. WILSON. 3 vols. 8vo. THIRD EDITION, cloth bds. 42*s*

Diez (F.) Romance Dictionary. An Etymological Dictionary of the Romance Languages, from the German of FR. DIEZ, with Additions by T. C. DONKIN, B.A. 8vo. cloth, 15*s*

In this work the whole Dictionary, which in the original is divided into four parts, has been, for greater convenience in reference, reduced to one Alphabet; and at the end is added a Vocabulary of all English Words connected with any of the Romance Words treated of throughout the work.

Diez (F.) Introduction to the Grammar of the Romance Languages, translated by C. B. CAYLEY, B.A. 8vo. cloth, 4*s* 6*d*

Homer's Iliad, translated into dramatic blank verse. By the Rev. T. S. NORGATE. Post 8vo. cloth, 15*s*

Homer's Odyssey, translated into dramatic blank verse. By the Rev. T. S. NORGATE. Post 8vo. cloth, 12*s*

Batrachomyomachia. The Battle of the Frogs and Mice, reproduced in dramatic blank verse. By the Rev. T. S. NORGATE. Post 8vo. sewed, 1*s*

Observations of the Spots of the Sun, from November 9, 1853, to March 24, 1861, made at Redhill. By R. C. CARRINGTON, F.R.S. Illustrated by 166 plates, royal 4to. cloth boards, 25*s*

Comparative Osteology. An Elementary Atlas of Comparative Osteology. Consisting of 12 Plates, drawn on Stone by B. WATERHOUSE HAWKINS, F.L.S. The Figures selected and arranged (from objects in the Museum of the Royal College of Surgeons) by Professor T. H. HUXLEY, F.R.S. Folio, cloth, 25*s*

Evidence as to Man's Place in Nature, or Essays upon—I. The Natural History of the Man-like Apes. II. The Relation of Man to the Lower Animals. III. Fossil Remains of Man. By T. H. HUXLEY, F.R.S. With woodcut Illustrations. *Third Thousand.* 8vo. *cloth*, 6*s*

The Genesis of the Earth and of Man; or, the History of Creation and the Antiquity and Races of Mankind considered on Biblical and other grounds. Edited by REGINALD STUART POOLE, M.R.S.L., etc. of the British Museum. Second edition, revised and enlarged. Crown 8vo. cloth, 6*s*

The Religion of the Universe, with consolatory Views of a Future State, and suggestions on the most beneficial topics of Theological Instruction. By ROBERT FELLOWES, LL.D. Third edition, revised with additions from the author's MS. and a preface by the Editor. Post 8vo. cloth, 6*s*

Mackay (R. W.) The Tübingen School and its Antecedents. A Review of the History and present Condition of Modern Theology. By R. W. MACKAY, M.A., Author of "The Progress of the Intellect," "A Sketch of the History of Christianity," etc. 8vo. cloth, 10*s* 6*d*

Arabic Chrestomathy, with complete Glossary, by W. WRIGHT, MS. Department, British Museum. (1 vol. 8vo.) [*In the press.*

Lane's Arabic-English Lexicon, derived from the best and most copious Eastern Sources, comprising a very large collection of words and significations omitted in the Kámoos, with Supplements to its abridged and defective explanations, ample grammatical and critical comments, and examples in prose and verse. Parts 1 and 2 (to consist of eight parts and a supplement.) Roy. 4to. cloth, each 25*s*

Arabic Grammar, founded on the German work of Caspari, with many additions and corrections. By WILLIAM WRIGHT, MS. Department, British Museum. Complete in 1 vol. 8vo. cloth, 15*s*

—— Vol. II. comprising the Syntax and an introduction to Prosody, may be had separately, price 7*s* 6*d*

Koran, newly translated from the Arabic; with Preface, Notes and Index. The Suras arranged in chronological order. By the Rev. J. M. RODWELL, M.A., Rector of St. Ethelburga, Bishopsgate. Crown 8vo. cloth, 10*s* 6*d*

Moor's Hindu Pantheon. A new Edition from the original copper-plates. 104 plates, with descriptive letter-press, by the Rev. A. P. MOOR. Royal 4to. cloth boards, gilt, 31*s* 6*d*

Legends and Theories of the Buddhists, compared with History and Modern Science. By R. SPENCE HARDY, author of "Eastern Monachism," "A Manual of Buddhism," etc. 1 vol. 8vo. [*In the press.*

Ancient Danish Ballads, translated from the originals, with Notes and Introduction by R. C. ALEXANDER PRIOR, M.D. 3 vols. 8vo. cloth, 31*s* 6*d*

Grammar of the Egyptian Language, as contained in the Coptic, Sahidic, and Bashmuric Dialects; together with Alphabets and Numerals in the Hieroglyphic and Enchorial Characters by the Rev. Henry Tattam, D.D., F.R.S. 2nd edition, revised and corrected. 8vo. cloth, 9*s*

Cowper's Syriac Grammar. The Principles of Syriac Grammar, translated and abridged from that of Dr. Hoffman, with additions by B. Harris Cowper. 8vo. cloth, 7*s* 6*d*

Garnett's Linguistic Essays. The Philological Essays of the late Rev. Richard Garnett, of the British Museum. Edited with a Memoir, by his Son. 8vo. cloth bds. 10*s* 6*d*

The Book of Ruth in Hebrew, with a critically revised Text, various readings, including an entirely new collation of Twenty-eight Hebrew MSS. (most of them not previously collated) and a Grammatical and Critical Commentary; to which is appended the Chaldee Targum, with various readings, Grammatical Notes, and a Chaldee Glossary. By Rev. Ch. H. H. Wright, M.A., of Trinity College, Dublin, and Exeter College, Oxford. 8vo. cloth, 7*s* 6*d*.

Schnorr's Bible Pictures. Scripture History Illustrated in a Series of 180 Engravings on Wood, from Original Designs by Julius Schnorr. (With English Texts.) Royal 4to. handsomely bound in cloth gilt extra, 42*s*

—— Or, the same in 3 vols. (each containing 60 plates) *cloth boards, extra gilt*, 15*s* each.

Nibelungenlied. The Fall of the Nibelungers, otherwise the Book of Kriembild: a translation of the Nibelunge Nôt, or Nibelungenlied. By William Nanson Lettsom. Post 8vo. cloth, 10*s* 6*d*

Natural History Review. A Quarterly Journal of Biological Science. Edited by Dr. W. B. Carpenter, F.R.S., Dr. R. McDonnell, Dr. E. P. Wright, F.L.S., G. Busk, F.R.S., Professor Huxley, F.R.S., Sir John Lubbock, Bart., F.R.S., Professor J. R. Greene, P. L. Sclater, F.R.S., Sec. Z.S., F.L.S., D. Oliver, F.R.S., F.L.S., F. Currey, F.R.S., and Wyville Thomson, LL.D., F.R.S.E., with illustrations. Quarterly, 4*s*. Annual subscription paid in advance, 12*s*

Journal of Sacred Literature and Biblical Record. Edited by B. H. Cowper (Editor of the New Testament in Greek from Codex A; a Syriac Grammar, &c.) Published Quarterly, price 5*s*—Annual Subscription prepaid, 17*s*, post free.

The Churchman and the Free Thinker; or, a Friendly Address to the Orthodox. By the Rev. Thomas Shore, M.A., formerly fellow of Wadham College, Oxford. 8vo. sewed, 2*s* 6*d*

Morgan (J. F.) England under the Norman Occupation. By James F. Morgan, M.A.

Contents: Domesday and the Conqueror's Policy—Measurement of Land—Agricultural Affairs, Rent, &c.—Condition of Tenants and Peasantry—Boroughs, Cities, Hundreds, Wapentakes, and Shires—Titles and Offices—Extinction of Villenage.

Schroen's Logarithms by Professor De Morgan. Seven-Figure Logarithms of Numbers from 1 to 108,000, and of Sines, Cosines, Tangents, Cotangents to every 10 Seconds of the Quadrant, with a Table of of Proportional Parts by Dr. Ludw. Schroen, Director of the Jena Observatory, &c. Fifth Edition, Corrected, and Stereotyped. With a Description of the Tables added by A. De Morgan, Professor of Mathematics, University College, London. 1 vol. impl. 8vo. Price 7*s* 6*d* sewed, 9*s* in cloth boards

BOOKS REDUCED IN PRICE.

Donaldson's Jashar. Second Edition, with important Additions.—Jashar. Fragmenta Archetypa Carminum Hebraicorum in Masorethico Veteris Testamenti Textu passim tessellata collegit, restituit, Latinè exhibuit, commentario instruxit J. G. Donaldson, S.T.D. Editio Secunda, aucta et emendata. 8vo. cloth, (pub. at 10*s*) 6*s*

Donaldson's Christian Orthodoxy reconciled with the Conclusions of Modern Biblical Learning. By J. W. Donaldson, D.D., late Fellow of Trinity College, Cambridge. 8vo. cloth, (pub. at 10*s*) 6*s*

Codex Alexandrinus.—Novum Testamentum, Graecè, ex antiquissimo Codice Alexandrino à C. G. Woide olim descriptum: ad fidem ipsius Codicis denuo accuratius edidit B. H. Cowper. 8vo. cloth (pub. at 12*s*), 6*s*

Proper Names of the Old Testament arranged Alphabetically from the original Text, with Historical and Geographical Illustrations, for the use of Hebrew Students and Teachers, with an Appendix of the Hebrew and Aramaic Names in the New Testament. 8vo. cloth (pub. at 7*s* 6*d*) 4*s* 6*d*

Ewald's Grammar of the Hebrew Language of the Old Testament, translated and enriched with later Additions and Improvements of the Author, by Dr. J. Nicholson. 8vo. boards (pub. at 10s 6d) 7s 6d

The Book of Genesis in Hebrew, with a critically-revised Text, various Readings, and Grammatical and Critical Notes, &c. By the Rev. C. H. H. Wright, M.A. 8vo. cloth boards (pub. at 10s 6d) 5s

The Book of Jonah, in Four Semitic Versions, viz., Chaldee, Syriac, Aethiopic, and Arabic, with Corresponding Glossaries. By W. Wright. 8vo. boards (pub. at 7s 6d) 4s

Latham's Philological, Ethnographical, and other Essays. Opuscula. By R. G. Latham, M.D., F.R.S., &c. 8vo. cloth (pub. at 10s 6d) 5s

Kennedy (James).—Essays, Ethnological and Linguistic. By the late James Kennedy, formerly H.B.M. Judge at the Havana. 8vo. cloth (pub. at 7s 6d) 4s

Davy (J.)–Physiological Researches. By John Davy, M.D. F.R.S. &c. 8vo. cloth, 1863 (pub. at 15s) 9s

Davy (J.)—Army Diseases.—On some of the more Important Diseases of the Army, with Contributions to Pathology. By John Davy, M.D. F.R.S. Lond. and Ed., Inspector-General of Army Hospitals, &c. 8vo. cloth (pub. at 15s) 9s

Frerichs.—Diseases of the Liver.—An Atlas of Pathological Anatomy, illustrative of a Clinical Treatise on the Diseases of the Liver. Translated and edited by Dr. Charles Murchison. Two Parts, 26 carefully coloured Plates. Royal 4to. 1861-62 (pub. at 33s) 24s

Pincoffs (P.)—Experiences in Eastern Military Hospitals; with Observations on the English, French, and other Medical Departments, the Organization of Military Medical Schools and Hospitals. 8vo. cloth (pub. at 4s) 2s

Hardy (Rev. Spence). — Eastern Monachism (Budhism).—An Account of the Origin, Laws, Discipline, Sacred Writings, &c. of the Order of Mendicants founded by Gotama Budha. 8vo. cloth (pub. at 12s) 7s 6d

Turkish Dictionary.—A Pocket Dictionary of the English and Turkish Languages. By G. Sauerwein. 12mo. cloth (pub. at 5s) 2s

Lorimer (James). — Political Progress not necessarily Democratic; or, Relative Equality the True Foundation of Civil Liberty. Crown 8vo. cloth (pub. at 5s) 2s

Frederick Rivers, Independent Parson. By Mrs. Florence Williamson. Post 8vo. cloth (pub. at 10s 6d) 6s

Home and Foreign Review, complete in eight Parts (July, 1862, to April, 1864), forming 4 vols. 8vo. sewed (pub. at 48s) 24s

Single Numbers, to complete sets, may be had at 3s each (pub. at 6s)

Natural History Review. (First Series.)—A Quarterly Journal of Zoology, Botany, Geology, and Palæontology. Edited by A. H. Halliday, W. H. Harvey, S. Haughton, E. Perceval Wright, &c. The complete First Series, 7 vols. 8vo. (pub. at £4. 18s) 42s

---

NEW ELEMENTARY BOOKS.

Richon (V.) Exercices Epistolaires à l'Usage des Etrangers qui désirent se perfectionner dans la pratique de la correspondance française, suivis d'un choix de lettres tirées des meilleurs Ecrivains contemporains. Par V. Richon, Bachelier-ès-Lettres à l'Université de Paris. 12mo. cloth, 2s 6d

Richon (V.) Exercices de Conversation, ou Recueil de Scènes tirées des œuvres de nos meilleurs auteurs dramatiques contemporains. 12mo. cloth, 4s

Exercises on the French Past Participles. By M. Bonneau, adapted for the use of English Students by G. A. Neveu. Second Edition, revised and enlarged by idiomatic notes. Post 8vo. cloth, 1s

Neveu (G. A.) Letters and Conversations, selected from the best writers, for the use of English Students, to facilitate the practice of translating from English into French, with Notes, by G. A. Neveu, Author of "Exercises on Past Participles, adapted from the French for the use of English Students." Post 8vo. cloth, 3s 6d

This work is divided into two parts; the first containing selections from French authors, literally translated into English for the purpose of retranslation; the second consisting solely of selections from the works of English Authors.

Neveu (G. A.) Key to the Letters and Conversations, forming also a French Reading Book. Cloth bds. 3s 6d

Noel and Chapsal's French Grammar, translated into English by A. Barnett. 12mo. bds. 3*s*

Mariette (Professor, King's College) A Key to the "Half Hours of French Translation." Crown 8vo. cloth, 6*s*

By the same Author,

Mariette's Half Hours of French Translation. New Edition. Crown 8vo. cloth, 4*s* 6*d*

Cottin's Elisabeth, ou les Exilés de Sibérie. A new edition, with English Vocabulary, by M. Bertrand (Bertrand's French School Classics, No. IV.) 12mo. cloth, 2*s*

Saint-Pierre (B. de) Paul et Virginie. A new edition, with English Vocabulary, by M. Bertrand (Bertrand's French School Classics, No. V.) 12mo. cloth, 2*s*

Voltaire's Histoire de Charles XII. A New Edition for the Use of Schools, with an English Vocabulary. By M. Bertrand. (Bertrand's French School Classics, No. I.) 12mo. cloth boards, 2*s* 6*d*

Voltaire's Histoire de Pierre le Grand. With an English Vocabulary. By M. Bertrand (Bertrand's French School Classics, No. II.) 12mo. cloth boards, 2*s* 6*d*

Fenelon.—Les Aventures de Telemaque. With an English Vocabulary. By M. Bertrand (Bertrand's French School Classics, No. III.) 12mo. cloth boards, 2*s* 6*d*

Euripidis Ion, Greek Text, with Notes for Beginners, Introduction, and Questions for Examination, by the Rev. Ch. Badham, D.D., Head Master of the Edgbaston Proprietary School. 8vo. cloth, 3*s* 6*d*

This edition has already been adopted at Eton, Rugby, Birmingham, and several other Grammar Schools.

Ihne's Short Latin Syntax, with copious Exercises and Vocabulary, by Dr. W. Ihne, Principal of Carlton Terrace School, Liverpool. 12mo. cloth. Second edition, carefully revised, 3*s* 6*d*

Nouveau Théatre Francais. Modern French Plays, edited for Schools, with idiomatic notes and a complete Vocabulary. By Dr. A. Buchheim. Part I. Les deux petits Savoyards—Le Mousse. 12mo. cloth, 2*s* 6*d*

Nouveau Théatre Francais. Part II. Le Testament de Madame Patural.—Le Revenant, ou le Trompeur trompé.—Le Vieux Garçon et la Petite fille. 12mo. cloth, 2*s* 6*d*

—— Parts I. II. together in one vol. Cloth, 4*s* 6*d*

Beaumont (H.) French for Children. The Complete Primer, containing Easy Lessons in Spelling and Reading, with Tales in Prose and Verse, with Interlinear Translation. 12mo. cloth, 2*s*

Fleury's Histoire de France racontée a la Jeunesse, edited for the use of English students, with notes by A. Beljame. 12mo. Cloth, 3*s* 6*d*

Aus Goethe's Italienischer Reise. Sketches of Travels in Italy by Goethe. The German Text, with Idiomatic and Grammatical Notes, Questions for Conversation, and a complete Vocabulary by Dr. A. Buchheim, Professor of German, King's College, London. 12mo. Cloth, 2*s* 6*d*

Buchheim's Deutsches Theater. Modern German Plays for Schools. Part I. 1. Eigensinn (Obstinacy). 2. Dichter und Page (the Poet and the Page), with idiomatic Notes and a complete Vocabulary, by Dr. Buchheim, Professor of German, King's College, London. 12mo. Cloth, 2*s* 6*d*.

Buchheim's Deutsches Theater. Part II. Contents: 1. Der Prozess (The Lawsuit). 2. Ein theurer Spass (a dear Joke). 3. List und Phlegma. With Notes, etc. 12mo. Cloth, 2*s* 6*d*

—— Parts I. II. together in 1 vol. Cloth, 4*s* 6*d*

Buchheim's French Prose and Poetical Reader, [Ahn's French Method, part 3] 2nd edition. 12mo. Cloth, 1*s* 6*d*

Barrère (P.) les Ecrivains Français, leur vie et leurs œuvres; ou l'histoire de la Littérature Française. Par P. Barrère, Membre de l'Université de France, ancien professeur de Français à l'Academie Royale Militaire de Woolwich, etc. etc. 8vo. Cloth, 6*s* 6*d*

Ahn's French School Grammar and Exercises. Complete Theoretical and Practical French Grammar, with Exercises. Improved and adapted for the Use of English Schools, with Notes by Professor A. Buchheim, Editor of Ahn's Complete French Course, etc. Crown 8vo. Cloth, 5*s*

Or separately—

—— Grammar. Cloth, 3*s*—Exercises. Cloth, 2*s* 6*d*

Ahn's Practical French Method. [Buchheim's Edition.] A new, practical, and Easy Method of Learning the French Language, adapted for the Use of English Students. By Professor A. Buchheim. First Course. Third Edition. 12mo. Cloth, 1*s* 6*d*

Ahn's French Method [Buchheim's Edition.] 2nd Course. Exercises, Dialogues, Tales, Letters, a Play, and Vocabularies. 12mo. Cloth, 1*s* 6*d*

—— Course I. II. together in 1 vol. Cloth, 3*s*

—— Key to Exercises in Course I. II. each 8*d*

Ahn's French Method. Part 3. A French Prose and Poetical Reader by Dr. A. Buchheim. Second Edition. 12mo. Cloth, 1*s* 6*d*

Ahn's French Familiar Dialogues, and French-English Vocabulary for English Schools. 12mo. Cloth, 1*s* 6*d*

Ahn's German Method by Rose. A new Edition of the Genuine Book, with a Supplement, consisting of Models of Conjugations, a Table of all regular dissonant and irregular verbs, Rules on the Prepositions, &c. &c. by A. V. Rose. First Course. 12mo. Cloth, 1*s* 6*d*

——— the same, the two Courses in one. Cloth, 3*s*

Rose (A. V.) English into German. A Selection of Stories and Anecdotes arranged in a Course, gradually increasing in difficulty, with notes and grammatical explanations for translating into German. 12mo. Boards. 1*s* 6*d*

Iffland, das Gewissen: a Tragedy. The German Text, edited for the use of Schools, with Grammatical and Idiomatic Notes, and a complete Vocabulary, by J. W. Fraedersdorff, of the Taylor Institution, Oxford. 12mo. Cloth, 2*s* 6*d*

Apel's German School Grammar, according to Dr. Becker's views; with a complete Course of Exercises. Fourth Edition, thoroughly revised. 12mo. Cloth, 6*s*

——— A Key to the Exercises in Apel's German Grammar. 12mo. Cloth, 4*s*

Apel's Short and Practical German Grammar for Beginners, with copious Examples and Exercises. 12mo. Cloth, 2*s* 6*d*

Becker's German Grammar. Third Edition, carefully revised, and adapted to the use of the English Student, by Dr. J. W. Fraedersdorff. 12mo. Cloth, 5*s*

German for Children. The Primer. Easy Lessons in Spelling and Reading, and Entertaining Tales in Prose and Verse, with the Interlinear Translation, by F. F. Moritz Foerster. 12mo. Cloth, 2*s*

Ollendorff's German Method. A new Translation (unabridged) from the Original Edition, by H. W. Dulcken. Second Edition. 12mo. Cloth boards, 5*s* 6*d*.

——— A Key to the Exercises. 12mo. Cloth, 3*s* 6*d*

Bojesen's Danish Speaker. Pronunciation of the Danish Language, Vocabulary, Dialogues and Idioms for the use of Students and Travellers in Denmark and Norway. By Madame M. Bojesen. 12mo. Cloth, 4*s*

Introduction to Danish or Norwegian; a Collection of Useful Phrases and Sentences, arranged in grammatical order, with references to Rask's Grammar, and Extracts from Danish and Norwegian historians, &c. with explanatory notes and a Vocabulary. By J. W. Fraedersdorff, Professor of Modern Languages at Queen's College, Belfast. 12mo. Cloth, 4*s*

Schmidt's German Reading Book for Beginners. A companion to the German Guide. 1*s* 6*d*

Schmidt (J. A. F.) German Guide, a Practical and Easy German Method for Beginners; Rules, Exercises, Grammatical Questions and Vocabulary. Course I. II. 2nd Edition. In 1 vol. 12mo. Cloth, 3*s*

——— the same. 1st Course. 2nd Edition. Cloth, 1*s* 6*d*

——— the same. 2nd Course. 2nd Edition, 12mo. Cloth, 1*s* 6*d*

——— the same. 3rd Course, for more advanced Students. 12mo. Cloth, 1*s* 6*d*

A Key to the 1st and 2nd Course. 2*s*.
A Key to the 3rd Course, 2*s*

The author of the above works has been for a long time a successful teacher in this country, and they are the results of many years experience and labour.

Schmidt. The Boy and the Bible, a Tale by L. Storch. German Text, and an interlinear translation on the Hamiltonian System. 2nd Edition. Cloth, 2*s* 6*d*

Weisse's Systematic Conversational Exercises for translating into German, adapted to his Grammar, by T. Heinrich Weisse, 12mo. Cloth, 5*s* (*In the press*)

Weisse (T. H.) German Grammar. A Grammar of the German Language, based on its natural relation to the English, for Schools and Private Study. Second edition, with important practical improvements. 12mo. Cloth, 5*s*

Schlütter's German Class Book. A Course of Instruction based on Becker's System, and so arranged as to exhibit the Self-Development of the Language, and its Affinities with the English. By Fr. Schlutter, Royal Military Academy, Woolwich. 408 pp., cloth boards, 5*s*

www.ingramcontent.com/pod-product-compliance
Lightning Source LLC
Chambersburg PA
CBHW020406030726
47496CB00007B/2324

* 9 7 8 3 3 3 7 1 2 3 4 3 7 *